RUSSIAN CURRENCY AND FINANCE

RUSSIAN CURRENCY AND FINANCE

A currency board approach to reform

Steve H. Hanke, Lars Jonung, and Kurt Schuler

London and New York

First published 1993
by Routledge
11 New Fetter Lane, London EC4P 4EE

Simultaneously published in the USA and Canada
by Routledge
29 West 35th Street, New York, NY 10001

Typeset in Garamond by Intype, London

Printed and bound in Great Britain by
T.J. Press (Padstow) Ltd.,
Padstow, Cornwall

British Library Cataloguing in Publication Data

A catalogue record for this book is available from the British
Library

ISBN 0–415–09651–0

Library of Congress Cataloging in Publication Data

Hanke, Steve H.
  Russian currency and finance : a currency board approach
to reform / Steve H. Hanke, Lars Jonung, and Kurt
Schuler.
      p.   cm.
  Includes bibliographical references and index.
  ISBN 0–415–09651–0
  1. Money--Russia (Federation) 2. Currency question--
Russia (Federation) 3. Economic stabilization--Russia
(Federation)
I. Jonung, Lars. II. Schuler, Kurt. III. Title.
HG1080.2.H34   1993
332.4'947--dc20   93–4355
                                                          CIP

CONTENTS

CONTENTS

ABOUT THE AUTHORS

Steve H. Hanke is Professor of Applied Economics at The Johns Hopkins University in Baltimore, chairman of MERiT Group, Inc. in Baltimore, and vice president of FMCI Financial Corporation in Toronto. He was a senior economist on President Reagan's Council of Economic Advisors from 1981 to 1982. He served as personal economic advisor to Zivko Pregl, the deputy prime minister of the Socialist Federal Republic of Yugoslavia, from 1990 until Mr Pregl resigned on 30 June 1991. He is the editor (with Alan A. Walters) of *Capital Markets and Development* (1991).

Lars Jonung is Professor of Economics and Economic Policy at the Stockholm School of Economics, and chief economic advisor to the prime minister of Sweden. Monetary economics, Swedish macroeconomic policy, and inflationary expectations are his main fields of research. His writings include *The Long Run Behavior of the Velocity of Money* (with Michael D. Bordo, 1987), *The Political Economy of Price Controls: The Swedish Experience 1970–1987* (1990), and, as editor, *The Stockholm School of Economics Revisited* (1991) and *Swedish Economic Thought: Explorations and Advances* (1993). He recently finished a study of Swedish central bank policy from 1945 to 1990. He has also served as economic advisor to the Skandinaviska Enskilda Banken and as editor of the *Skandinaviska Enskilda Banken Quarterly Review*.

Kurt Schuler is a postdoctoral fellow at The Johns Hopkins University in Baltimore. As a Summer Fellow at G.T. Management (Asia) Ltd in Hong Kong in 1989, he worked with John Greenwood, who guided the return of Hong Kong to the currency board system in 1983.

FIGURES

TABLES

1

THE CASE FOR A CURRENCY BOARD IN RUSSIA

EXTREME INFLATION AND MONETARY REFORM

Russia has experienced 'extreme inflation'[2] of at least 15 per cent a month since 1991. Russia is now on the verge of hyperinflation, that is, increases in the consumer price index of at least 50 per cent a month for at least three consecutive months. Extreme inflation has become the most important problem in Russia today and is largely responsible for the recent economic decline, social unrest, and political conflict in Russia. If extreme inflation continues, it will jeopardize Russia's progress towards a market economy and stable representative government.

Russia's inflation is caused by the Central Bank of Russia. The Central Bank finances the government budget deficit – which comprises the deficit of the government itself and of state enterprises – by increasing the money supply. For approximately two decades until 1986, the budget deficit of the Soviet government was 2–3 per cent of gross domestic product (GDP).[3] Consequently, inflation was present, but low (Birman 1980). To most observers, inflation seemed even lower than it was, because it was repressed by price controls imposed by the Soviet government. Repressed inflation manifested itself as shortages of goods at official prices or as increases in prices for goods and services in the black market.

A combination of more government spending and less tax revenue from a declining economy caused the budget deficit of the Soviet government to increase to 6 per cent of GDP in 1986, 6.9 per cent in 1987, 10.3 per cent in 1988, 9.9 per cent in 1989, 5.7 per cent in 1990, and 25.5 per cent in 1991. (The reduction in the deficit in 1990 is deceptive because many expenses were shifted to 1991.) The trend continued in Russia and other former Soviet republics after the breakup of the Soviet Union in December 1991. The budget deficit of the Russian government, including Russia's share of the Soviet deficit, was estimated to be 30.9 per cent of Russia's GDP in 1991 and perhaps 12 per cent in 1992 (Åslund 1991: 192; see also Table 3.2 in this book).[4]

To finance the budget deficits of the Soviet and Russian governments,

the State Bank of the USSR and its successor, the Central Bank of Russia, have created new roubles in increasing quantities. As the quantity of roubles created by the Central Bank has increased, inflation has accelerated and the value of the rouble has plummeted. Consumer price inflation was 5.6 per cent in 1990, 90.4 per cent in 1991, and 2,600 per cent in 1992 (see Table 3.2). The exchange rate of the rouble was 22.88 roubles per US dollar at the end of 1990, 169.20 roubles at the end of 1991, and 414.50 roubles at the end of 1992 (see Table 3.1). (Some recent inflation and depreciation are effects of partial liberalization of prices and of the foreign-exchange market, which have brought previously repressed inflation and depreciation into the open.)

Russia is now beginning a sequence of events typical of hyperinflations (for case studies, see Yeager *et al.* 1981 and Capie 1991; see also Bernholz and Gersbach 1992). Rouble prices not controlled by the government are becoming indexed to the rouble–US dollar exchange rate, which is the most up-to-date indicator of inflation. When indexation is complete, nominal prices for goods not controlled by the government will increase proportionally to the depreciation of the rouble against the dollar. The *relative* prices of such goods will cease to indicate their relative scarcity, so rouble prices will cease to convey information about real changes in supply and demand.

The destruction of price information that extreme inflation causes will be worsened because many prices remain controlled by the Russian government and by local governments. Consequently, Russia will have two broad categories of goods and services. The 'real-price-rigid' category will be goods whose rouble prices increase as the rouble depreciates, but are rigid in relation to one another. In real terms, the prices of real-price-rigid goods will be approximately constant. The 'nominal-price-rigid' category of goods will be those whose prices are fixed in nominal terms because of price controls. In real terms, the prices of nominal-price-rigid goods will decrease because of extreme inflation. (Nominal prices are prices in current roubles, whereas real prices are prices in inflation-adjusted roubles.)

Extreme inflation will distort prices within each category of goods and between the two categories. Within each category of goods, relative prices will not adjust. Within the real-price-rigid category, relative prices will not adjust because they will be indexed to the exchange rate. Within the nominal-price-rigid category, relative prices will not adjust because they will remain controlled. Extreme inflation will also create perverse distortions of prices between the real-price-rigid category and the nominal-price-rigid category. The nominal-price-rigid category of goods will become cheaper and cheaper in real terms, causing shortages.

The effects of extreme inflation will be even worse than they would be in a full-fledged market economy because the structure of prices in Russia is still largely that inherited from the period when Russia was a centrally

planned economy. Just when flexible relative prices would be most beneficial as indicators of the relative scarcity of goods and services, extreme
inflation and price controls are obstructing flexibility. Consequently, in
Russia the price system does not accurately indicate which uses of resources
are most valuable to economic agents. Extreme inflation and institutions
inherited from the centrally planned economy are hindering Russia's progress towards a full-fledged market economy.

If extreme inflation continues, it will render the rouble unusable. Goods
will continue to be readily purchasable with US dollars and other relatively
stable foreign currencies, but not with roubles. That will create further
hardship in Russia, where the range of goods purchasable with roubles has
already shrunk in recent months. Russians who lack easy access to foreign
currency, such as those who do not live in the largest Russian cities, will
suffer most. The Russian economy will decline even further.

Given that extreme inflation has contributed to the collapse of the
Russian economy and that the decline in the standard of living caused by
extreme inflation is unpopular, why does extreme inflation persist in
Russia? The answer can be found in the characteristics of the current
political situation in Russia. There are four actors in this drama: the Russian
parliament, the executive branch of the Russian government, the Central
Bank of Russia, and the Russian public. Although the executive branch
contests the parliament's control of the Central Bank of Russia, currently
the Central Bank must finance spending ordered by the parliament. (The
parliament can override vetoes by Russia's president of spending ordered
by the parliament.) Elements of the Russian public demand continued
government spending on subsidies: workers and managers in unprofitable
state enterprises demand subsidies to keep the enterprises open, and consumers demand subsidies for the prices of certain goods. By continuing
the subsidies, the parliament obtains political support from those interest
groups, but it is unable to pay for the subsidies by noninflationary borrowing, and unwilling to impose higher taxes, which would be politically
unpopular. Instead, it orders the Central Bank of Russia to finance the
government budget deficit that results. To finance the deficit, the Central
Bank creates large new quantities of roubles, which causes inflation.

Inflation is unpopular with most of the Russian public. The parliament,
however, seems to have convinced most of the public that the executive
branch rather than the parliament is responsible for extreme inflation. In
reality, partial price liberalization and other economic reforms enacted by
the executive branch have converted repressed inflation into open inflation,
and the executive branch has caused little inflation except to the extent
that it has agreed to laws passed by the parliament to continue deficit
spending. The parliament benefits from extreme inflation by obtaining
political support from interest groups that favour continued subsidies, and
by blaming the executive branch for extreme inflation.

3

The current situation is unsustainable, however, and extreme inflation contains the source of its own destruction. The rouble is decreasing in importance in the Russian economy as relatively stable foreign currencies displace it. The extensive displacement of the rouble by foreign currency in the Russian economy will ultimately cause real (inflation-adjusted) revenue from creating new roubles to diminish almost to zero. When that happens, the parliament will no longer be able to continue most subsidies that now exist. Unprofitable state enterprises will have to fire workers and consumers will have to pay higher real prices for formerly subsidized goods. At that point, a political upheaval will probably result. It is unclear whether the Russian public will blame the parliament, the executive branch, or both for extreme inflation, but whatever the case, the result will be a new configuration of political forces.

Political conditions may then be appropriate to make monetary reforms as far-reaching as the political reforms that resulted from the 1991 revolution. Just as Russia astounded the world then by moving decisively from Communist Party rule and socialism towards representative government and a market economy, it may have the opportunity to astound the world again by moving decisively from extreme inflation and economic decline to low inflation and economic growth.

To end extreme inflation and provide one of the necessary conditions for rapid, sustainable economic growth, Russia needs a sound currency. A sound currency is one that is stable, credible, and fully convertible. Stability means that current annual inflation is relatively low, usually in single digits. Credibility means that the issuer creates confidence that it will keep future inflation low. Full convertibility means that the currency can buy domestic and foreign goods and services, including buying foreign currencies at market rates without restriction. The Central Bank of Russia, despite its professed intent to make the rouble a sound currency, and despite help from Western governments and international organizations, seems to be no nearer that goal today than it was a year ago or than the Soviet central bank was five years ago.

Accordingly, we propose that Russia reform its monetary system by establishing a currency board rather than by continuing to rely on the Central Bank of Russia.

CURRENCY BOARD VERSUS CENTRAL BANK

Central banking is familiar to Russians and to the inhabitants of most other countries, at least on a practical level, as the monetary system of their country. A central bank is a monetary authority that has discretionary monopoly control of the supply of the reserves of commercial banks. Usually this implies a monopoly of the supply of notes (paper currency) and coins.[5] Discretionary control means the ability to choose a monetary policy at will, at least partly unconstrained by rules; it is discussed in more detail later in this section. Reserves mean the medium of settlement of payments. Often, a monetary system uses two types of media to settle payments: one type that is used primarily domestically, such as notes issued by the monetary authority, and foreign reserves (ultimate reserves) used in international trade, such as gold, foreign bonds, or notes issued by a foreign central bank. A commercial bank means any bank other than a central bank, including cooperative banks, investment banks, and savings banks.

Unlike central banking, the currency board system is unfamiliar to most people. It has existed in more than seventy countries, including Russia, but today remains in only a few countries, most notably Hong Kong (see Appendix C). A currency board is a monetary institution that issues notes and coins (and, in some cases, deposits) fully backed by a foreign 'reserve' currency and fully convertible into the reserve currency at a fixed exchange rate on demand. The reserve currency is a convertible foreign currency or a commodity chosen for its expected stability. The country that issues the reserve currency is called the reserve country. (If the reserve currency is a commodity, the country that has the currency board is considered the reserve country.)

As reserves, a currency board holds low-risk, interest-earning securities and other assets payable in the reserve currency, equal to 100 per cent or slightly more of its notes and coins in circulation, as set by law. A currency board usually accepts no deposits; if it does, they too must be backed 100 per cent or slightly more by assets payable in the reserve currency. A currency board earns profits from the difference between the return on the reserve-currency securities it holds and the expense of maintaining its notes and coins in circulation. It remits to the government (or to its owner, if not the government) profits beyond what it needs to pay its expenses and maintain its reserves at the level set by law. A currency board does not have discretionary control over the quantity of notes, coins, and deposits it supplies. Market forces determine the quantity of notes, coins, and deposits it supplies, and hence the overall money supply in a currency board system.

A currency board is only a part of the monetary system in any country that has commercial banks and other financial institutions. The currency board *system* comprises the currency board, commercial banks, and other financial institutions. It also comprises certain rules of behaviour by them and the government concerning exchange rates, convertibility, government finance, and so on, which this book describes.

Table 1.1 lists differences between a typical currency board and a typical central bank. This section briefly explains each difference. Later chapters discuss the differences in detail. We emphasize that the descriptions are accurate for a typical actual currency board or central banks, past or present. The description of a currency board does not describe a theoretically ideal currency board, nor does it describe an exceptionally good

5

actual currency board. It describes a typical actual currency board, though the actual performance of currency boards has been close to the ideal they have been established to strive for (see chapter 4). Similarly, the description of a central bank does not describe a theoretically ideal central bank. Nor does it describe an exceptionally good actual central bank such as the US Federal Reserve System or the German Bundesbank. It describes a typical actual central bank, because the Central Bank of Russia currently is, at best, a typical central bank, and will remain one for the foreseeable future. The description also fits most other central banks, especially those in developing countries, which are a substantial majority of central banks in existence today.[6]

Table 1.1 A typical currency board versus a typical central bank

Typical currency board	Typical central bank
Usually supplies notes and coins only	Supplies notes, coins, and deposits
Fixed exchange rate with reserve currency	Pegged or floating exchange rate
Foreign reserves of 100 per cent	Variable foreign reserves
Full convertibility	Limited convertibility
Rule-bound monetary policy	Discretionary monetary policy
Not a lender of last resort	Lender of last resort
Does not regulate commercial banks	Often regulates commercial banks
Transparent	Opaque
Protected from political pressure	Politicized
High credibility	Low credibility
Earns seigniorage only from interest	Earns seigniorage from interest and inflation
Cannot create inflation	Can create inflation
Cannot finance spending by domestic government	Can finance spending by domestic government
Requires no 'preconditions' for monetary reform	Requires 'preconditions' for monetary reform
Rapid monetary reform	Slow monetary reform
Small staff	Large staff

Note: The characteristics listed are those of a typical actual currency board or central bank, especially one in a developing country, not those of a theoretically ideal or exceptionally good currency board or central bank.

To begin at the top of the list in Table 1.1, a typical currency board *usually supplies notes and coins only*, whereas a typical central bank also supplies deposits. Some past currency boards have accepted deposits, however. The deposits of a typical currency board are subject to the same reserve requirement as its notes and coins. To simplify exposition of the currency board system, this book usually discusses currency boards as if they issue notes and coins only. The additional complications that result from deposits are minor and do not significantly change the analysis.

Notes and coins issued by a currency board or central bank, and deposits held by commercial banks at the currency board or central bank, constitute the monetary base. The monetary base counts as reserves of commercial banks when held by them, but not when held by the public. Deposits of the public at commercial banks and notes and coins held by the public constitute the money supply.[7] Notes and coins in circulation, whether held by the public or by commercial banks, constitute cash.

Deposits at the central bank are the main form of reserves for commercial banks in a typical central banking system. In a typical currency board system, commercial banks have no deposits at the currency board; instead, reserve-currency assets are their main form of reserves. In both a currency board system and a central banking system, commercial banks hold 'vault cash' – notes and coins of the currency board or central bank – to satisfy their depositors' requests to convert those deposits into notes and coins.

A typical currency board maintains a truly *fixed exchange rate with the reserve currency*. The exchange rate is permanent, or at most can be altered only in emergencies. The exchange rate may be written into the constitution that describes the legal obligations of the currency board. The record of currency boards in maintaining fixed exchange rates has been excellent (see chapter 4). A typical central bank, in contrast, maintains a pegged or floating exchange rate rather than a truly fixed rate. A pegged exchange rate is constant for the time being in terms of a reserve currency, but carries no credible long-term guarantee of remaining at its current rate. A floating exchange rate is not maintained constant in terms of any reserve currency. The exchange rate maintained by a central bank is typically not written into law, and can be altered at the will of the central bank or the government. When a typical central bank suffers heavy political or speculative pressure to devalue the currency, it devalues. Allegedly fixed exchange rates maintained by central banks have in reality typically been pegged exchange rates. Chapter 2 elaborates on the distinction between fixed and pegged exchange rates.

As reserve assets against its liabilities (its notes and coins in circulation), a typical currency board holds securities in the reserve currency; it may also hold bank deposits and a small amount of notes in the reserve currency. It holds *foreign reserves of 100 per cent* or slightly more of its note, coin, and deposit liabilities, as set by law. Many currency boards have held a maximum of 105 or 110 per cent foreign reserves to have a margin of protection in case the reserve-currency securities they held lost value. A typical central bank, in contrast, has variable foreign reserves: it is not required to maintain any fixed, binding ratio of foreign reserves to liabilities. Even where a minimum ratio exists, a typical central bank can hold any ratio in excess of that. For example, a central bank required to hold at least 20 per cent foreign reserves may hold 30, 130, or even 330 per cent foreign reserves. A typical central bank also holds domestic-currency assets, which a typical currency board does not.

A typical currency board has *full convertibility* of its currency: it exchanges its notes and coins for reserve currency at its stated fixed exchange rate without limit. Anybody who has reserve currency can exchange it for currency board notes and coins at the fixed rate, and anybody who has currency board notes and coins can exchange them for reserve currency at the fixed rate. However, a currency board does not guarantee that deposits at commercial banks are convertible into currency board notes and coins. Commercial banks are responsible for holding enough notes and coins as vault cash to satisfy their contractual obligations to their depositors to convert deposits into notes and coins on demand. If the government imposes no minimum reserve requirement on commercial banks, commercial banks may hold any quantity, or ratio of reserves to liabilities, that they think is prudent; they are not required to hold 100 per cent foreign reserves like the currency board, nor 100 per cent currency board notes and coins against deposits. (In other words, M0 is backed 100 per cent by foreign reserves in a currency board system, but broader measures of the money supply such as M1, M2, and M3 are not.) Deposits denominated in the currency board currency at solvent commercial banks are fully convertible at a fixed exchange rate into currency board notes and coins, and currency board notes and coins are fully convertible at a fixed exchange rate into the reserve currency. As for foreign currencies other than the reserve currency, the currency board has no direct role in determining exchange rates with them. Commercial banks trade them at market-determined exchange rates, which may be fixed, pegged, or floating against the reserve currency and hence against the currency board currency.

A typical central bank, in contrast, has limited convertibility of its currency. Central banks in the majority of developed countries and in a few developing countries have fully convertible currencies, but most central banks, including the Central Bank of Russia, have inconvertible or only partly convertible currencies. They restrict or forbid certain transactions, particularly purchases of foreign securities or real estate (see chapter 2 and IMF 1992e).

A typical currency board has a *rule-bound monetary policy:* it is not allowed to alter the exchange rate, except perhaps in emergencies (chapter 6 proposes rules for defining such emergencies), nor is it allowed to alter its reserve ratio or the regulations affecting commercial banks. A currency board merely exchanges its notes and coins for reserve currency at a fixed rate in such quantities as commercial banks and the public demand. When the demand for money changes, the role of a currency board is passive. Market forces alone determine the money supply through a self-adjusting process (see chapter 4).

A typical central bank, in contrast, has a partly or completely discretionary monetary policy. A central bank can alter at will, or with the approval of the government, the exchange rate, its ratio of foreign reserves, or the regulations affecting commercial banks. It is not subject to strict rules like a typical currency board. Chapters 2 and 4 discuss the effects of discretionary monetary policy by a central bank.

A typical currency board is *not a lender of last resort*, that is, it does not lend to commercial banks or other enterprises to help them avoid bankruptcy. Commercial banks in a currency board system must rely on alternatives to a lender of last resort (see chapter 8). A typical central bank, in contrast, is a lender of last resort.

A typical currency board *does not regulate commercial banks*. Banking regulations in a currency board system are usually few, and are enforced by the ministry of finance or an office of bank regulation. A typical central bank, in contrast, often regulates commercial banks. Perhaps the most common form of regulation is the imposition of reserve requirements on commercial banks. The required reserves, which are held in the form of deposits at the central bank and vault cash, typically exceed the prudential reserves that commercial banks would hold if no reserve requirements existed.

The activities of a typical currency board are *transparent*, because a currency board is a very simple institution. It is merely a sort of warehouse for reserve-currency securities that back its notes and coins in circulation. The activities of a typical central bank are opaque. A central bank is not a warehouse; it is a speculating institution whose effectiveness partly depends on the ability to act secretly sometimes. For example, the Central Bank of Russia does not announce how much it will increase the supply of rouble notes next month; at most, it announces how much it increased the supply of rouble notes in the past.[8]

Because a typical currency board is rule-bound and transparent, it is *protected from political pressure*. It is protected by implicit rules of political behaviour, or, better yet, by an explicit constitution such as that of Appendix A. A typical central bank is politicized. Some central banks, such as the German Bundesbank and the US Federal Reserve System, are politically independent in the sense that their governors, once appointed, have sole control of the monetary base and cannot be fired by the executive or legislative branches of government during the governors' fixed terms of office. Even the most politically independent central banks sometimes yield to strong political pressure, though. The Central Bank of Russia and its predecessors have been very politicized (see chapter 3).

A typical currency board has *high credibility*. Its 100 per cent foreign reserve requirement, rule-bound monetary policy, transparency, and protection from political pressure enable it to maintain full convertibility and a fixed exchange rate with the reserve currency. An appropriately chosen reserve currency will be stable; therefore, the currency issued by the currency board will be stable. A typical central bank, in contrast, has low credibility. A few exceptionally good central banks, which exist mainly in developed countries, have high credibility, but the majority, including the

Central Bank of Russia, do not. Because a typical central bank has discretion in monetary policy, is opaque, and is politicized, it has the means and the incentive to break promises about the exchange rate or inflation whenever it wishes.

Readers may ask how credible a currency board can be if, as has been the case with most currency boards, its reserve currency is issued by a central bank. Might not the central bank of the reserve country create monetary instability in Russia, for example? No central bank has a perfect record of combating inflation and the central bank of the reserve country may export instability and inflation to Russia through the currency board.

We reply that one must think in terms of *relative* credibility. The reserve currency, if issued by a central bank, should be a currency issued by an exceptionally good central bank, such as the US Federal Reserve System or the German Bundesbank. The Federal Reserve and the Bundesbank are not perfect, but they have much more credibility than the Central Bank of Russia now has or will have in the foreseeable future. For the two periods 1965–1980 and 1980–1990, only six of the 101 developing countries reporting data to the World Bank had lower average annual inflation in consumer prices than the United States, and only two had lower average annual inflation than Germany. (World Bank 1992a: 218–19). The US dollar and the German mark have exceptionally good records and good prospects for future stability, whereas the rouble issued by the Central Bank of Russia has a bad record and bad prospects for future stability. A currency board will transmit the relative credibility of the reserve country's central bank to the currency board rouble, whereas no such effect will occur if Russia continues with a central bank. By means of a fixed exchange rate to a currency issued by an exceptionally good central bank, a currency board can 'import' the monetary policy of that central bank.

A typical currency board *earns seigniorage* (income from issue) *only from interest*. The currency board earns interest from its holdings of reserve-currency securities (its main assets), yet pays no interest on its notes and coins (its liabilities). Gross seigniorage is the income from issuing notes and coins. It can be explicit interest income or implicit income in the form of goods acquired by spending money. Net seigniorage (profit) is gross seigniorage minus the cost of putting and maintaining notes and coins in circulation.

A typical central bank also earns seigniorage on its notes and coins in circulation *and* on the deposits that commercial banks hold with it and its loans. The deposits, like notes and coins, usually pay no interest. But a more important source of seigniorage for a typical central bank is inflation. To define inflation precisely, it is a general increase in prices, typically caused by an increase in the nominal money supply that is not the result of increased voluntary saving. A typical currency board cannot create inflation because it does not control the ultimate reserves of the monetary system. For instance, the currency board system of Hong Kong uses the US dollar as its reserve currency. The ultimate reserves of the Hong Kong currency board system are the US dollar monetary base, which is supplied by the US Federal Reserve System rather than by the Hong Kong Exchange Fund (currency board). Like any system of fixed exchange rates, a currency board system may *transmit* inflation from the reserve country, but a currency board cannot *create* inflation because it cannot increase the monetary base independently of the monetary authority of the reserve country. A typical central bank, in contrast, can create inflation at its discretion by increasing the domestic monetary base, as the Central Bank of Russia is now doing.

A typical currency board *cannot finance spending by the domestic government* or domestic state enterprises because it is not allowed to lend to them. A typical central bank finances spending by the domestic government, whether to a relatively small extent (as in the United States) or to a large extent (as in Russia).

A typical currency board *requires no 'preconditions' for monetary reform*. Government finances, state enterprises, or trade need not be already reformed before the currency board can begin to issue a sound currency. A typical central bank cannot issue a sound currency unless the 'fiscal precondition' exists, that is, the government no longer needs to finance budget deficits by means of inflation. Once governments start to depend on central banks for financing deficits, they usually have trouble stopping.

A typical currency board is conducive to *rapid monetary reform*. For example, the North Russian currency board described in chapter 9 opened only eleven weeks after the plan for it was first conceived. A typical central bank is a hindrance to rapid monetary reform, as the next section explains.

Finally, a typical currency board needs only a *small staff* of a few persons who perform routine functions that are easily learned. A typical central bank needs a large staff trained in the intricacies of monetary theory and policy. The Central Bank of Russia has more than 5,000 employees.

A CURRENCY BOARD AS THE KEY TO ECONOMIC REFORM IN RUSSIA

The conventional approach to economic reform in Russia and other emerging market economies assumes that they must have central banks.[9] The conventional approach is a distillation of experience since the early 1980s with International Monetary Fund (IMF) stabilization programmes in many countries that have experienced extreme inflation, large government sectors, and economic decline. This approach has the support of the IMF, the World Bank, Western governments that give aid to Russia, and many Western and Russian economists, and is exemplified by the economic reforms that have occurred in Poland since 1 January 1990.[10] As with any body of economic opinion, the conventional approach to economic reform in Russia and other emerging market economies is not monolithic, but it has the general characteristics described here.

The Russian government's current programme of economic reforms implements the conventional approach only in part. Contrary to a widespread misconception, the government's current economic programme has many vestiges of central planning and is not a consistent programme of 'shock therapy'. In monetary policy, for example, the Russian government and the Central Bank of Russia are following neither the conventional approach nor the alternative approach that we advocate here, both of which advocate monetary restraint rather than extreme inflation. We think, however, that the conventional approach would not work well even if it were fully implemented in Russia. The conventional approach would rely on the Central Bank of Russia to provide a sound currency, but as chapters 2 and 3 explain, the Central Bank of Russia is unlikely to provide a sound currency in the near future. Hence the conventional approach would risk failure by relying on the Central Bank of Russia.

A currency board is an important part of an alternative approach to economic reform. The alternative approach shares the goals of the conventional approach but achieves them by different means.[11]

Both approaches to economic reform have two main goals: macroeconomic stabilization to stop economic decline and microeconomic restructuring to achieve a full-fledged market economy. Macroeconomic stabilization deals with economic forces that affect the economy as a whole: inflation, interest rates, price controls, and trade. Microeconomic restructuring deals with the ownership of resources and the structure of particular sectors of the economy, such as agriculture, communications, and retail sales. Macroeconomic stabilization can be accomplished by the government acting alone, whereas microeconomic restructuring also requires the involvement of local and foreign entrepreneurs. Table 1.2 summarizes the goals and means of the alternative approach and the conventional approach to economic reform in Russia and other emerging market economies.

Let us now compare the two approaches. The alternative approach achieves *macroeconomic stabilization* by means of deregulation of prices and trade, and by means of a currency board with a fixed exchange rate. The conventional approach tries to achieve macroeconomic stabilization by means of liberalization of prices and trade, and by means of a central bank with a pegged exchange rate. The means appear similar, but have quite different effects.

The alternative approach advocates *deregulation of prices and trade*. It abolishes all price controls except perhaps those applying to monopoly utilities such as electricity, gas, and water, whose prices can be regulated by special agencies as they are in many full-fledged market economies. (Even for monopoly utilities, eliminating legal barriers to competition may

12

Table 1.2 Goals and means of achieving economic reform in Russia

Goals	Means	
	Alternative approach	*Conventional approach*
Macroeconomic stabilization	Deregulation of prices and trade	Liberalization of prices and trade
	Currency board with a fixed exchange rate	Central bank with a pegged exchange rate
Microeconomic restructuring	'Market infrastructure'	'Market infrastructure'
	Corporatization and privatization of state property	Rapid privatization of state property

produce better results than conventional price regulation.) The alternative approach also abolishes all trade quotas and, ideally, abolishes all tariffs. In reality, tariffs may be retained because they are among the most easily collected taxes, but if so, tariffs should be used only to produce tax revenue, not to protect favoured domestic industries from foreign competition. The tariff rate should be low and uniform. The alternative approach does not need quotas or tariffs to enforce foreign-exchange controls, since the currency is fully convertible.

The conventional approach, in contrast, advocates *liberalization of prices and trade*. It abolishes many price controls, trade quotas, and tariffs, but retains others. In the conventional approach, full deregulation of prices and trade is not possible because the central bank allows the government and state enterprises to operate with soft budget constraints. Soft budget constraints mean that because economic agents receive subsidies, they can spend more than the sum of their earnings and their unsubsidized borrowing. The opposite of soft budget constraints is hard budget constraints, which mean that economic agents cannot spend more than the sum of their earnings and their unsubsidized borrowing.[12]

Here is an example of how soft budget constraints work. Many state enterprises in Russia are unprofitable. However, they continue to grant wage increases to workers and accumulate materials for hoarding because they expect that the government will subsidize their losses, either directly or through the Central Bank of Russia. Instead of restructuring or closing the enterprises, the Russian government orders the Central Bank of Russia to lend to them at steeply negative real interest rates through state commercial banks (interest rates less than the inflation rate).[13] The government uses the loans to subsidize the unprofitable state enterprises. Workers at the unprofitable state enterprises, the enterprises themselves, and the government all have soft budget constraints in this example.

Loans made by the Central Bank of Russia to finance soft budget constraints increase the monetary base, and overly rapid increases in the monetary base cause inflation. To try to forestall inflation, the conventional approach requires the government to retain centralized price controls on state enterprises, limiting the wages they pay workers, the materials they are allowed to buy, and their debts to commercial banks.[14] The government also retains some trade quotas, tariffs, and foreign-exchange controls to prevent soft budget constraints from emerging in foreign trade conducted by state enterprises. To the extent that the government lacks the ability or the willpower to enforce price and other controls, soft budget constraints persist.

In the alternative approach, the means for imposing the hard budget constraints essential to macroeconomic stabilization is a *currency board with a fixed exchange rate*. A typical currency board tends to impose hard budget constraints because it cannot create inflation to finance the government budget deficit. A currency board does not lend to the domestic government or to state enterprises, whether directly, or through domestic commercial banks, or through the government budget. The hard budget constraint that a currency board tends to impose on the government limits the nominal and real amount of subsidies that the government can grant to state enterprises. That creates pressure on the government to restructure or close unprofitable state enterprises. Restructuring or closing state enterprises hardens their budget constraints. In the alternative approach, centralized price controls are unnecessary, from a strictly economic standpoint. The determination of prices can be left to market forces within the framework of hard budget constraints, because state enterprises that are unprofitable will tend to be closed or restructured by the government.

In the conventional approach, in contrast, the means for trying to impose hard budget constraints is a *central bank with a pegged exchange rate*. (Currently, the rouble has controlled floating exchange rate, not a pegged rate.) However, to the extent that the exchange rate is pegged rather than fixed, budget constraints are soft. The defect of a pegged exchange rate is that it allows devaluation. Devaluation softens budget constraints by allowing the central bank to continue to finance the government budget deficit with no ultimate nominal limit. When lending by the central bank increases the monetary base so much that the central bank loses large amounts of foreign reserves at the existing pegged exchange rate, the central bank can devalue the currency, re-pegging at a new rate that holds until it devalues again. If fully implemented in Russia, the conventional approach would probably result in frequent devaluations of the pegged exchange rate of the rouble. Soft budget constraints would tend to persist because Russians would know that there would be no ultimate nominal limit to the ability of the Central Bank of Russia to finance the government budget deficit (see chapter 2).

In the conventional approach, the Central Bank of Russia would tend to remain a lender of last resort not only to commercial banks, like central banks in developed countries, but to state enterprises and to the government. In most developed countries, access to the central bank as a lender of last resort is limited to commercial banks. The central bank is not a lender of last resort to state enterprises. Central banks in most developed countries act as lenders of last resort infrequently, such as when it appears that failures by commercial banks may reduce confidence in the stability of the monetary system. The Central Bank of Russia, like the central banks of many other developing countries, is a lender of last resort in a broader and more dangerous way, and would tend to remain so if the conventional approach to economic reform in Russia were fully implemented. In Russia, state enterprises as well as commercial banks have access to the Central Bank of Russia as a lender of last resort and the Central Bank frequently acts as a lender of last resort to them. One might even say that in the past few years, the Central Bank of Russia has become their lender of *first* resort. The soft budget constraints allowed by the Central Bank of Russia create for the Russian monetary system problems of moral hazard (incentives to behave imprudently). Soft budget constraints would tend to persist if the conventional approach were fully implemented, because the exchange rate of the rouble would be pegged rather than fixed.

Both the alternative approach and the conventional approach agree that *microeconomic restructuring* can begin before macroeconomic stabilization, but differ concerning the relationship between microeconomic restructuring and macroeconomic stabilization. The alternative approach tends to impose hard budget constraints rapidly.[15] In the alternative approach, the government tends to finance itself by levying taxes and by borrowing at positive real interest rates. It may continue to subsidize some state enterprises, so that their budget constraints remain soft, but it is forced to choose which unprofitable state enterprises it will continue to subsidize and will tend to harden the budget constraints of the rest by restructuring or closing them. State commercial banks tend to increase interest rates to positive real levels and cease being conduits for subsidies to state enterprises, because in the alternative approach no central bank exists as a lender of last resort to subsidize state commercial banks or state enterprises. Commercial banks tend to become monitors of the performance of enterprises, which in turn tends to make enterprises more market-oriented, for example by limited wage increases to levels justified by the productivity of workers.

The alternative approach has no preconditions, fiscal or otherwise; rather, by tending to impose hard budget constraints, it solves the fiscal preconditions for economic reform and simultaneously introduces a sound currency immediately. It tends to achieve macroeconomic stability more rapidly and allows other economic reforms to proceed sooner than in the conventional approach.[16] The experience of some currency board systems in implementing similar economic reforms after the Second World War

15

(see chapter 4) suggests that the alternative approach can be successful in Russia.

The conventional approach, in contrast, is unlikely to harden budget constraints rapidly because it would rely on the Central Bank of Russia as a means of macroeconomic stabilization. Instead, the soft budget constraints that are now pervasive in the Russian economy would probably continue. The Central Bank of Russia has financed government budget deficits rather than creating pressure to reduce them. The government budget, therefore, has become the focus of efforts to reform the Russian economy; a balanced budget is the fiscal precondition for establishing a sound currency in the conventional approach (Federov 1991: 281; Greene and Isard 1991: 8–11; McKinnon 1991: 4; IMF 1992c: 30–1; World Bank 1992b: 29–31). Without hard budget constraints, however, budget deficits will tend to remain large because deficit spending is a way of buying temporary political peace.

Recent experience with the difficulty of achieving rapid macroeconomic stabilization by means of a central bank in Russia and other former Soviet republics seems to have changed the thinking of IMF officials about the relationship of microeconomic restructuring and macroeconomic stabilization there. The IMF is now concentrating on microeconomic restructuring, which it hopes will eventually create conditions for macroeconomic stabilization (Balls 1993). This variant of the conventional approach is unlikely to succeed. Unless hard budget constraints are imposed by means of macroeconomic stabilization, enterprises, particularly large state enterprises, will tend to continue to have soft budget constraints and will not behave like enterprises in a full-fledged market economy. Unprofitable large state enterprises in particular will probably continue to exert strong political pressure for subsidies as long as inflation can continue to extract significant real resources for them from the rest of the Russian economy. Therefore, extreme inflation would probably continue even if the Russian government fully implemented the conventional approach.

To achieve microeconomic stabilization, both the alternative approach and the conventional approach advocate establishing *market infrastructure* – institutions and innovations such as private ownership of property, a comprehensive body of business law, a reformed system of accounting that follows generally accepted Western standards, and appropriately trained accountants (see Niskanen 1991). Both the alternative approach and the conventional approach also advocate *privatization* of state property. Privatization improves productivity by making the connection between effort and reward more direct. Governments in several emerging market economies have successfully privatized farmland, housing, and small businesses rapidly; local governments in Russia have also begun to privatize those types of small state property. Experience has shown that rapid privatization

16

of small state property is economically feasible and can be politically popular.

Privatization of large state enterprises is different. The experience of other emerging market economies suggests that for political reasons, privatization of large state enterprises in Russia will be long and slow. The alternative approach, therefore, includes an interim policy, *corporatization* – restructuring or closing state enterprises by changing their management and their organizational structure. The hard budget constraints that a currency board tends to impose create strong political pressure for corporatization and eventual privatization.

The conventional approach, in contrast, emphasizes the importance of *rapid privatization*.[17] Rapid privatization of small state property tends to impose hard budget constraints on the new owners because they are too numerous and diffuse to exert strong political pressure for subsidies. However, rapid privatization of large state enterprises, even if politically feasible, may not impose hard budget constraints on the new owners and hence on managers and workers. The enterprises may continue to receive subsidies because the owners, managers, and workers can exert strong political pressure. Privatization of large state enterprises will not necessarily harden their budget constraints unless the government itself has a hard budget constraint and cannot easily subsidize them. If the government has a soft budget constraint, the budget constraints of large, unprofitable enterprises will tend to remain soft and an important cause of extreme inflation will continue. Therefore, official privatization of large state enterprises in Russia will probably not actually privatize many of them rapidly unless a currency board exists.

In recent writings about the conventional approach, questions of sequencing, that is, the proper order in which reforms should occur, have caused much discussion.[18] To us, the credibility of the overall programme of reforms is more important than the order in which reforms occur. The emerging market economy in Russia can achieve progress even if the order of reforms is less than ideal, provided that reforms do not seriously contradict one another and are part of a programme comprehensive enough to change fundamental economic relations. Piecemeal reforms are meaningless and doomed to fail. A comprehensive programme of reforms to establish a full-fledged market economy in Russia should include the following policies.

1 Reform the monetary system by means of a currency board.
2 Abolish remaining vestiges of central planning. (Approximately 40 per cent of trade among state enterprises remains subject to central allocation [Åslund 1992].)
3 Abolish remaining price controls and subsidies.
4 Corporatize state enterprises.

5 Privatize much more state property, particularly housing and farm land. Eliminate the system of residence permits, which restricts labour movement and is unnecessary where a free market in housing exists.
6 Continue to deregulate trade. (Lower barriers to importing goods will help to prevent domestic monopolies from prevailing.) Abolish export quotas.
7 Reduce tax rates, to encourage entrepreneurial activity.
8 Avoid giving unions or industries special privileges that protect them from competitive market forces.
9 Enact laws that secure rights to private property, assure the enforcement of contracts, and make it easy to establish new businesses.
10 Publicize the economic changes to make the Russian people and foreigners understand the course and probable consequences of reforms.

We have written elsewhere about the elements of a comprehensive programme of economic reforms generally applicable to emerging market economies (Hanke and Walters 1991a). A recent report by the World Bank (World Bank 1992b) contains many detailed suggestions for reforming the Russian economy; although we do not agree with all of its recommendations, it is a good starting point for thinking about comprehensive economic reform in Russia. Accordingly, we will not elaborate further here our ideas about microeconomic restructuring or about deregulation of prices and trade as an aspect of macroeconomic stabilization. Instead, this book concentrates on the monetary reform aspect of macroeconomic stabilization, because that is the key to rapid overall economic reform in Russia.

A currency board established according to this proposal will be beneficial for the Russian economy. It will issue a sound currency from the day it opens. Its fixed exchange rate with its reserve currency will be an 'anchor' for wages and prices that will keep inflation and real interest rates relatively low, as they are in Western countries. Rouble prices will become useful for accurate economic calculation, which they now are largely not.

A currency board will tend to eliminate exchange risk with the reserve currency. (Exchange risk is the possibility of losses or gains from fluctuations in exchange rates.) Domestic and foreign investment in Russia and foreign trade will therefore tend to be higher than if Russia continues with central banking. Higher investment will increase the ratio of capital to labour, raising labour productivity and real wages. Economic growth will tend to be higher and emigration of skilled workers from Russia lower than otherwise.[19] Successful monetary reform will also strengthen the political legitimacy of representative government in Russia. The Russian government has achieved few economic reforms that are both necessary and popular. A sound currency provided by a currency board will be an accomplishment that the Russian government can display as evidence that market-oriented economic reforms can quickly yield beneficial results. A currency board will create credibility for the Russian government, which will help the government make the further economic reforms necessary to establish a full-fledged market economy in Russia. By breaking decisively with existing monetary institutions, a currency board will reduce the possibility that they will be used to strengthen vestiges of central planning.

OUTLINE OF THE REMAINDER OF THIS BOOK

This book explains how a currency board system works and how to establish a currency board in Russia. Chapter 2 states general theoretical and practical arguments against using the Central Bank of Russia as a means of trying to provide a sound currency. Chapter 3 sketches the historical record of central banking in Russia, describes how central banking has shaped the current Russian monetary system, and identifies some of the main problems with the current system.

Chapter 4 explains how the money supply is determined in a currency board system, and contrasts it with how the money supply is determined in a central banking system. Chapter 5 describes two approaches to establishing a currency board. One approach is to convert the Central Bank of Russia into a currency board. The other approach is to establish the currency board as the issuer of a parallel currency to the Central Bank rouble. (A parallel currency is one that circulates extensively alongside another currency. The parallel currency can have a fixed, pegged, or floating exchange rate with the other currency, and can circulate legally or illegally.[20]) If the currency board is the issuer of a parallel currency, its currency will circulate officially alongside the Central Bank rouble at the market rate of exchange, much as foreign currency now does unofficially. This book calls the currency issued by the currency board the currency board rouble, though it can be called something else if the name 'rouble' is disadvantageous.

The proposed Russian currency board will issue notes and coins backed 100 per cent by foreign reserves in a reserve currency such as the US dollar, the German mark, or gold, and will exchange its roubles for the reserve currency at a truly fixed exchange rate. It can obtain its initial foreign reserves in several ways. Chapter 5 describes how to calculate the appropriate size of the initial foreign reserves of the currency board and how to obtain the initial foreign reserves.

Chapter 6 explains how to operate a currency board. It also contains ideas about ways to protect the currency board from political pressure, in particular from pressure to convert the currency board into a central bank. Furthermore, it suggests how a currency board system can deal with a reserve currency that becomes unstable. Chapter 7 discusses problems with the Russian monetary system that need to be solved in any comprehensive monetary reform, and explains how establishing a currency board will provide a framework within which Russians can solve the problems. Chapter 8 responds to objections to a currency board in Russia. Chapter 9 describes how Russian governments have achieved successful monetary reforms in the past by using approaches like those we advocate. Chapter 10 summarizes our proposals.

The appendices contain a model constitution for the proposed Russian currency board, a more detailed explanation than chapter 4 of how the money supply is determined in a currency board system, and a list of countries that have had currency boards.

Our proposals are designed for the particular conditions of Russia today, but the essentials of the currency board approach are also applicable in other former Soviet republics, most of which are suffering the same combination of extreme inflation and severe economic decline now afflicting Russia.

2

THE CASE AGAINST THE CENTRAL BANK OF RUSSIA

The previous chapter argued that relying on the Central Bank of Russia is likely to result in slower, less successful reform of the Russian economy than would occur if Russia had a currency board. This chapter and the next add detail to the argument. This chapter considers general theoretical and practical arguments against using the Central Bank of Russia as a means of trying to provide a sound currency now and in the foreseeable future. The arguments apply to any typical central bank, not only the Central Bank of Russia. This chapter also untangles some confusions that have arisen because economists and politicians assumed that a central bank is the only means by which macroeconomic stabilization can be achieved. Many problems of stabilization that occur in a typical central banking system do not occur in a typical currency board system. The next chapter considers historical factors particular to central banking in Russia that have created additional problems in the current Russian monetary system not found in many typical central banking systems.

THE FUNCTIONS OF MONEY, AND HOW WELL THE ROUBLE PERFORMS THEM

Consideration of the performance of a monetary system must begin with consideration of the functions of money. Money functions as a medium of exchange, store of value, and unit of account. A sound currency fulfils all three functions satisfactorily and enables participants in a market economy to make decentralized exchanges efficiently. A sound domestic currency is crucial for Russia today because the Russian government is trying to replace the vestiges of central planning with decentralized exchange in markets. Without a sound currency, decentralized exchange cannot reach its full potential. A currency that suffers extreme inflation reduces the efficiency of decentralized exchange and hence decreases the efficiency of a market economy.

The rouble is at present an unsound currency that fulfils none of the three functions of money satisfactorily. It is an inadequate medium of

21

exchange: the outside world refuses to accept the rouble. That impedes foreign investment and trade, and hence the growth of the Russian economy. And within Russia, the inefficiency of the Central Bank of Russia in transferring payments between deposit accounts has resulted in a proliferation of commodity exchanges, which allow enterprises to conduct trade in barter and avoid the banking system.

The rouble is an unreliable store of value: extreme inflation makes its precise value unpredictable, though it is currently depreciating rapidly. As a result, Russians save by hoarding commodities or relatively stable foreign currencies, which retain value better than the rouble. Such hoarding is rational because of the rapid depreciation of the rouble, but costly compared to being able to use a sound domestic currency. Hoarding of commodities diverts goods from use by their ultimate consumers into the stockpiles of enterprises and middlemen. Hoarded bricks, for instance, could be used to build apartments instead of piling up at construction sites. Hoarding existed in the centrally planned economy because central planning created shortages of goods (Shmelev and Popov 1989: 133–5, 305); it persists in the emerging market economy because the rouble is not a reliable store of value. Even vodka has become a substitute store of value (Albright 1991).

As for hoarding of foreign currency, the Soviet central bank estimated in November 1991 that Soviet citizens, mainly persons in Moscow and St Petersburg, held approximately US$3 billion[21] of foreign notes, mainly US dollars and German marks. Because of the extreme inflation in the rouble that has persisted since, Russians now almost certainly hold more than $6 billion in foreign notes, which exceeds the value of the supply of rouble notes. Acquiring foreign notes requires Russians to give up goods and services to obtain pieces of paper that Western central banks print at almost no cost. It creates a perverse form of foreign aid that flows from Russia to Western central banks. Besides holding foreign notes in Russia, Russian enterprises and individual persons hold bank deposits, securities, and real estate abroad, usually in violation of existing foreign-exchange controls. As much as $19 billion of foreign-currency earnings may have left Russia in 1991 alone (Institute of International Finance 1992). (An alternative estimate places the flight at $2 billion from January to September 1991, or $2.7 billion on an annual basis [IMF 1992b: 33 n. 33].) Foreign bank deposits earn interest, so unlike holding foreign notes they do not generate a perverse form of foreign aid, but they reduce the capital available in Russia to help modernize the Russian economy.

The rouble is an unsatisfactory unit of account: extreme inflation is distorting the structure of prices in Russia and is making economic calculation very difficult. Most nominal prices are not yet indexed to inflation or to the exchange rate of the rouble. Consequently, real prices fluctuate widely because sellers have difficulty estimating the effect of inflation, not because of underlying real changes in supply and demand. The competitiveness of Russian industrial products in world markets consequently experiences large fluctuations caused entirely by inflation, making it difficult for Russian industries to plan production for export markets and to earn foreign currency. An example of the effect of extreme inflation is that prices of energy, which are still controlled by the government, have followed a sawtooth pattern in real terms. The government steeply increases the nominal prices of energy at irregular intervals, but the real prices then diminish as extreme inflation continues (World Bank 1992b: 178, 314). Another example of the effect of extreme inflation is that prices for the same good vary widely within the same city in Russia, and by as much as ten times across regions (IMF 1992c: 10).[22] Large fluctuations in real prices caused by extreme inflation provide inconsistent signals, making it very difficult for Russians to make accurate accounting calculations and for participants in the emerging market economy to allocate resources efficiently.

Despite extreme inflation in the rouble, Russians continue to use the rouble to some extent, mainly because the Russian government uses the rouble in payments and accounts, and requires most payments to the government to be made in roubles. The rouble no longer serves as a store of value, but supported by the government, it continues to serve as a medium of exchange and unit of account. Even for those functions, foreign currency has partly displaced the rouble. However, the convenience of the rouble as a medium of exchange is such that Russians have until now been willing to bear a tax in the form of depreciation. If the rouble is used only as a medium of exchange, and not as a store of value, the tax is not as high as it may first seem. For example, if the rouble depreciates 20 per cent a month (that is, inflation is 25 per cent a month), by holding roubles for only a week on average, Russians can confine the depreciation tax to approximately 5 per cent per transaction, since a week is approximately one-quarter of a month (see Keynes 1971 [1923]: 44). It is worth paying 5 per cent per transaction rather than resort to barter, which usually has wider spreads than 5 per cent between prices bid and prices offered. It may not be worth paying 10 or 15 per cent per transaction to use roubles, though, so if inflation continues to increase, the rouble will cease to be used as a medium of exchange. When that happens, it will also cease to be used as a unit of account, just as it has already ceased to be used as a store of value.

STABILITY AND CREDIBILITY

The rouble is not now a sound currency. To understand more precisely how a sound domestic currency would benefit the Russian economy, the next few sections elaborate the connection between each of the qualities of a sound currency enumerated in the previous chapter – full convertibility, credibility, and stability – and the corresponding functions of money – as a medium of exchange, store of value, and unit of account, respectively.

A currency's usefulness as a unit of account depends on its stability. Stability means that current annual inflation in consumer and wholesale prices is relatively low, usually in single digits. We will combine discussion of stability with discussion of credibility. Credibility means that the issuer creates confidence that it will keep future inflation low. The concept of credibility in a sense compresses expectations of the future stability of the currency into the present. A currency's usefulness as a store of value depends on its credibility. (A later section in this chapter discusses the connection between the third function of money – a currency's usefulness as a medium of exchange – and full convertibility.)

Central banks everywhere have difficulty achieving credibility. The difficulty is especially severe in developing countries, because central banks there experience very strong political pressure for inflation. For the 101 developing countries reporting to the World Bank, average annual inflation in consumer prices was 16.7 per cent from 1965 to 1980 and 61.8 per cent from 1980 to 1990. The comparable figures for the 24 developed countries reporting to the World Bank were 7.7 and 4.5 per cent (World Bank 1992a: 219). From 1971 to 1990, 26 developing countries had inflation of 20 to 80 per cent a year for at least five years, 14 had inflation exceeding 80 per cent a year for at least two years, and 14 had inflation exceeding 200 per cent a year for at least one year (Goldstein *et al.* 1992: 7). No developed country except Israel had similar levels of inflation.

The Central Bank of Russia faces special problems achieving credibility because it and its predecessors have longstanding records, extending back to the mid-1800s, of providing an unsound currency (see chapter 3 and Solimano 1991). The Central Bank of Russia also suffers from the low esteem the Russian public has for existing government institutions, which under Soviet rule were tools for oppressing most of the population. The officials in charge of the Central Bank of Russia are former Communist Party officials, and the powers of the Central Bank are much the same today as they were during the last days of Soviet rule. Extreme inflation and other recent monetary events have reinforced the Russian public's distrust of the Central Bank.

Lack of credibility typically contributes to high open inflation and high real interest rates (in monetary systems without price or foreign-exchange controls) or repressed inflation and artificially low real interest rates that cause shortages of credit (in monetary systems with price controls or restrictions on convertibility, such as Russia). For example, because attempts by the Central Bank of Russia to stabilize the rouble have not been credible, prices in Russia have increased rapidly. Workers have based their demands for wages on the expectation that the Central Bank would depreciate the rouble. State enterprises and government ministries have incurred deficits because they have expected that the Russian parliament and the executive branch of the Russian government would rescue them by pressuring or passing laws ordering the Central Bank to finance the deficits. Such behaviour has created momentum for continued inflation.

In a typical central banking system without price controls or restrictions on convertibility, high real interest rates accompany high inflation. To compensate investors for the exchange risk of using a currency prone to depreciation, real interest rates for borrowers without access to subsidized credit typically must be high. High real interest rates stifle economic activity by increasing the cost of borrowing. In a typical central banking system with price or foreign-exchange controls, such as Russia, the central bank keeps domestic real interest rates artificially low, discouraging saving and causing shortages of credit at existing, controlled nominal rates of interest. Ideally, real interest rates in truly unrestricted markets for credit should typically be positive but low, to encourage savings yet not stifle economic growth.

In contrast to a typical central bank, a typical currency board has high credibility, for reasons explained in the previous chapter. A typical currency board system tends to have low inflation because its reserve currency has low inflation. Also, because a fixed exchange rate with the reserve currency eliminates exchange risk with that currency, a typical currency board system tends to have interest rates similar to the levels prevailing in the reserve currency, plus an allowance for political risk (the risk that private property rights will not be enforced or that the government will seize private property), taxes, and transactions fees.[23]

CREDIBILITY AND EXCHANGE RATES

The degree of credibility of a monetary system affects the type of exchange-rate arrangements that are sustainable for it. An exchange-rate arrangement that is not credible tends not to be sustainable because it imposes high costs on the economy.

There are three basic types of exchange-rate arrangements. To reiterate terms introduced in the previous chapter, a pegged exchange rate is constant for the time being in terms of a reserve currency, but carries no credible long-term guarantee of remaining at its current rate. A pegged exchange rate should not be confused with a fixed exchange rate.[24] A fixed exchange rate is permanent, or at most can be altered only in emergencies. A floating exchange rate is not maintained constant in terms of any reserve currency.[25]

The main difference between a fixed exchange rate and a pegged exchange rate is credibility. A typical central bank cannot maintain a truly fixed exchange rate because it has low credibility. A declaration by a typical central bank that it maintains a fixed exchange rate is not credible because the monetary rule of a fixed exchange rate conflicts with discretionary monetary policy. The only period when a large number of central banks has maintained truly fixed exchange rates was during the 'classical' gold standard (1880 or before to 1914). At the time, central banking was still relatively uncommon among the monetary systems of the world, and many central banks were owned privately rather than by governments (Conant 1969 [1927]; Schuler 1992a: 21, 40–5). Those conditions, which induced central banks to maintain fixed exchange rates, no longer apply.

Since 1914, almost all central banks that have claimed to maintain fixed exchange rates, including exceptionally good central banks, have in reality maintained pegged exchange rates. Almost all central banks depreciated their currencies against gold or silver during the First World War, the Great Depression, the Second World War, and the breakup of the Bretton Woods system in the early 1970s. Most central banks with pegged exchange rates have also depreciated their currencies individually at other times (for a history, see Yeager 1976: 295–610).

The main purpose of a pegged exchange rate is to make hard budget constraints credible. In practice, though, a pegged rate is typically a depreciating exchange rate, involving devaluation or foreign-exchange controls to accommodate soft budget constraints. The bias towards depreciation creates perverse consequences, which were mentioned briefly in the previous section. As compensation for the perceived risk of depreciation of a pegged exchange rate, lenders and investors demand higher real rates of interest than would exist with a truly fixed exchange rate (Walters 1990: 14–15). It may take years for a typical central bank to achieve substantial credibility for a pegged exchange rate. In the meantime, high real interest rates used to defend a pegged exchange rate create high costs, which are particularly painful to capital-intensive industries and export industries competing against foreign counterparts based in countries with more credible monetary authorities.

High real interest rates (or shortages of credit at artificially low real interest rates) are one perverse consequence of pegged exchange rates; overvalued real exchange rates are another. The real exchange rate is the ratio of the prices of traded goods to the prices of nontraded goods. Traded goods are exports and imports. Nontraded goods are goods such as land and labour, which for various reasons cannot easily be moved from one country to another. There are several ways to calculate price ratios of traded to nontraded goods, but the important thing is that all are intended to show whether exchange rates are systematically affecting the competitiveness of export industries. Overvalued real exchange rates mean that export industries are relatively uncompetitive, whereas undervalued real exchange rates mean that export industries are relatively competitive.[26]

Overvalued real exchange rates in a country with a pegged exchange rate can result from sudden increases in foreign investment, which are discussed in the next section, or, more commonly, from domestic inflation. A typical central bank maintaining a pegged exchange rate tends to inflate, which causes the monetary base to increase faster than its foreign reserves. Consequently, the domestic price level increases. Imports become less expensive and exports decrease because they become more expensive in world markets. The central bank loses foreign reserves as people buy more imports and as currency speculators bet that the loss of foreign reserves will induce the central bank to depreciate the currency.[27] To avoid losing more foreign reserves and to revive exports, the central bank imposes foreign-exchange controls. Alternatively, the central bank devalues the currency, re-pegging it at an exchange rate sufficiently undervalued that for a while the central bank can safely continue to inflate. An undervalued exchange rate revives exports by making them suddenly inexpensive and chokes imports by making them suddenly expensive, but as inflation continues and the exchange rate later becomes overvalued, the opposite effects occur.

For an economy with a typical central bank maintaining a pegged exchange rate, therefore, a pegged rate tends to alternately depress and overstimulate economic activity. Export industries often experience high real interest rate and high costs for the nontraded goods that they use to help produce traded goods. Rather than increase their productivity to remain competitive, export industries often take the easier course of pressuring the central bank to devalue the currency. Political pressure to devalue the currency or impose foreign-exchange controls also comes from government ministries and state enterprises, who desire their soft budget constraints to continue. The incentives facing a typical central bank are such that it usually benefits more by depreciating the currency than by maintaining the existing exchange rate. The clash between the long-term goals and the short-term incentives of central banks is so pervasive that it has a name: 'time consistency' (or 'time inconsistency'; see Kydland and Prescott 1977).

The European Monetary System (EMS) is an example of the problem of time consistency. The EMS is the most ambitious attempt to maintain pegged exchange rates since the Bretton Woods system (which lasted from 1945 to 1973, but which had current-account convertibility of most major currencies only after 1958). In the EMS, member central banks promise to maintain exchange rates within narrow bands against one another's currencies. The EMS began operating on 13 March 1979. As of June 1993, it has had seventeen realignments of rates, most recently in September 1992 (twice), November 1992, and January and May 1993.[28] The realignments have usually been devaluations of other currencies against the German mark, the strongest currency in the system. In the most recent realignments, which occurred after severe speculative attacks, the Italian lira and the pound sterling were floated, in effect devaluing them, and the Spanish peseta, Portuguese escudo, and Irish punt were devalued. The Finnish markka, Swedish krona, and the Norwegian krone, which were outside the EMS but which 'shadowed' the EMS, were also devalued. The Swedish krona was devalued even though the Bank of Sweden at one point increased overnight interest rates to the equivalent of 500 per cent a year to defend the peg (Norman 1992; Norman and Barber 1992). West European central banks lost an estimated $6 billion in September 1992 alone supporting pegged exchange rates (Sesit 1992).

Even better-than-average central banks, such as those of the EMS, have had difficulty maintaining a 'hard' peg, which allows no systematic depreciation. This has induced some central banks to experiment with a 'crawling' peg.[29] A crawling peg is a limited appreciation or depreciation of the currency according to a schedule. For example, a central bank may promise not to depreciate its currency against the US dollar by more than 20 per cent a year. With a decelerating crawling peg, depreciation slows year by year and perhaps eventually stops. A decelerating crawl is implicitly a promise by the central bank to reduce the growth of the monetary base.

A possible advantage of a crawling peg compared to a hard peg is that a crawling peg may be less costly to the economy because it does not try to achieve credibility immediately; instead, the crawl can decelerate to a hard peg when the central bank seems to have enough credibility to maintain a hard peg without high real interest rates or extensive foreign-exchange controls. Another way in which a crawling peg may be less costly to the economy than a hard peg is that if expectations of inflation pervade behaviour and long-term contracts, a crawling peg reduces the shifts of real wealth that occur with a suddenly imposed hard peg.

The main disadvantage of a crawling peg is that it can accelerate, rather than decelerate to a hard peg. Countries that have tried crawling pegs have generally had higher inflation than other countries in their regions that have maintained harder pegs punctuated by occasional devaluations (Connolly 1985). A crawling peg does not change the governance or the incentives of the central bank, so it is little more credible than a hard peg. In addition, countries with extreme inflation, such as Russia, tend to have no long-term contracts in domestic currency because the domestic currency is not a reliable unit of account, so a sudden, credible end to inflation would not cause huge shifts of real wealth.[30] Consequently, a crawling peg has no significant advantage for Russia even compared to a hard peg.

Because most central banks, including most better-than-average central banks, have lacked the credibility to maintain fixed or pegged exchange rates, many economists have advocated floating exchange rates for them. An advantage of a floating exchange rate compared to a pegged rate is that a floating rate requires little credibility, because the central bank makes no promise concerning the exchange rate. The central bank need not worry that lack of credibility will cause it to lose foreign reserves supporting the exchange rate, because it need not support the exchange rate at all.

Another advantage of a floating exchange rate is that in theory, full convertibility can be allowed. There need be no fear that full convertibility will create the perverse consequences that can occur with a pegged exchange rate. In practice, though, most countries with floating exchange rates impose foreign-exchange controls (IMF 1992e: 570–5).

A floating exchange rate can be 'clean' or 'dirty'. In a clean float, the central bank does not try to influence the exchange rate systematically. It is possible to for a central bank to hold zero foreign reserves if it allows a clean float. The Reserve Bank of New Zealand, which has allowed a clean float since 1985 (Moore 1992: 111–12), is apparently the only central bank that has ever allowed a clean float for an extended period. A central bank operating a floating rate typically practises a dirty float, in which it tries to influence the exchange rate systematically by buying or selling foreign currency. Dirty floating could be beneficial if central banks intervened with the goal of making profits, so that they acted as stabilizing speculators in foreign-exchange markets. However, they do not, and they tend to lose huge sums of money trying to counteract depreciation. The Central Bank of Russia, for example, lost $650 million from January to September 1992 (Hays 1992b). Its losses should be seen as part of a long-term pattern on the part of central banks (Taylor 1982).

Even a clean floating exchange rate has disadvantages, as described in more detail in chapter 8. The main disadvantage is that it does not counteract political pressure for inflation from interest groups and ambitious politicians who favour soft budget constraints and short-term considerations. Since the early 1980s, some central banks in developing countries have successfully combined floating exchange rates with low inflation, low real interest rates, and full convertibility, but almost none of them have done so over long periods (Collier and Joshi 1989: 103). The dirty, controlled float of the rouble now maintained by the Central Bank of Russia fits that pattern, combining extreme inflation with extensive restrictions on convertibility.

Another disadvantage of a floating exchange rate is that real interest rates can be high, as they tend to be with a pegged exchange rate, if high inflation appears likely. A typical central bank maintaining a floating exchange rate may encounter difficulties like those of a typical central bank maintaining a pegged exchange rate. A low inflation rate is a 'price-level peg' similar to an exchange-rate peg. Although a central bank needs little credibility to operate a floating exchange rate, it needs substantial credibility to combine low inflation with low real interest rates and full convertibility of the currency. If its credibility is low, real interest rates will be high, although probably not so high as with a pegged exchange rate that has low credibility. (The reason that real interest rates will probably be lower with a floating exchange rate is that speculative pressure on the central bank tends to be less with a floating exchange rate than with a pegged exchange rate, because the central bank has no obligation to maintain a particular exchange rate. With a floating rate, speculators typically engage more in offsetting speculation against each other and less in speculation against the central bank than with a pegged rate.)

Yet another disadvantage of a floating exchange rate is that it requires the central bank to target something other than the nominal exchange rate. However, other targets have problems of definition, control, and appropriateness. Suppose the central bank decides to target the money supply. The central bank must define which measure of the money supply it wishes to control – the monetary base, or broader measures that include components beyond its direct control, such as deposits at commercial banks. The central bank must try to control the measure it has chosen, setting targets and achieving them. It must revise targets to compensate for leads and lags in economic activity and for other factors, such as changes in banking technology and people's habits of holding money that can change the money supply unpredictably. The central bank must also frequently evaluate whether the target it has chosen is appropriate, or whether another target would be more appropriate for encouraging economic growth and price stability. Problems of defining and achieving appropriate targets caused most Western central banks to abandon strict adherence to money supply targets after experimenting with them in the 1980s. However, price levels, interest rates, real growth rates, and nominal income also have problems as targets (see Lindsey and Wallich 1987).[31] The exchange rate is the easiest target to define, control, and evaluate.

Because a typical currency board has high credibility, it can maintain a truly fixed exchange rate. A fixed exchange rate maintained by a currency board avoids the disadvantages of a pegged or floating exchange rate maintained by a typical central bank. A typical currency board need never worry that its foreign reserves are inadequate, because they are equal to 100 per cent or slightly more of its notes and coins in circulation. Because the exchange rate is fixed, lenders and investors tend not to demand high real interest rates as compensation for a perceived risk of depreciation against the reserve currency. A well-chosen reserve currency will be stable, credible, and fully convertible. (Chapter 5 discusses how to choose a reserve currency.) A typical currency board system therefore does not experience the high real interest rates (or, alternatively, shortages of credit at artificially low real interest rates) caused by perceived risk of devaluation in a typical central banking system with a pegged exchange rate and even in some central banking systems with floating exchange rates.

CONVERTIBILITY AND FOREIGN-EXCHANGE CONTROLS

A currency's usefulness as a medium of exchange depends on its convertibility. Convertibility means that the currency can buy domestic and foreign goods and services, including foreign currencies. A centrally planned economy can function with an inconvertible currency because, at least in theory, central planning rather than decentralized exchange in markets coordinates economic activity. A market economy, however, needs a convertible currency to function efficiently. Without a convertible currency, people cannot easily make the decentralized exchanges using money that make a market economy more efficient than a centrally planned economy.[32]

Convertibility has three gradations corresponding to the extent to which a government allows a currency to function as a medium of exchange. The most basic type of convertibility is cash convertibility – the ability to exchange a rouble of bank deposits for a rouble of notes and coins on demand. Cash convertibility is so much taken for granted in market economies that it is seldom discussed, except when bank runs occur. Nevertheless, it does not exist in Russia for enterprise deposits at commercial banks, for reasons explained in the next chapter.

The second type of convertibility is commodity convertibility – the ability to buy domestic goods and services. This, too, is so much taken for granted in market economies that it is seldom discussed. In countries with commodity convertibility, all that is usually required to buy domestic goods and services is cash or credit to pay a domestic seller; domestic trade is little restricted compared to a centrally planned economy. The exchange of goods and services is much more extensive, rapid, and efficient where commodity convertibility exists than where it does not. Russia has been moving towards full commodity convertibility for the rouble, but has not yet achieved it because energy and some other important goods are still largely allocated by quotas rather than prices.

The third type of convertibility is foreign-exchange convertibility – the ability to buy foreign goods and services, including foreign currencies. If no restrictions exist on buying foreign goods and services, including foreign currencies, at market rates of exchange, a currency is said to have full foreign-exchange convertibility. A currency with cash, commodity, and full foreign-exchange convertibility has full convertibility. Foreign-exchange convertibility almost always implies cash and commodity convertibility, so henceforth in this book, full convertibility will be synonymous with unrestricted foreign-exchange convertibility. The currencies of most developed countries are fully convertible, but the currencies of most developing countries are partly convertible or inconvertible. The Hungarian forint and the Polish zloty, for example, are convertible for most current-account purchases, in which residents use domestic currency to buy foreign goods and services for import, but inconvertible for many capital-account purchases, in which residents use domestic currency to buy foreign financial assets such as foreign currencies and securities, and certain nonfinancial assets such as real estate.[33] Restrictions on capital-account transactions are called capital controls. The rouble is at present inconvertible both for current-account and capital-account transactions.

Current-account convertibility exposes domestic producers to foreign competition if trade quotas and tariffs are minor. Hungary, Poland, and other emerging market economies that have introduced partial current-account convertibility have found that it tends to reduce the market power of state enterprises, inherited from the centrally planned economy. Current-account convertibility tends to introduce into the domestic economy the structure of prices that prevails in world markets. World prices are signals that help people to determine which areas of production to specialize in. By specializing in the goods they produce most efficiently, then trading those goods for other goods, wealth increases globally.

Current-account convertibility is helpful for foreign trade, but is insufficient for attracting substantial foreign investment; for that, capital-account convertibility is necessary. Unless foreigners can repatriate some profits, they will usually be reluctant to make large investments.

Almost universal agreement exists that cash and commodity convertibility are desirable in Russia immediately. (Chapter 7 proposes ways of achieving cash convertibility, as well as commodity convertibility with respect to energy prices.) However, many economists have advised Russia to delay full foreign-exchange convertibility (for example, Brada *et al.* 1990: 117–20; Greene and Isard 1991: 12–13, 16; McKinnon 1991: 156; Williamson 1991b: 379). One argument against immediate full convertibility is that it would worsen capital flight, that is, domestic investment would leave Russia on a large scale. Another argument, inconsistent with the first argument, is that immediate full convertibility would allow excessive foreign investment into Russia and would thereby make uncompetitive many Russian export goods produced by existing enterprises. Foreign investment increases the prices of land, labour, and other nontraded goods. Prices of exported goods would then increase because they are made partly from nontraded goods. A large, sudden appreciation of the real exchange rate could make exports uncompetitive, causing a depression (as Ronald McKinnon argues in Hanke and Walters 1991c: 187–9). A third argument against immediate full convertibility is that it would create problems of moral hazard. Chile, Argentina, and Uruguay suffered banking crises in the 1980s after they abolished some restrictions on convertibility. Many enterprises and commercial banks borrowed heavily abroad. Their liabilities were payable in foreign currency but their income was mainly in domestic currency. As real exchange rates appreciated, political pressure from export industries and economic pressure from currency speculators induced the central banks of those countries to devalue. Devaluation steeply increased the burden of debt repayment for enterprises and commercial banks that had borrowed in foreign currency, and bankrupted many. Their governments or central banks rescued them and assumed responsibility for repaying their debts.

These arguments against full convertibility, and the low probability that central banks in most former Soviet republics will soon issue fully convertible currencies, have led some economists to propose that the former Soviet republics establish a clearing or payments union (Brabant 1991a, b; Williamson 1992: 29–30). The proposals envision that the rouble and the currencies of other republics would continue to be partly inconvertible, even for current-account transactions, for at least several more years. In a clearing union, central banks accumulate credits against each other for trades made by residents of their countries, and settle the balances periodically, usually in a fully convertible (hard) foreign currency or gold. A clearing union reduces the foreign currency that a central bank needs to hold because it settles a combined balance with the other members of the union instead of settling many bilateral balances individually. A payments union is like a clearing union except that some member central banks can incur deficits (overdrafts) for consecutive clearing periods instead of fully settling balances in foreign currency or gold at the end of each period. To discourage members of a payments union from incurring persistent deficits, deficits usually must be repaid within a limited period with interest.

A clearing or payments union has historical precedents, most notably the European Payments Union that operated in Western Europe from 1950 to 1958. Advocates of a payments union have claimed that the reserves necessary to establish a payments union among former Soviet republics may be as little as $1.3 billion (Havrylyshyn and Williamson 1991: 58).

The arguments against full convertibility, although perhaps valid for a typical central banking system, are not valid for a typical currency board system. Immediate full convertibility in a typical currency board system is credible, so it tends to encourage a net inflow of capital rather than capital flight. Although foreign investment increases the prices of labour, land, and other nontraded goods, if the investment is used productively, the new higher prices will reflect the increased productivity of those nontraded goods (Schmieding 1992: 196). The experience of currency board systems has been that foreign investment does not cause large, sudden appreciations of the real exchange rate that make exports uncompetitive and cause depressions. International capital movements, like interregional capital movements, tend to be self-correcting if they overreact to opportunities for arbitrage. Immediate full convertibility tends not to create problems of moral hazard in a typical currency board system because a typical currency board is not a lender of last resort. The unhappy experience of Chile, Argentina, and Uruguay with fuller convertibility illustrates the moral hazard created when a central bank is implicitly a lender of last resort to commercial banks and private and state enterprises; it does not illustrate inherent problems of convertibility (Corbo *et al.* 1986: 620–30).

Because the arguments against immediate full convertibility are not applicable to a typical currency board system, a clearing or payments union for Russia and other former Soviet republics seems less advantageous than currency boards in the republics. A clearing or payments union would be cumbersome to operate. It would require continuing restrictions on trade and, compared to a currency board system, would hinder the Russian economy from becoming open to world markets. A clearing or payments union for former Soviet republics would be less useful than the European Payments Union was for Western Europe because in coming years, former Soviet republics will probably reduce their trade with one another and increase their trade with the rest of the world. The rest of the world will not belong to the clearing or payments union and will demand payment in fully convertible currency, gold, or barter (Kenen 1991; Pollak 1991). Furthermore, it would be difficult to devise a suitable form of governance for a clearing or payments union in the former Soviet Union because Russia is larger than the other former republics combined. It has a justifiable claim to dominate a clearing or payments union, while the other republics are understandably wary of Russian domination.

Establishing sound, fully convertible currencies by means of currency boards would avoid those problems, would tend to preserve whatever part of interrepublican trade remains worthwhile for the emerging market economies of the former Soviet republics, and would facilitate trade with the rest of the world (compare Michalopoulos and Tarr 1992: 15).

The historical experience of currency boards supports the view that problems with full convertibility in a typical central banking system are caused by central banking rather than by full convertibility. The North Russian currency board maintained full convertibility from the day it opened, even though Russia was in the midst of civil war (see chapter 9). The currency boards of Hong Kong, Malaya, and the Philippines resumed convertibility into their reserve currencies soon after Japanese occupation during the Second World War ended (King 1957: 23, 109). No mass flight from local currencies into reserve currencies occurred; instead, convertibility encouraged foreign investment. The postwar experience of Hong Kong, the most notable currency board system still in existence, has been that large, uncontrolled increases in foreign investment have not hurt export industries; rather, they have equipped export industries with the tools necessary for growth (Schuler 1992b: 159–61).

The experience of these currency board systems, and the contrast with the typical experience of central banking systems, is part of a pattern. The IMF's *Annual Report on Exchange Arrangements and Exchange Restrictions*, published since 1950, describes restrictions on convertibility in its member countries and some of their colonies. Never have the majority of central banking systems reporting to it had full convertibility. In 1991, only 34 of the 158 countries with central banks that reported to the IMF had full convertibility. Of those, 18 were among the 24 developed countries reporting to the IMF. Only 16 of the 124 developing countries reporting to the IMF had full convertibility (IMF 1992e: 570–5).[34] In contrast, 5 of the 6 currency board systems in existence had full convertibility. One – Hong Kong – reported to the IMF. Of the rest – Bermuda, Gibraltar, the Cayman Islands, the Falkland Islands, and the Faroe Islands – only the modified, atypical currency board system of Bermuda had foreign-exchange controls. Bermuda limits the amount of funds that Bermudians may transfer abroad each year. It is apparently the only currency board system that has ever restricted convertibility into its reserve currency.[35]

CENTRAL BANKING AND DEFICIT FINANCE

The lack of stability, lack of credibility, and restricted convertibility of a currency issued by a typical central bank results from its subordination to financing government budget deficits. In recent years, government budget deficits have been typical of developed and developing countries alike. In 1990, 44 of the 57 developing countries and 15 of the 22 developed countries reporting government budget data to the World Bank had deficits (World Bank 1992a: 238–9). (Countries with currency boards have been exceptions: their government budgets have typically been in surplus.)

Most developed countries have fully convertible currencies and well-developed financial markets, so their governments can finance budget deficits by issuing debt that financial markets hold voluntarily. For example, Italy's government budget deficit has for many years been approximately 10 per cent of GDP. Italy's government budget deficit is approximately 2.5 times as large a share of GDP as the federal government budget deficit in the United States, and is a larger share of GDP than in all but a few developing countries, yet Italy has had much lower inflation than most developing countries (see World Bank 1992a: 218–19, 238–9). Financial markets have so far been willing to hold increasing amounts of Italian government bonds payable in lire.[36] The Bank of Italy has been spared from creating high inflation to finance government budget deficits, so it has had some scope for discretionary monetary policy.

Russia is not like Italy. The market for Russian government bonds is small. The commercial banking system in Russia, as in many other developing countries, is an appendage of government finance. To obtain funds cheaply, the government pays negative real interest rates. Negative real interest rates on rouble savings have caused Russians to abandon the rouble as a store of value and to use foreign currency and commodities instead.

Because financial markets are backward in Russia and other developing countries, their capacity to absorb government debt, even when compelled to do so, is small. That leaves inflation as the main method of financing government budget deficits. The Central Bank of Russia and other central banks in developing countries have almost no scope for discretionary monetary policy because they must create inflation sufficient to finance budget deficits. In Russia, 94 per cent of all loans by the Central Bank from January to mid-September 1992 were made on the instructions of the Russian parliament or of the executive branch of the government (FBIS 1992l). Most of the loans went to finance the deficits of the government and state enterprises. The average interest rate on loans by the Central Bank of Russia to the Russian government in 1992 was 8 per cent (FBIS 1993f).[37] The subordination of the Central Bank and the banking system to government finance keeps the Russian financial system backward, over-regulated ('repressed'), and incapable of mobilizing savings efficiently to encourage economic growth (like financial systems discussed by Fry 1988: 13–16).

The main argument that economists make for preferring a central bank to a currency board in Russia or elsewhere is that a central bank has more flexibility. On theoretical grounds the advantages of central bank flexibility are doubtful, as is explained later in this chapter. But even if the theoretical case for central bank flexibility were correct, a typical central bank in a developing country has little flexibility because it is subordinate to government deficit finance.

A typical currency board cannot finance spending by the domestic government or by domestic state enterprises because it cannot lend to them. It cannot finance domestic government budget deficits, so it avoids subordinating the monetary system to deficit finance.

POLITICAL INDEPENDENCE: AN UNATTAINABLE GOAL

To help the Central Bank of Russia and other central banks to resist political pressure to finance government budget deficits, the IMF and many economists have suggested that they be politically independent (Bofinger 1992: 128; Camdessus 1992: 342; Sachs and Lipton 1992: 46–7). Political independence for a central bank means that its governors, once appointed, have sole control of the monetary base and cannot be fired by the executive or legislative branches of government during their fixed terms of office. It also usually means that the central bank finances itself from seigniorage and lending, rather than depending on the executive or legislative branches of government for funds, and that the executive and legislative branches cannot dictate lending by the central bank. For developed countries, the more politically independent the central bank, the lower inflation tends to be (Alesina 1989).

The Central Bank of Russia is not now politically independent, nor has

Russia ever had a politically independent central bank. But suppose the Central Bank of Russia became politically independent. Evidence suggests that it would not be well protected from political pressure even so. It has been impossible to fully protect central banks from political pressure even in developed countries with long traditions of representative government and separation of powers among the branches of government.[38] Developing countries such as Russia that are still trying to achieve fully representative government and that have no indigenous tradition of separation of powers have found the task even more difficult. Furthermore, political independence does not seem to result in lower inflation for central banks in developing countries (Cukierman *et al.* 1992: 369–76).

A typical currency board, in contrast, can be protected from political pressure, as past currency boards have been. Chapter 6 proposes safeguards to provide maximum protection from political pressure for a currency board in Russia.

INADEQUATE STAFF

Besides the difficulty of protecting the Central Bank of Russia from political pressure, there is also the problem of finding sufficient qualified staff for the Central Bank. Russia has many people who are knowledgeable about central banking in a centrally planned economy, but few people who are knowledgeable about central banking in an emerging market economy. Although staff of the IMF and Western central banks have been teaching techniques of central banking in a market economy to the staff of the Central Bank of Russia (Norman 1991; IMF 1992d: 114), it is doubtful that the staff of the Central Bank could administer an appropriate monetary policy even if they were protected from political pressure.

A typical currency board needs only a small staff. Even though Russia is a huge country, a currency board in Russia will probably need only a few dozen employees, compared to more than 5,000 employees for the Central Bank of Russia.[39] The tasks that the staff of a currency board performs are simple and do not require as much skill as the tasks performed by the staff of a central bank.

FLEXIBILITY: A PROBLEM EVEN IN THEORY

This chapter has emphasized the practical problems encountered by the Central Bank of Russia and other typical central banks. There are also strong arguments against discretionary monetary policy, and hence against a typical central bank, on theoretical grounds. Their gist is that even a central bank that has the flexibility to act according to its best judgment, rather than in response to political pressure, is likely on average to destabilize the economy.

Theoretical arguments against discretionary monetary policy come from three sources. The 'monetarist' school of economic thought emphasizes that long and variable lags can make the effects of discretionary monetary policy unpredictable. Unless the central bank knows approximately how long a lag exists between changes in the monetary base and changes in prices, for example, it can destabilize rather than stabilize the economy by trying to influence economic activity. Hence there is reason to think that discretionary policy on average will have worse results than rule-bound policy, even though in particular cases discretionary policy may get lucky and do better than rule-bound policy (Friedman 1948, 1960; Laidler 1982: 25–34, 153–63, 187–92; Meltzer 1992).

The 'rational expectations' school of economic thought emphasizes that whatever systematic discretionary policy a central bank can administer, people can anticipate and counteract. In fact, many people, such as traders and commercial bankers, can make profits by correctly anticipating the policy of the central bank. Their actions create problems for the central bank because much of the effectiveness of its policies depends on surprise. If people correctly anticipate that the central bank will create higher inflation, they adjust prices and interest rates accordingly, and inflation has no temporary stimulative effect on the economy. The rational expectations school claims that to the extent that a central bank has a systematic policy, people tend to anticipate the policy even if the central bank tries to hide it. The only type of central bank policy that is consistently effective, then, is one of random surprises. On average, random surprises destabilize the economy because they create unwelcome uncertainty. Monetary rules are the best attainable policy given the ability of people to anticipate and counteract the policies of the central bank. Discretionary monetary policy can easily result in higher inflation and lower economic growth than rule-bound policy (Barro and Gordon 1983, Kydland and Prescott 1977, Persson and Tabellini 1990: 19–33).

A related criticism of discretionary monetary policy, made by the 'Austrian' school of economic thought, is that discretionary monetary policy is a type of central planning. Central banking has the same disadvantages as, say, central planning of agricultural production.[40] Central planning suppresses price and quantity signals that convey information to people who have the skill to interpret them correctly. In the monetary system, among the most important signals are changes in reserves. Changes in the balance of payments or in the public's holdings of notes and coins can cause changes in reserves and, through them, changes in the money supply, interest rates, and income (see chapter 4 and Appendix B). Discretionary monetary policy, to be worthy of the name, must try to fight markets as they adjust toward a new set of market-clearing (equilibrium) prices. By doing so, it usually makes adjustment more prolonged and costly. Luck may occasionally enable discretionary monetary policy to have beneficial effects. On average, though, discretionary monetary policy is harmful, because a central bank has no way of knowing in advance, or often even in retrospect, which discretionary policies are beneficial and which are harmful (Selgin 1988b: 85–125).

The monetarist school and the Austrian school emphasize aspects of a central bank's ignorance, whereas the rational expectations school emphasizes a central bank's inability to surprise people with systematic policy. Although none of the three schools has ever considered in detail a currency board as a monetary rule, the arguments of all three schools lend support to the case for currency boards, since currency boards are rule-bound and have no discretion in monetary policy.

Advocates of discretionary monetary policy consider it undesirable for governments to renounce discretionary monetary policy as a possible tool for making real adjustments in national economies. As an example of the benefits that discretionary monetary policy can bring, they appeal to cases in which nominal wages are too high for full employment, yet rigid, so that some people who wish to work cannot find jobs. A central bank, they say, can increase employment by creating inflation. Inflation can reduce real wages and make the domestic currency depreciate against foreign currencies, causing a temporary increase in exports.

When considering the validity of these examples, one must ask why nominal wages are rigid. The reasons are usually that people expect that the central bank will inflate, and that laws give workers who already have jobs special privileges protecting them from competition by unemployed workers. If the central bank and special privileges for already employed workers were abolished, greater incentives would exist for nominal wages to become flexible. Central banking is the problem rather than the solution in the example. Nominal wages have been flexible in Hong Kong and other currency board systems, even though currency board systems have rarely needed flexibility because strong economic growth has resulted in generally increasing real and nominal wages.

A currency board cannot administer a discretionary monetary policy, so its policy is inflexible. Rather than being a disadvantage, though, the inflexibility of a currency board tends to protect an economy from the destabilizing effects of discretionary monetary policy and tends to force wages and prices to be flexible. The case for establishing a currency board or other monetary rule is much the same as the case for establishing a constitution that limits the powers of government. Constraints external to day-to-day politics are necessary to prevent most governments from abridging political freedoms. It is possible for a government to agree to bind itself to constitutional constraints, and to create institutions that successfully enforce the constraints, even though the government would not behave in the same manner if no constitutional constraints existed. Constitutions are desirable because even a government that respects political freedoms at one time may later abridge them unless a constitution establishes them as durable features of political life. The experience of constitutions is far from perfect, but it does support the claim that a constitution is typically more effective than no constitution constraining the powers of representative (democratic) governments.

A currency board is a form of monetary constitution that prevents the domestic government from abridging economic freedoms by levying a high inflation tax not desired by the public. Because a currency board cannot finance budget deficits of the domestic government, the currency board system establishes an implicit low-inflation fiscal constitution. A clever, very determined government can probably find ways to subvert a currency board, just as it can subvert a political constitution, but safeguards proposed in chapter 6 will secure the proposed Russian currency board maximum protection from such scheming and should be sufficient to deter a less than very determined government.[41]

THE EXPERIENCE OF YUGOSLAVIA

The monetary experience of Yugoslavia since 1989 illustrates the problems just enumerated of providing a sound currency in Russia or in any country that has a typical central bank. Yugoslavia designed its 1989 monetary reform with the help of the IMF, of which it had been a member since 1945. The reform was intended to control inflation, which in 1989, long before the Yugoslav civil war began, was 2,720 per cent. On 18 December 1989, Yugoslavia pegged its currency, the dinar, to the West German mark at seven dinars per mark. It allowed partial convertibility of the dinar beginning on 1 January 1990. To maintain the peg, real interest rates on loans by commercial banks increased to approximately 40 per cent per year, compared with 3–4 per cent per year in Germany, because people thought that the National Bank of Yugoslavia would be unable to maintain the exchange rate.

By June 1990, monthly inflation was almost zero. However, inflation in 1990 as a whole was 300 per cent, or approximately a hundred times more than in Germany, because the dinar monetary base increased 169 per cent. The real effective exchange rate (a version of the real exchange rate) of the dinar increased 85 per cent, according to the IMF. The overvaluation of the dinar caused real GDP to decrease 7.6 per cent (IMF 1991: 37; National Bank of Yugoslavia 1991: 10, 31, 34, 36).

The weakest point of the monetary reform was its policy towards bankrupt worker-owned and -managed enterprises and the commercial banks that the enterprises owned. Because the Yugoslav government was unwilling to restructure the enterprises and because their managers could not fire workers, who were the owners, the government ordered the National Bank of Yugoslavia to increase subsidized loans to worker-owned enterprises and their associated commercial banks. Another weak point of the reform was that the law establishing the exchange rate did not make institutional changes to prevent state enterprises and lower levels of government from obtaining credit and depleting the foreign reserves of the central bank. As a result of Yugoslavia's federal structure of government, the National Bank of Yugoslavia was not subject to unified control. Its foreign reserves increased from 50 billion dinars in December 1989 to 88 billion dinars in September 1990, but then decreased to 59 billion dinars by December 1990 (National Bank of Yugoslavia 1991: 22). To prevent a further loss of foreign reserves, on 28 December 1990 the Yugoslav government announced that effective from 1 January 1991 the dinar would be devalued to nine dinars per German mark. Coincidentally, also on 28 December 1990, the Serbian parliament secretly and illegally ordered Serbian state commercial banks to lend 18.3 billion dinars (approximately $1.8 billion) to Serbian state enterprises (Sudetic 1991). When the story of the Serbian action became public on 8 January 1991, the National Bank of Yugoslavia lost its remaining credibility. The Yugoslav government and the National Bank of Yugoslavia did not punish the Serbian government by seizing the assets of Serbian state commercial banks or Serbian state enterprises. Instead, the National Bank of Yugoslavia unsuccessfully tried to support the exchange rate of the dinar against massive sales of dinars for marks and then devalued the dinar from 9 to 13 per German mark on 19 April 1991. Since then, the National Bank of Yugoslavia has devalued the dinar many other times; the market exchange rate of the dinar in the present, smaller Yugoslavia (Serbia and Montenegro) is approximately 500,000 dinars per mark as of early June 1993, and inflation in consumer prices exceeds 200 per cent a month.[42]

The monetary experience of Yugoslavia indicates the path that Russia may follow unless it establishes a currency board. Russia and Yugoslavia share a history of centrally planned economies, communist politics, and a culture atomized by years of government oppression. Like Yugoslavia then, Russia today has a federal structure of government and an unclear division of property and powers of taxation between the central government and lower levels. All of these factors create immense political pressure for continued inflation to finance the soft budget constraints of state enterprises and the government.

3

CENTRAL BANKING AND THE RUSSIAN MONETARY SYSTEM

The previous chapters discussed the Central Bank of Russia as if it were a typical central bank. That is a generous assessment; if anything, the Central Bank of Russia and its predecessors have been worse than average. The history of central banking in Russia is one of currency depreciation and inconvertibility, which have been the dominant monetary traditions. The origin of the present monetary system in those traditions damages the credibility of the Central Bank of Russia and diminishes the likelihood that it can reduce inflation without making real interest rates very high. This chapter sketches the history of central banking in Russia, describes how central banking has shaped the current Russian monetary system, and identifies some of the main problems of the system.

THE HISTORY OF CENTRAL BANKING IN RUSSIA

Central banking began in Russia in 1860, when the government founded the State Bank of Russia by consolidating several bankrupt state commercial banks. As time passed, the State Bank reduced its direct lending to industry and agriculture and became a standard central bank, dealing mainly with the many privately owned banks that came into existence in the late 1800s.

The State Bank also became responsible for issuing rouble notes. Previously, the Ministry of Finance had issued notes. From the time that rouble notes were first issued in 1769, the rouble had maintained a pegged exchange rate with copper or silver only from 1769 to 1777 and 1839 to 1853. The rest of the time the rouble was a depreciated floating currency. Initially the State Bank maintained no pegged exchange rate either. In 1862 the State Bank pegged the exchange rate of the rouble to gold, but returned to a depreciated float for the rouble the next year. The State Bank did not re-establish a pegged exchange rate with gold until 1897 (Arnold 1937: 3–15).

The period of the pegged exchange rate from 1897 to 1914 was one of substantial economic progress, although it was interrupted from 1904 to 1906 by the Russo-Japanese War and the political disturbances that followed. From 1905 to 1906, the Russian government became perhaps the first government to impose modern capital controls (Bloomfield 1939: 58–9). Industrial production increased rapidly during the period of the pegged exchange rate, but agricultural production, which was still the greater share of the Russian economy, increased slowly. Overall production per person and per worker seem to have grown at rates that were average compared to rates in industrial countries, but no faster, so Russia did not begin to catch up with Britain, Germany, or the United States, unlike less agricultural, more heavily industrialized countries such as Sweden and Japan.[43]

The pegged exchange rate ended when the State Bank imposed current- and capital-account controls on the rouble on 9 August 1914, twelve days after the First World War began.[44] The rouble has not been fully convertible since. The czarist government and the provisional (Kerensky) government that replaced it as of 15 March 1917 relied much on inflation to finance their wartime deficit spending. At the time of the Bolshevik Revolution, the purchasing power of the rouble in domestic markets had fallen to 14 per cent of its pre-war level (Arnold 1937: 30, 49).

The Bolshevik Revolution occurred on 6–7 November 1917. On 8 November the Bolsheviks posted soldiers at the State Bank and on 20 November the Bolshevik government seized the State Bank, which had refused to print rouble notes to finance new government spending. On 27 December the government sent soldiers to occupy privately owned banks, decreed banking to be a state monopoly, and decreed that all privately owned banks would be merged into the State Bank. By other decrees of December 1917 and January and February 1918, the government defaulted on all government debt, nationalized foreign banks, confiscated the capital of all privately owned banks, and declared that government officials could open safe deposit boxes and seize the contents (Arnold 1937: 53–71; Nove 1989: 41).

During the civil war that followed the Bolshevik Revolution, all factions, except the White Guard (anti-Bolshevik) government of North Russia, issued currencies that depreciated rapidly. The North Russian government established a currency board (see chapter 9). The monetary policy of the Bolsheviks during the civil war was part of a more comprehensive economic strategy, called, in retrospect, War Communism. It is unclear to what extent War Communism was an improvised wartime programme and to what extent it was a deliberate attempt to immediately establish an ideal socialist economy. Some Bolsheviks claimed that Russia could not establish socialism without passing through a further period of capitalism. Radical Bolsheviks, in contrast, saw War Communism as an opportunity to implement immediately the longstanding socialist goal of replacing money with barter and book-entry credits. The government abolished the State Bank on 19 January 1920 and introduced aspects of a moneyless economy, paying many wages in barter and distributing many goods and services free of charge. At the same time, the government continued to issue rouble notes to finance its spending (Arnold 1937: 70, 88–9; Nove 1990: 55–6, 64–72). (Technically, the government called the Soviet rouble the sovznak, meaning 'Soviet token'.)

Whatever the motives behind War Communism, the economic results were clearly disastrous. To reverse economic collapse, the government in 1921 introduced the New Economic Policy, a partial return to a market economy. The State Bank was re-established on 16 November 1921 and local governments were allowed to establish commercial and cooperative banks. A crucial part of the New Economic Policy was a relatively stable new currency, the chervonets, which the government introduced at a floating exchange rate alongside the existing, depreciating sovznak currency on 28 November 1924. The chervonets was equivalent to ten pre-war czarist gold roubles. It soon became the dominant currency in circulation. The government retired the sovznak from circulation from 7 March 1924 at a rate of 50 billion sovznaks per chervonets, which was equal to 5 billion sovznaks per pre-war rouble. The chervonets was briefly convertible into foreign currency for some purposes (Arnold 1937: 119, 146–215, 262–3, 281–8; see also chapter 9 of this book).

The government reversed the reforms of the New Economic Policy as Stalin and Trotsky gained power. The limited foreign-exchange convertibility of the chervonets (ten new-style roubles) ceased on 9 July 1926, when the government forbade exports of Soviet currency. By a law of 30 January 1930, during the First Five-Year Plan, the commercial and co-operative banks were forbidden to deal with one another without permission from the State Bank, and in effect became no more than branches of it (Arnold 1937: 263, 351–8). The monetary system became a 'monobank', combining the functions of issuing notes and coins, holding the savings deposits of households, and lending to state enterprises.[45] At times the monobank was split into separate banks, but they were no more than administrative subdivisions of it.

The reforms resulting from the 1930 law remain the foundation of the Russian monetary system today.[46] The reforms in effect split the rouble into two types of currency by dividing the monetary system into two financial circuits that had few points of contact. The cash circuit (*nalichnyi*) comprised rouble cash itself (notes and coins) and rouble household savings deposits at the state savings bank. Budget constraints were usually hard in the cash circuit. Rouble cash and household savings deposits were freely spendable on consumer goods, although people usually also needed rationing coupons, permission from the authorities, or a favourable spot in a queue to obtain the goods at official prices. Most producer goods could not legally be purchased with cash, but consumer goods in short supply and producer goods could be obtained in the black market at high prices with cash. No system of chequing accounts existed for state enterprises or households; enterprise payments were made by book-entry transfers, and households usually received wages in cash and paid for goods with cash. The noncash circuit (*beznalichnyi*) comprised rouble deposits of state enterprises and government ministries at state banks, which were not freely spendable funds, but an accounting check for the convenience of central planners. On the one hand, state enterprises could not spend deposits without permission from planners, but on the other hand, planners often created additional funds for state enterprises to buy goods when necessary, so the budget constraints of state enterprises were somewhat soft.

Central planners tried to keep the cash and noncash circuits separate. Household savings deposits were readily convertible into notes and coins. State enterprises, however, typically were not allowed to hold large amounts of notes and coins except to pay workers, nor could they convert their deposits into notes and coins without permission from planners. Enterprise deposits were not as useful as cash for many transactions, so they traded at a discount to cash in the black market. The cash and noncash circuits remain separate today, although the 1987 Soviet Law on State Enterprise and the collapse of central planning have made it easier for state enterprises to evade restrictions on converting enterprise deposits into cash (Aven 1991: 191). As of April 1993 the unofficial exchange rate, although quite variable, is approximately 1.3 noncash roubles per cash rouble.

After the 1930 reform, the next important Soviet monetary reform was the currency conversion of 14 December 1947.[47] The conversion in effect confiscated part of the savings of the Soviet people to eliminate repressed inflation that the State Bank had created during the Second World War. Notes and coins were converted at 10 old roubles per new rouble. Household savings deposits were converted at one old rouble per new rouble up to 3,000 roubles, 1.5 old roubles per new rouble for the next 7,000 roubles, and 2 old roubles per new rouble for roubles after that. Government bonds were converted at 3 old roubles per new rouble. Wages and prices did not change; the average monthly wage at the time was approximately 3,000 roubles (Brabant 1992; Holzman 1955: 206, 232). (Another reform, on 1 January 1961, converted notes and coins, household deposits, enterprise deposits, wages, and prices at 10 old roubles per new rouble, leaving real magnitudes unchanged except that the rouble was, in effect, devalued for purposes of foreign trade [Kuschpèta 1978: 44; Nove 1990: 391].)

Official prices remained relatively stable until 1991. Of course, many official prices did not reflect real supply and demand, so they did not have the same meaning as in a market economy. Because official prices set by central planners were stable, inflation remained repressed in the state sector of the Russian economy; inflation did, however, increase prices in the private sector, such as in the black market. (Even in the black market, the rouble could not readily buy as many goods as foreign currency could.)

Repressed inflation accumulated in the Soviet economy until it became open inflation in 1991.

THE GOVERNMENT BUDGET AND EXTREME INFLATION

Extreme inflation began in 1991, caused by a combination of increasing supply and diminishing real demand for roubles. The Soviet government was unwilling or unable to reduce inflation by reducing its budget deficit. Instead, it tried to reduce inflation by confiscating roubles. On 22 January 1991 the government required the public to convert 50- and 100-rouble notes, then the largest denominations in circulation, into smaller denominations. It was declared that the large-denomination notes were no longer money. Conversions were limited to 1,000 roubles a person, and people with extensive holdings of large notes were questioned about the source of their incomes. Many holders of large notes had apparently been forewarned of the conversion, and had already exchanged large notes for smaller denominations, or got relatives to convert large notes for them. The confiscation did not uncover as many people engaged in illegal activity as the government had hoped, nor did it reduce inflation much: only 3 per cent of the large notes, or 1 per cent of the 140 billion roubles of notes and coins in circulation, were not converted into smaller denominations and returned to circulation (IMF 1992b: 16, 70).

The attempted confiscation of rouble savings by means of the conversion destroyed demand for the rouble as a store of value and began the steep decline of public confidence in the rouble that continues today. The statistics of Tables 3.1, 3.2, and 3.3 summarize the decline of the Russian economy that has accompanied the decline of confidence in the rouble. The trend of economic decline is continuing and the minister of the economy has predicted that industrial production will decrease 10 per cent more in the first half of 1993 (Rubinfien 1992).

The Central Bank of Russia has been at the centre of high inflation and the decline of the economy. It was founded by the Russian government in 1990 as a means for the Russian government to assert autonomy from the Soviet government, but had almost no real power until November 1991, when it acquired most of the staff and the Russian offices of the Soviet central bank, the State Bank of the USSR (Gosbank). It became the owner of the Russian assets of the State Bank when the State Bank was dissolved on 21 December 1991. The Central Bank of Russia issues notes and coins, lends to commercial banks and the Russian government, and regulates the Russian monetary system.

The Central Bank of Russia is not now politically independent, nor has Russia ever had a politically independent central bank. The chairman of the Central Bank of Russia serves at the pleasure of the parliament,

Table 3.1 Exchange rate of the rouble, 1990–3

Roubles per US dollar			
January 1990	10.27	October	73.10
February	12.32	November	110.00
March	no auction	December	169.20
April	13.52	January 1992	230
May	15.91	February	170
June	20.59	March	160
July	24.17	April	143.50
August	24.17	May	113.00
September	no auction	June	144.00
October	22.29	July	161.20
November	20.18	August	205.00
December	22.88	September	254.00
January 1991	26.40	October	398.00
February	36.96	November	447.00
March	36.08	December	414.50
April	37.10	January 1993	572.00
May	37.90	February	593.00
June	42.00	March	692.00
July	50.00	April	823.00
August	51.90	May	1,024.00
September	56.00	June	1,060.00

Note: Exchange rates are those established at the last Moscow interbank auction of each month for noncash roubles. They are controlled rates. Unofficial, uncontrolled exchange rates value the rouble at less than interbank rate.
Sources: IMF (1992b: 84–5), World Bank (1992b: 310–11), press reports.

although in March 1993 the chairman was made a member of the Council of Ministers (the cabinet). The parliament claims ultimate authority over the Central Bank, and can also order it to create credit. (To be precise, 'the parliament' means either of two bodies. The Congress of People's Deputies, which has more than 1,000 members, meets occasionally to vote on important issues. It selects approximately a quarter of its members to form the Supreme Soviet, which meets in the interim and does most of the day-to-day legislative work.) The accountability of the Central Bank is fiercely contested by the executive branch and the parliament, each of which desires the Central Bank to be accountable to (and controlled by) it rather than the other branch.

The monetary policy of the Central Bank has always been subordinate to the finances of the Russian government. As has been mentioned, 94 per cent of all loans by the Central Bank from January to mid-September 1992 were made on the instructions of the parliament or at the request of the executive branch of the government (FBIS 1992l). From January to mid-September 1992, the Central Bank lent the government 822.5 billion roubles to finance the government budget deficit. The average interest rate of the

Table 3.2 Important Russian economic statistics, 1990–3

	December 1990	September 1991	December 1991	March 1992	June 1992	September 1992	December 1992	March 1993
Cash outside bank (billion roubles)	76.4	123.5	167	240	575	898.6	1,650	
Rouble deposits (billion roubles)	425.4	608.5	827	1,075				
Foreign-currency deposits (billion roubles)	8.1*	9.5*	203	319				
Total money supply (billion roubles)	509.9	741.5	1,201	1,633			7,100	
Roubles per US dollar	22.88	56	169.2	160	144	254	414.50	692
Money supply (billion US$)	22.3	13.2	7.1	10.2			17.1	
Enterprise arrears (billion roubles)			39	780	3,200	600	29	6,000
Average wage (roubles/month)	275.2	600	1,200		4,400	7,200	16,000	
Average wage (US$/month)	14.73	10.71	7.07		30.55	28.35	38.60	
Nominal annual GDP (billion roubles)	626.3		727.8				15,000	
Real GDP growth (per cent, year over year)	0		– 13.0				–18.8	–17
Consumer price inflation (per cent, year over year)	5.6		90.4	612	1,300		2,600	
Wholesale price inflation (per cent, year over year)	3.0		138.0	1,740	1,460		3,400	
Government spending (per cent of GDP)	30.6**		47.9				43	
Budget deficit (per cent of GDP)	5.7		30.9				12	

Sources: FBIS (1992b, 1993b), IMF (1992b, 30, 41, 58, 67, 84; IMF 1992n, 1993b), Whitlock (1992: 33–4), World Bank (1992b: viii-ix, 291, 297–8, 307, 310–11, 314), press reports. The original sources for most of these statistics are reports by Goskomstat and Roskomstat.
Notes: Statistics may not be reliable. Statistics of real GDP growth exaggerate the decline of the Russian economy because they omit much undetected activity. Budget deficit includes the deficit of the government itself and of state enterprises.
*Foreign-currency deposits are valued at the official rate of 1.8 roubles = $1 for December 1990 and September 1991.
** Soviet Union as a whole.

Table 3.3 Important monetary events in Russia, 1991–3

22 January 1991	Government withdraws 50- and 100-rouble notes from circulation.
9 April	Moscow Interbank Currency Exchange opens.
1 May	Russian government establishes alternative banking system to Soviet system.
19 June	Official of State Bank of the USSR (Gosbank) says government will be unable to make rouble internally convertible in January 1992.
19–21 August	Attempted military coup.
10 October	IMF managing director urges long-term aid for Russia.
27–28 October	Western countries meet with prime ministers of Soviet republics on foreign debt of Soviet Union.
2 December	Bank for Foreign Economic Affairs of the USSR (Vneshekombank) halts sales of foreign currency to Soviet citizens.
19 December	Bank for Foreign Economic Affairs depletes foreign reserves.
21 December	State Bank of the USSR is dissolved; replaced in Russia by Central Bank of Russia.
2 January 1992	Many prices liberalized or deregulated in Russia.
4 January	Western creditors agree to defer repayment of principal on debt of former Soviet Union.
24 February	Russian minister of the economy predicts rouble will continue to strengthen (as it has recently on selling of dollars by Central Bank of Russia).
1 March	Temporary 'coupon' currency of Ukraine enters widespread circulation.
1 April	Western countries announce $24 billion aid package for Russia, including $6 billion rouble stabilization fund administered by IMF.
23 April	IMF warns Russian government not to delay reform, since that may delay ability to draw on rouble stabilization fund.
5 May	Senior Russian government official says rouble will be fully convertible by 1 August, pegged at 80 roubles per dollar with help of IMF rouble stabilization fund.
10 May	Chairman of Central Bank of Russia says full convertibility of rouble will be delayed from planned date of 1 August until autumn.
1 June	Russia becomes a member of IMF. Chairman of the Central Bank of Russia resigns.
20 June	Estonia becomes first former Soviet republic to completely replace the rouble with a domestic currency.
1 July	Official multiple exchange rates end as rouble begins a controlled float. Central banks of former Soviet Union adopt system of bilateral accounts as rouble zone collapses.
5 July	IMF lends Russia $1 billion.
12 July	IMF says rouble stabilization fund will not be established until early 1993.
14 July	Law on Currency Regulation, adopted by Russian parliament, legalizes payment in foreign currency for some purposes.
August–September	Central Bank of Russia lends hundreds of billions of roubles to cancel arrears of state enterprises.

Table 3.3 continued

2 September	Central Bank of Russia says it has spent $650 million in 1992 to support the rouble and will spend only $100 million more.
13 September	IMF official urges more loans for Russia.
6 October	American law signed allowing American quota increase at IMF to be used to establish currency boards.
12 November	Ukraine completely replaces the rouble with 'coupon' currency.
16 March 1993	Chairman of Central Bank of Russia becomes a member of Council of Ministers.
2 April	Western governments agree to delay payment of $15 billion of foreign debt of Russian government.
April	Russian government announces plans to index wages, pensions, and savings deposits.
15 April	Western countries announce $43 billion aid package for Russia.
May	IMF reverses position on rouble zone and now favours introducing independent national currencies in former Soviet republics.

Sources: IMF (1992b) *Financial Times Index*, National Newspaper Index (United States).

loans in 1992 was 8 per cent, and more than half of the loans were made for longer than ten years, making them virtually a gift (FBIS 1993f).

ENTERPRISE ARREARS

Besides financing the deficit of the Russian government (and some deficits of local governments [Wallich 1992]), the Central Bank of Russia has financed the other component of the overall government budget deficit, the deficits of unprofitable state enterprises. Some of the deficits of state enterprises have been in the form of enterprise arrears, which in Russia are defined as debts to other state enterprises that are more than two months overdue.

Enterprise arrears were not a problem until 1992. They were tiny in the centrally planned economy. The Soviet banking reform of 1930 forbade state enterprises to extend credit to one another without the permission of the State Bank of the USSR (Arnold 1937: 351). The purpose of the reform was to enable central planners to exert more control over state enterprises. The reform was quite effective in achieving its purpose.

However, enterprise arrears have become a problem recently because the Russian economy is neither a tightly controlled centrally planned economy nor a full-fledged market economy. In a full-fledged market economy, enterprises grant credit to other enterprises at their own risk. In Russia, in contrast, the government implicitly guarantees enterprise credits because state enterprises currently are not treated as autonomous from the government. State enterprises in Russia have granted credit to one another with little regard for the credit-worthiness of the debtors, confident that the Russian government would eventually pay the debts of other state enterprises. Because the government implicitly guarantees enterprise credits, state enterprises that produce goods for which demand has decreased, such as military goods, extend credit to one another as a way of temporarily maintaining demand. Enterprise credits enable state enterprises to bypass credit limits that the government imposes on state commercial banks. The government has eventually paid uncollectable enterprise arrears, by ordering the Central Bank of Russia to lend to state commercial banks at negative real rates of interest. The state commercial banks have then re-lent the funds to state enterprises, also at negative real rates of interest. Enterprise arrears have therefore become an important source of soft budget constraints in the Russian economy, because the Central Bank has been a lender of last resort to state enterprises through state commercial banks.

Another reason that enterprise arrears exist is that they are a means of bypassing the payments system. By bypassing the payments system, state enterprises evade collection of value-added and profits taxes, which the government collects by diverting funds from enterprise deposits in state commercial banks to its own account. State enterprises cannot bypass the banking system completely, though: they must convert some of their deposits into notes to pay workers, so the government is able to collect some taxes through state commercial banks (Ickes and Ryterman 1992: 2, 21; Whitlock 1992: 35; World Bank 1992b: 19–20). The payments system is discussed in more detail later in this chapter.

Enterprise credits in their present form, implicitly guaranteed by the Russian government, promote waste of resources. Demand at the end of the chain of production by consumers or the government no longer exists for goods produced by many state enterprises, but the resources used to make the goods are being withheld by state enterprises in the beginning or the middle of the chain of production because enterprise credits are artificially maintaining demand. Withholding of resources from the market decreases supplies, creating artificial shortages that increase prices (Ickes and Ryterman 1992: 354).

The moral hazard implicit in the Central Bank of Russia's role as a lender of last resort and the desire of state enterprises to avoid the banking and payments system have caused rapid growth in enterprise arrears, which increased from 39 billion roubles at the beginning of 1992 to 3,200 billion roubles by the summer (Whitlock 1992: 35). The Central Bank responded by lending at least 500 billion roubles in August and September 1992 to state enterprises to cancel the arrears (Whitlock 1992).[48] The loans were made to state commercial banks, which were obliged to re-lend them to state enterprises. Interest rates on the loans were no more than 83 per cent, which was much below the rate of inflation. The loans merely replaced enterprise credits with Central Bank credits. In the autumn of 1992 and the winter of 1992–3, enterprise arrears resumed rapid growth; as of April 1993, enterprise arrears perhaps exceed 6,000 billion roubles.

The complexity of the web of state enterprise credits is one factor that makes it difficult to determine accurately the financial condition of state enterprises. (Other factors are the inefficiency of the payments system, existing standards of accounting in Russia, and lack of unrestricted markets for some goods.) Consequently, it is difficult for the Russian government to know which state enterprises make profits and should remain open, and which make the worst losses and should be closed (Ickes and Ryterman 1992: 27). Declaring an unprofitable state enterprise bankrupt could cause a chain of bankruptcies to profitable state enterprises that are creditors to the unprofitable enterprise and to one another. Bankruptcy could also affect private enterprises that supply state enterprises. Problems with the arrears of large state enterprises hinder corporatization and privatization of the enterprises.

COMMERCIAL BANKING

Commercial banks are the only significant financial intermediaries in Russia; large, well-established mortgage companies, pension funds, mutual funds, and insurance companies are lacking.[49] Russia has five state commercial banks and more than 1,500 nonstate commercial banks.

In the centrally planned economy, no nonstate commercial banks existed. Each state commercial bank served a specialized clientele, and had a monopoly within its own sector. State commercial banks extended credit almost automatically to state enterprises, if the enterprises had proper documentation that goods had been shipped to other state enterprises that were supposed to pay for the goods. They did not assess the credit-worthiness of borrowers because all loans were guaranteed by the government. State commercial banks were little more than accounting bureaux.

Three former Russian divisions of Soviet state commercial banks remain in existence today as Russian state commercial banks. They are successors to the Soviet banks created during reforms of 1987, which divided the old monobank into somewhat independent parts. The largest state commercial bank, the Savings Bank (Sberbank), formerly had a monopoly of household deposits. The Savings Bank was and still is in the cash circuit of the economy. The Industrial Construction Bank (Promstroibank) and the Agricultural Bank (Rosselkhozbank) served state enterprises in the sectors of the economy indicated in their names. They were and still are in the noncash circuit of the economy, and they accept deposits and make loans.

The Russian government has founded two other state commercial banks. The Bank for Foreign Trade (Vneshtorgbank) was founded in 1991 as a rival to the Soviet Bank for Foreign Economic Affairs (Vneshekombank). Although large, it has no special importance, because the monopoly of foreign-exchange dealing that the Bank for Foreign Economic Affairs formerly had has been abolished; dozens of nonstate commercial banks are now allowed to deal in foreign exchange (IMF 1992c: 92–4). Legislation to establish the Russian Bank for Reconstruction and Development became law on 31 December 1992. The purpose of the Bank for Reconstruction and Development is to finance sectors of the economy favoured by the government (FBIS 1993a).

Two former Soviet state commercial banks no longer exist in their previous form. The Social Housing Bank (Zhilsotsbank) was broken up into several smaller nonstate banks in mid–1991. The Bank for Foreign Economic Affairs (Vneshekombank), which formerly had a monopoly of foreign-exchange dealing, is in liquidation; it continues as the manager of the foreign debt of the former Soviet Union, but seeks no new business. Its deposits have been frozen since December 1991, when the Soviet government in effect seized the foreign currency belonging to depositors to pay the government's foreign debt. The Russian government has promised to issue foreign-currency bonds paying 3 per cent interest a year to the depositors (Boulton 1993).

Competition among state commercial banks remains limited because they have retained their old relationships with many customers and have not aggressively sought new customers. The Agricultural Bank has begun to compete with the Savings Bank for deposits, but most of the Agricultural Bank's branches are in the countryside, where only a minority of the population lives (World Bank 1992b: 109). As of April 1993, interest rates paid by the Savings Bank and the Agricultural Bank on time deposits are 20–60 per cent a year, although the Russian government has promised to index the rates to inflation. The State Bank formerly lent its deposits to the Ministry of Finance for centralized allocation, but since late 1991 it has lent its new deposits to households or to other commercial banks in the interbank market.

The Central Bank of Russia lends to state commercial banks at steeply negative real interest rates. As of April 1993, the Central Bank's maximum nominal interest rate for loans to state commercial banks is 100 per cent a year. State commercial banks must re-lend the loans from the Central Bank at a premium not more than 3 per cent above the Central Bank rate. Old relationships between state commercial banks and state enterprises are solidified by the access of the state commercial banks to credit from the Central Bank at negative real rates of interest. State commercial banks remain little more than conduits for subsidies to state enterprises. Officially, individuals and private companies receive few loans from state commercial banks (IMF 1992c: 17–18), but by paying bribes, the private sector can divert some loans from state enterprises.

More than 1,500 nonstate commercial and cooperative banks have been established in Russia according to the provisions of the 1988 Soviet Law on Cooperatives and the 1990 Soviet Law on Banks and Banking Activity. Some nonstate commercial banks are former branches of state commercial banks. Many nonstate banks have state enterprises as their largest stockholders, depositors, and borrowers, so although they are not directly owned by the government, they are not privately owned in the sense that most Western commercial banks are. The rules separating state from nonstate financial activity are unclear, and the commercial banking system remains in effect socialized. State enterprises use the commercial banks they own to obtain loans from the Central Bank at negative real interest rates and to evade the separation between the cash and noncash financial circuits. Nonstate commercial banks are not clearly in either circuit, though they tend more towards the noncash circuit.

The government abolished interest rate ceilings on 1 January 1992, so nonstate commercial banks can offer depositors and charge borrowers higher interest rates than state commercial banks. As of April 1993, state and nonstate commercial banks pay no or very low interest on demand deposits. Annualized interest rates on interbank loans are 100–150 per cent, which is at least 1,000 per cent less than the rate of inflation. This suggests a lack of effective competition among commercial banks. Regulations imposed by the Central Bank of Russia reduce competition, for example by hindering nonstate banks from opening branches (IMF 1992c: 18; World Bank 1992b: 106–12; Aukutsionek and Belyanova 1993). Opportunities for lending are limited for nonstate banks because prospective borrowers have little collateral to offer, since most property remains owned by the state. Nonstate commercial banks are mainly vehicles for speculation in commodities, property, or whatever other short-term investments seem attractive. They do not make long-term loans because of the high and variable rate of inflation. Perhaps 80 per cent of all commercial banks in Russia have capital of less than 50 million roubles, and the real value of their capital is shrinking as extreme inflation continues (Whitlock 1993: 27).

The Central Bank of Russia imposes a reserve requirement of 20 per cent on all commercial banks except the Savings Bank, which is subject to a different reserve requirement. Commercial banks hold the reserves as noninterest-earning deposits at the Central Bank (World Bank 1992b: 113).

Commercial banking techniques in Russia are primitive. Cheques were only introduced recently and account for less than 5 per cent of transactions (World Bank 1992b: 115); no system of household chequing accounts exists. Russia has few persons with the training to operate Western-style banks. It also has few accountants with Western-type skills; according to Russian estimates (which seem too high to us), there are 2 million accountants who need to retrain from scratch, and Russia needs 100,000 chartered accountants (Jack 1992; World Bank 1992b: 258). International organizations and Western governments are making extensive efforts to train the staff of the Central Bank of Russia and commercial banks in the rudiments of credit assessment, Western standards of accounting, and management (Norman 1991; IMF 1992d: 114).

THE PAYMENTS SYSTEM

The system for making monetary payments, which is operated by the Central Bank of Russia, is very inefficient. In many banking systems, such as that of Canada, commercial banks settle payments without involving the central bank, except perhaps at the final stage. Suppose depositors at Bank A deposit $100 million of cheques or other payment orders payable on Bank B, and depositors at Bank B deposit $90 million of cheques payable on Bank A. The banks exchange cheques and Bank B pays Bank A $10 million, the difference in their settlement (clearing) balance. If there are other banks – call them C, D, and E – all may settle their balances multilaterally, with each bank calculating what it owes to the others as a group. To take a simple case, suppose the situation between Banks A and B is the same as before, but Bank A owes Bank C, D and E a total of $10 million, whereas Bank B is owed a total of $10 million by Banks C, D and E. Then Bank B pays Bank A nothing, which saves Bank B from holding $10 million of reserves. The Central Bank has a role in settlement only at the end, if at all. To make settlement, commercial banks may instruct the Central Bank to transfer deposits at the central bank (commercial bank reserves) from the account of one commercial bank to the account of another.

Central banks in some countries are more intimately involved in the payments system than they are in the foregoing example, without significant bad effects. The Central Bank of Russia, however, is too much involved in the payments system. It settles book-entry payments made between state enterprises as well as regular payments made to or from household savings accounts, such as rent payments. Most payments throughout Russia, except payments between depositors at the same branch of a commercial bank, are made through the Central Bank. Every branch of every commercial bank must have a separate clearing account with the Central Bank. In the Western payments system, in contrast, commercial banks have a single clearing account for the whole bank, which makes settlement or payments more efficient and rapid.

The volume of payments has increased as the number of private firms has increased, state enterprises have been divided into smaller units, and the number of commercial banks has increased. The capacity of the payments system has not kept pace. Consequently, payments between banks in Moscow take several days to more than three weeks. Payments between banks not in the same region are routed through Moscow. They can take months, by which time inflation has destroyed much of their real value (Sachs and Lipton 1992: 45; World Bank 1992b: 115, 138 n. 4). For example, with inflation of 25 per cent a month, at the end of three months a fixed nominal payment loses 58 per cent of its initial real value. The inefficiency of the payments system gives Russians an incentive to delay payments and claim that the payments are in transit. In contrast, in the United States, Canada, and Brazil, the largest Western countries, all payments clear within two days. Western payments systems are so much faster in part because they rely on electronic transfer of funds rather than relying on the mail like the Russian payments system (IMF 1992a: 8–9; Summers 1992: 10).

The inefficiency of the payments system has also made the system vulnerable to fraud (FBIS 1992i). But despite losses from fraud, the Central Bank of Russia refuses to change payments procedures drastically or relinquish control of the payments system because it retains an old-style mentality about control of the financial affairs of state enterprises. Furthermore, by slowing payments, the Central Bank increases the float credit outstanding, which it can then lend to the Russian government.

The inefficiency of the payments system is one factor causing demand for rouble notes to increase relative to demand for rouble deposits. Households and enterprises are converting more and more rouble deposits into rouble notes. They dislike payment to their deposit accounts because it may take months to occur. Enterprises are not depositing some rouble notes at state commercial banks because they cannot necessarily convert cash deposits back into cash, and because they wish to evade collection of taxes through the banking system. Enterprise deposits, and even to some extent the deposits of private firms, remain in the noncash financial circuit. Except for the Savings Bank, which remains separate from the noncash financial circuit and whose deposits have full cash convertibility, state commercial banks make no record of whether deposits were made in the form of noncash credit or cash, so even enterprises that deposit cash often cannot withdraw that cash from their bank accounts; instead, they must pay by cheque or other forms of deposit transfer (Sachs and Lipton 1992: 38). At times the supply of notes has not increased as much as the demand, so many state enterprises have occasionally skipped payment of wages to workers. In response to shortages of notes, some cities have at times issued their own notes as substitutes for Central Bank notes (FBIS 1992c). The notes are IOUs, with small or no reserves in roubles or commodities as backing. The inefficiency of the payments system is also inducing enterprises to resort to barter as an alternative to the payments system, by means of the many commodity exchanges that have been established in Russia and other former Soviet republics (Zhurek 1993). Like enterprise credits and use of notes rather than deposits, commodity exchanges also make tax evasion easier.

INTERREPUBLICAN EXCHANGE

The payments system between former Soviet republics is even more cumbersome than the payments system within Russia. Except for Estonia, whose monetary system is described in the next chapter, every former Soviet republic retains the separate cash and noncash financial circuits that existed in the centrally planned economy. The central bank of each republic controls the domestic noncash circuit, but some republics issue no notes themselves and continue to use rouble notes, which are printed only by the Central Bank of Russia. To obtain rouble notes, other republics must achieve surpluses in their bilateral accounts with Russia or obtain loans from the Central Bank of Russia. The Central Bank of Russia charges other republics that use rouble notes a fee of 1 per cent to pay the costs of printing and transporting the notes (IMF 1992a: 25 n. 6). (Rouble *coins* have tended to disappear from circulation because inflation has quickly made their value as metal exceed their face value.)

Trade between republics is paid for by transfers of noncash deposits in bilateral accounts maintained by the Central Banks of the republics. Before the Soviet Union broke up, each republic had a so-called Central Bank. In reality, they were branches of the State Bank of the USSR, with no independence from it. In 1990 and 1991, some republics, including Russia, also established powerless 'shadow' central banks as part of their struggle against the Soviet government. The shadow central banks took control of the branches of the State Bank after the State Bank was dissolved on 21 December 1991. In early 1992 the new central banks honoured all credits created by central banks in other republics, as if they were still subject to unified control. The result was a race to inflate, because republics whose central banks created credits fastest could attract goods from other republics. To prevent diversion of goods to republics that inflated faster, on 1 July 1992 binding bilateral accounts replaced the old system of honouring without limit credits created by central banks in other republics. Now Russian enterprises cannot sell 500 million noncash Russian roubles of goods to Ukraine unless Ukrainian enterprises sell the equivalent of 500 million noncash Russian roubles of goods to Russia within a limited period, for example. The system allows some leeway for balances between zero and set upper limits, in the form of 'technical credits' (overdrafts). Beyond the limits of the technical credits, creditor central banks refuse to honour credits of debtor central banks. Russia has a trade surplus with most other former Soviet republics. To enable them to buy Russian goods, it has lent many of them large amounts. Credits to other republics were as much as 25 per cent of the total loans made by the Central Bank of Russia in 1992 (Hiatt 1993b), although in late March 1993, the executive branch of the Russian government ordered the Central Bank to cease credits to other republics.

The changeover to binding bilateral accounts ended the former unified rouble zone. Notes and cash deposits of republics that do not use rouble notes have floating exchange rates against the rouble and against each other in unofficial markets. Noncash deposits, even of republics that use rouble notes, also have floating exchange rates against Russian and other republican noncash deposits in unofficial markets. Furthermore, noncash deposits in most republics even have floating exchange rates against *domestic* notes and cash deposits in unofficial markets. Some republics have officially established floating exchange rates with the currencies of other republics (*Economist* 1992a, c). The supposedly pegged exchange rates of the currencies of some other republics to the Russian rouble are merely an accounting fiction.

The bilateral accounts are necessary because, except for the Estonian kroon, all successor currencies to the Soviet rouble are at present inconvertible. The inconvertibility of the successor currencies is a cause of the collapse of interrepublican trade. The system of bilateral accounts hinders multilateral trade. In the former rouble zone, for example, Russia could buy 1 million roubles of coal from Ukraine, use the coal to make steel, and sell 1 million roubles of steel to Lithuania. Lithuania could use the steel to make machinery and sell 1 million roubles of machinery to Ukraine. Ukraine, Russia, and Lithuania would each receive 1 million roubles. If separate accounts for each republic had been kept, each would have had a bilateral payments surplus of 1 million roubles with one republic and a bilateral payments deficit of 1 million roubles with another republic, but a net, multilateral payments balance of zero. In the new system of bilateral accounts, if there is no other trade, the trade in the example cannot occur, because Ukraine buys nothing directly from Russia to offset Russia's purchase of coal from Ukraine. In reality, some offsetting trade does occur, but trade between any two republics is rarely perfectly balanced, so some multilateral trade is prevented from occurring. To help revive multilateral trade, Russia and some other former Soviet republics have discussed establishing an Inter-State Bank to operate a clearing or payments union (Boulton 1993).

The Soviet banking system had 81 regional centres and approximately 1,400 local cash settlement centres operated by the State Bank of the USSR to settle payments. As has been mentioned, the State Bank guaranteed all legitimate payments. Many payments formerly made through regional centres are now interrepublican transactions and hence must be settled through bilateral accounts maintained by the Central Bank of Russia in Moscow. That increases the strain on the payments system because it increases the number of steps necessary to make each payment. Russian commercial banks are allowed to accept correspondent accounts from banks in other republics for current-account purchases by people or enterprises in other republics, but they are forbidden to open correspondent accounts in other republics (FBIS 1992d, e; IMF 1992a: 8–9).

Bilateral accounts or a clearing or payments union are necessary in the former Soviet Union at present because people paid in inconvertible currency wish to exchange it quickly, lest it become utterly useless. Bilateral accounts or clearing or payments unions are unnecessary in countries with fully convertible currencies, such as those with currency boards. People paid in convertible currency have confidence that they will be able to use it if they wish to buy goods later.

FOREIGN EXCHANGE; FOREIGN DEBT

The Russian government has abolished many restrictions on exchange into foreign currency that existed during Soviet rule. (Foreign currency in this context means currency issued outside the former Soviet Union, particularly fully convertible currency.) Since 1 April 1991, authorized banks have been permitted to offer foreign-currency accounts and to trade foreign currency among themselves. The Moscow Interbank Currency Exchange opened on 9 April 1991. State enterprises have been allowed to deal in foreign exchange with one another since August 1991. On 1 July 1992 the government 'unified' the various exchange rates in existence and allowed the rouble to begin a controlled float (see Boulton 1992a). However, the rouble remains inconvertible. The government restricts current-account transactions through a system of export licences, though it has promised to abolish most export licences in 1993 (FBIS 1992o). The export licences exist because price controls remain on some goods, particularly energy. Unrestricted ability to export would enable people to buy those goods at controlled prices and sell them for higher world market prices. The government restricts capital-account transactions by limiting the amount of foreign currency that Russians can purchase and by prohibiting them from holding certain foreign assets (see IMF 1992c: 100). Many imports continued to be purchased through centralized agencies and sold at subsidized prices (World Bank 1992b: 18). Consequently, the exchange rate is not yet really unified and the controlled float of the rouble is not yet a real float.

As during the last few years of Soviet rule, exporters are required to sell some foreign-currency earnings for roubles to the Central Bank and to authorized commercial banks. As of April 1993, exporters are required to sell 30 per cent of foreign-currency earnings to the Central Bank and 20 per cent to other authorized banks (FBIS 1992b). The government has discussed making exporters sell all foreign-currency earnings for roubles (Lloyd and Volkov 1992). Sellers of foreign currency receive noncash roubles at the rate determined in auctions on the Moscow Interbank Currency Exchange, but the roubles they receive then accumulate in bank deposits that pay negative real interest rates, whereas foreign-currency deposits usually pay positive real interest rates. The Central Bank of Russia uses the foreign currency from forced sales by exporters to pay some of the foreign debt of the Russian government and to support the rouble on the Moscow Interbank Currency Exchange. The Central Bank has no other regular source of foreign exchange. Officially, all foreign-currency transactions must be made through authorized banks, but an active unofficial market exists in which the cash rouble is worth somewhat less than the noncash, controlled interbank exchange rate. The Moscow Interbank Currency Exchange trades foreign currency worth only 5 per cent of Russia's officially recorded export trade. Exporters hide much of their foreign-currency earnings in banks abroad (World Bank 1992a: 17–18; Hays 1992b).

The Russian government has taken responsibility for all of the foreign debt of the former Soviet Union, in exchange for ownership of certain former Soviet government assets. The Russian government is in default on most of the foreign debt, which totals $86 billion and is all payable in foreign currency.[50] The foreign currency that the government receives from required sales of foreign currency by exporters is insufficient to pay the current foreign debt. Foreign creditors have granted the Russian government several delays in repaying the debt, and the government is negotiating with them for a restructuring of the debt.

RUSSIA AND THE IMF

Western governments and the IMF have tried to help the Russian government and the Central Bank of Russia stabilize the rouble by offering advice and promising to establish a rouble stabilization fund if the Russian government fulfils certain conditions. The IMF has been advising the Russian government on economic reform since October 1991.[51] The Group of Seven (G–7) countries (the United States, Japan, Germany, France, Italy, Britain, and Canada) on 1 April 1992 pledged to lend Russia as much as $10 billion through the IMF.

The IMF offered Russia the opportunity to borrow a general-purpose fund of perhaps $3 billion and a rouble stabilization fund of as much as $6 billion if the Russian government fulfilled certain conditions specified in an agreement made with the IMF in July 1992. The conditions were that by the end of 1992, the government budget deficit should not exceed 5 per cent of Russia's GDP and that inflation should be less than 10 per cent a month (Odling-Smee 1992a: 4–5). The Russian government was unable to fulfil the rather lax conditions specified by the IMF. As of April 1993, the government is trying to negotiate another agreement with the IMF to borrow from the general-purpose fund and the rouble stabilization fund.

It is doubtful that the rouble stabilization fund would truly stabilize the rouble if administered by the Central Bank of Russia. If administered by the Central Bank, the purpose of the rouble stabilization fund would be to help maintain a pegged exchange rate for the rouble. However, as was argued in chapter 2, a pegged exchange rate would probably have perverse consequences because, like a typical central bank, the Central Bank of Russia has low credibility. With a pegged exchange rate, real interest rates would probably have to be very high to compensate lenders and investors for the perceived risk of devaluation of the rouble. The Central Bank would then face a dilemma. It could try to maintain the pegged exchange rate until the peg became credible, but the probable result in the meantime would be frequent speculative attacks on the rouble and low economic growth because of high real interest rates. Alternatively, the Central Bank could devalue the rouble to reduce real interest rates and temporarily increase economic growth, but the probable result would be that Russians would expect further depreciation. Inflation, wages, and prices would increase accordingly, and the Central Bank would validate expectations of inflation by continuing to allow soft budget constraints.

The Central Bank of Russia has already tried and failed to stabilize the exchange rate of the rouble on the Moscow Interbank Currency Exchange, where the Central Bank sells more than one-third of the US dollars traded. From January to early October 1992, the Central Bank lost $650 million supporting the rouble; in that period, the rouble depreciated from 150 per dollar to 342 per dollar (FBIS 1993g; Hays 1992b). Allowing the Central Bank to administer the rouble stabilization fund would probably have similar results. The Central Bank of Russia is an inefficient means of trying to stabilize the rouble. By relying on the Central Bank, the IMF and the Russian government forego the likelihood of rapidly achieving a sound currency, hard budget constraints, and macroeconomic stabilization.

A currency board, in contrast to the Central Bank of Russia, will stabilize the rouble permanently and will be credible. Accordingly, the IMF should focus its efforts on a Russian currency board rather than on the Central Bank. A currency board will tend to impose hard budget constraints on the Russian government and state enterprises. Establishing a currency board will end extreme inflation and will tend to reduce or eliminate the government budget deficit, which are the goals that the IMF desires. The currency board system will establish the credible monetary and fiscal constitution that Russia now lacks.

A currency board can also be a trustworthy monetary authority for other former Soviet republics that wish to use the same currency as Russia. A currency board established according to principles explained in this book will be unable to manipulate the supply of currency board roubles for the political advantage of any group. Republics that wish to form a 'currency board rouble zone' to replace the now-defunct Central Bank rouble zone can do so by establishing a currency board jointly with Russia. The joint currency board can issue a different brand of notes and coins for each participating republic. Each republic will then earn seigniorage from its own brand of notes and coins, but all brands will have a fixed exchange rate with the reserve currency and hence with one another. Alternatively, the republics can establish independent currency boards. Either way, the currency board system will facilitate trade between Russia and other former Soviet republics by creating sound currencies that are internationally acceptable and do not need the present cumbersome system of bilateral interrepublican exchange.

Authorization already exists for the IMF to lend funds to establish a currency board in Russia. The US Foreign Operation, Export Financing, and Related Programs Appropriations Act, 1993 (Public Law 102–391) stipulates that the increase of $12 billion in the American quota (capital subscription) at the IMF may be used to establish currency boards.[52] The funds may be used to establish currency boards in any IMF member country, not only Russia. The IMF would have to approve use of the funds to establish a currency board in Russia or elsewhere, but the Russian government should be able to gain the approval of the IMF to establish a currency board according to the principles explained in this book, especially since the United States is the largest contributor to the IMF.

To summarize the condition of the Russian monetary system, it is backward and uncompetitive. Current conditions offer Russians little incentive to save in roubles; foreign currency or commodities are much better stores of value. Hence, the financial system does not efficiently mobilize domestic savings and allocate them to borrowers. Russia has never had a sustained period of full currency convertibility, and depreciation of the currency has been the norm under czarism, communism, and representative government. Central banking in Russia has a long history of providing an unsound currency. The Central Bank of Russia suffers from the defects that affect any typical central bank and from additional defects peculiar to itself. It has no credibility, is unlikely to achieve credibility in the near future, and is therefore unlikely to be able to stabilize the rouble in the foreseeable future.

4

CURRENCY BOARDS, CENTRAL BANKS, AND THE MONEY SUPPLY PROCESS

Because the Central Bank of Russia is unlikely to stabilize the rouble, the next few chapters explain in detail a different approach to stabilization, an approach that calls for establishing a currency board in Russia. They show how the money supply is determined in a currency board system, how to establish a currency board in Russia, and how to operate the currency board and protect it from political pressure to convert it into a central bank. This chapter begins with a simplified exposition contrasting the money supply process in a currency board system with the money supply process in a central banking system.

THE MONEY SUPPLY PROCESS IN A CURRENCY BOARD SYSTEM

A typical currency board system relies entirely on market forces to determine the amount of notes and coins that the currency board supplies. Market forces also determine the other components of the money supply – in the examples in this book, the public's deposits at commercial banks – by processes described later in this section and in Appendix B.

In a currency board system and a central banking system alike, commercial banks are intermediaries between lenders and borrowers. A commercial bank cannot for long lend more to borrowers than depositors wish to lend to the bank, in the form of deposits held instead of spent by depositors. If a commercial bank lends excessively, the borrowers spend the excess, for instance by writing cheques. In the payments system, more funds flow out of the bank than flow into the bank. To prevent the outflow from bankrupting it, a commercial bank holds reserves. The loans of commercial banks are limited by their need to maintain sufficient reserves to enable depositors to convert deposits into reserves on demand and to withstand outflows of reserves through the payments system.

A typical currency board has no active role in determining the monetary base. A fixed exchange rate with the reserve currency and a fixed reserve ratio of 100 per cent or slightly more foreign reserves prevent a currency board from increasing or decreasing the monetary base at its own discretion. Nor does a typical currency board influence the relationship between the monetary base and the money supply by imposing reserve ratios or otherwise regulating commercial banks. The money supply in a typical currency board system, therefore, is determined entirely by market forces. A typical central bank, in contrast, can at its discretion increase or decrease the monetary base. For example, it can lend to commercial banks, creating reserves for them, even if its foreign reserves are decreasing. More reserves tend to enable commercial banks to make more loans, which they do by creating deposits for borrowers. The money supply then increases. Decreasing the monetary base tends to have the opposite effect. Besides changing the monetary base, a typical central bank can also influence the supply of loans by commercial banks by changing the reserve requirements for commercial banks.

Despite the inability of a typical currency board to create reserves for commercial banks at its own discretion, the money supply in a typical currency board system is quite elastic (responsive) to changes in demand, because the system can acquire foreign reserves. The elasticity of the money supply in a currency board system is one reason that Hong Kong is among the world's leading centres of ample, low-cost finance. The rules governing a currency board merely prevent it from creating reserves for commercial banks in an inflationary manner, as a central bank can. Other sources of elasticity in the money supply are variability in commercial banks' deposit-to-reserve ratio, the pooling of reserves among branches of commercial banks in the currency board country and the reserve country, interbank lending, and variability in the public's deposit-to-cash ratio. To simplify exposition, most of the discussion that follows omits mention of sources of elasticity other than the acquisition of foreign reserves.

The ultimate reserves in a currency board system are the monetary base of the reserve currency. The only way to acquire the ultimate reserves is to obtain them from the reserve country.[53] In its simplest form, that requires achieving a current-account surplus. Making certain assumptions about a currency board system (enumerated in Appendix B), changes in the current-account balance begin a sequence of events that change the money supply in the same direction. A current-account surplus ultimately increases the money supply, whereas a current-account deficit ultimately decreases the money supply. (The overall balance of payments is the gain or loss of reserves in a period. It consists of the current-account balance – trade in goods and services – plus the capital-account balance – investment and gifts. Assume for the time being that the capital-account balance is zero, so that the overall balance equals the current-account balance.)

The simplified flow diagrams that follow (Figures 4.1–4.2) illustrate the link between changes in the balance of payments and the money supply in a currency board system. Appendix B contains a more detailed discussion that supplements this chapter.

Figure 4.1 illustrates an initial situation where the current-account balance is zero: the value of exports equals the value of imports. Now assume that a current-account surplus occurs. The surplus works its way through the monetary system in the sequence depicted in Figure 4.1. The currency board plays an explicit (though passive) role in the sequence only at the stage labelled 'demand for goods in general, including currency board notes and coins, increases'. The system is self-adjusting, and it eventually achieves a new equilibrium, that is, the current-account balance returns to zero and the relevant markets clear.

When a current-account *deficit* occurs, the sequence is as in Figure 4.2. Market forces rather than discretionary action by the currency board cause the money supply to adjust to the current-account balance. The monetary system is self-adjusting. The currency board is passive in response to changes in demand for notes and coins; it merely supplies whatever quantity is demanded at the fixed exchange rate with the reserve currency. Notice also that because the exchange rate is fixed, arbitrage occurs through changes in the money supply, interest rates, and the current-account balance, rather than through the exchange rate. In that respect, the currency board system is like the 'classical' gold standard or gold-exchange standard practised by many central banks before the First World War, which had truly fixed exchange rates.

Arbitrage is the key to changes in the money supply of a currency board system. It works by making prices in the reserve country an 'anchor' for nominal prices in the currency board country.[54] The currency board maintains a fixed exchange rate with the reserve currency, but it controls no other nominal or real price in the economy. Instead, arbitrage determines those other prices. Arbitrage also occurs with a floating exchange rate, but exchange risk creates additional costs that tend to make arbitrage less efficient than it is with fixed exchange rates.[55]

Suppose the US dollar is the reserve currency for the proposed Russian currency board; then American prices will be the anchor for prices in currency board roubles. If disparities in prices exist, so that, for example, timber costs more in the United States than in Russia after making allowance for taxes and transportation, traders will tend to buy Russian timber and sell it in the United States. Overall price changes, as reflected in wholesale price indexes, will tend to be similar in Russia and the United States. If Russia establishes secure property rights, eliminates barriers to foreign investment, and has taxes no greater than those in the United States, interest rates will also tend towards American levels. Wages in Russia will tend to increase at approximately the same rate as in the United States, plus an allowance for gains in productivity. Real wages can thus increase quickly in the currency board system if productivity increases.

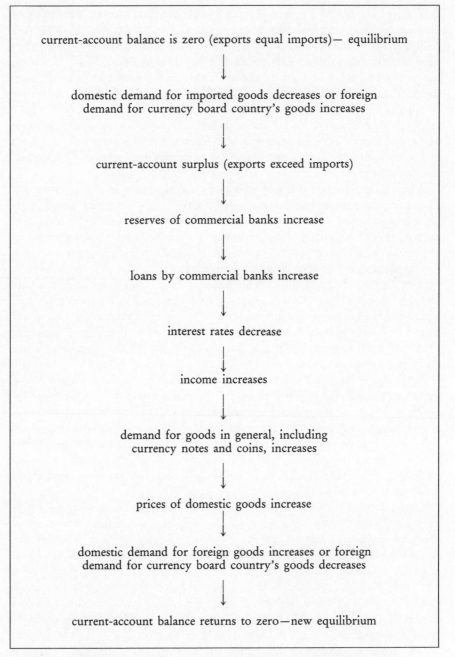

current-account balance is zero (exports equal imports) — equilibrium

↓

domestic demand for imported goods decreases or foreign
demand for currency board country's goods increases

↓

current-account surplus (exports exceed imports)

↓

reserves of commercial banks increase

↓

loans by commercial banks increase

↓

interest rates decrease

↓

income increases

↓

demand for goods in general, including
currency notes and coins, increases

↓

prices of domestic goods increase

↓

domestic demand for foreign goods increases or foreign
demand for currency board country's goods decreases

↓

current-account balance returns to zero — new equilibrium

Figure 4.1 Simplified money supply increase in a currency board system

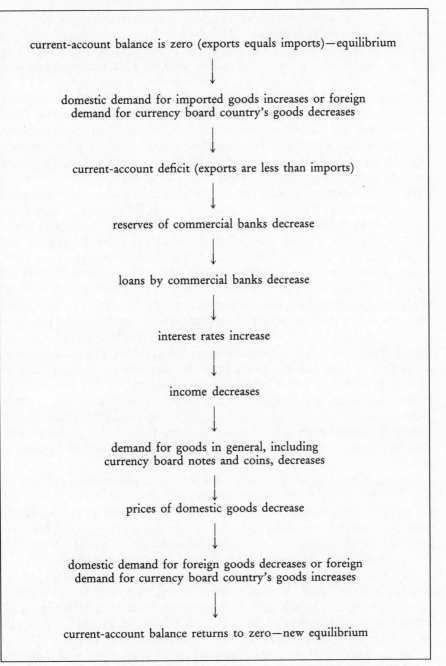

current-account balance is zero (exports equals imports)—equilibrium

domestic demand for imported goods increases or foreign
demand for currency board country's goods decreases

current-account deficit (exports are less than imports)

reserves of commercial banks decrease

loans by commercial banks decrease

interest rates increase

income decreases

demand for goods in general, including
currency board notes and coins, decreases

prices of domestic goods decrease

domestic demand for foreign goods decreases or foreign
demand for currency board country's goods increases

current-account balance returns to zero—new equilibrium

Figure 4.2 Simplified money supply decrease in a currency board system

An important exception to the foregoing remarks about arbitrage is that consumer price indexes can diverge between the currency board country and the reserve country. Divergence can occur because consumer price indexes contain many nontraded goods, such as rent and local services, whereas wholesale price indexes mainly contain traded goods, such as foodstuffs, minerals, and manufactures. Ultimately, prices of domestically produced traded goods reflect the cost of both the nontraded goods (particularly rent and wages) and the traded goods used to produce them. In a currency board system, prices of nontraded goods can persistently increase faster than prices of traded goods, although indirect arbitrage through traded goods tends to limit increases in the prices of nontraded goods to the extent justified by increases in productivity. For example, suppose that the productivity of labour in export industries increases 4 per cent a year in Russia and 0 per cent a year in the United States, the reserve country. Suppose further that inflation in the prices of Russian export goods is zero and that inflation in all American price indexes is zero. Consequently, real wages can increase 4 per cent a year in the export sector in Russia versus 0 per cent a year in the United States without affecting the competitiveness of Russian goods exported to the United States. Suppose that real wages in Russian export industries do increase 4 per cent a year. To avoid losing workers to export industries, other industries in Russia must increase real wages and the nominal prices they charge consumers. Wages and consumer prices in Russia then tend to increase faster than wholesale prices because average productivity is increasing. The Russian consumer price index increases, whereas the American consumer price index does not change. In these circumstances, the increase in the Russian consumer price index is a sign of a structural change in the Russian economy towards activities that add more value to production of tradeable goods.

The experience of currency board countries confirms both the effectiveness of arbitrage with the reserve country for prices of traded goods and the possibility of divergence in the rates of inflation for prices of wages, rents, and other nontraded goods. In Hong Kong, interest rates and the prices of exported goods have closely followed their counterparts in the United States since 1983, when Hong Kong returned to the currency board system and the US dollar became Hong Kong's reserve currency again. Average wages and the consumer price index, however, have increased more in Hong Kong than in the United States because productivity, and hence real GDP per person, have increased faster in Hong Kong (Culp and Hanke 1992; Hong Kong 1992: 10, 13; World Bank 1992a: 219).

For the sake of clarity, the foregoing exposition of how the money supply adjusts to the balance of payments in a currency board system made some simplifying assumptions. Real conditions are never so simple. It is, in fact, common in a currency board system for the money supply to change in the *opposite* direction from the current-account balance. One factor that can loosen or break the rigid link between the money supply and the current-account balance is foreign investment, which is part of the capital-account balance. Foreign investment can offset or exceed current-account deficits, resulting in a gain of reserves. Hong Kong had current-account deficits for decades at a time, yet its money supply increased because Hong Kong attracted large inflows of foreign investment. The pattern holds generally for fast-growing economies that maintain fixed exchange rates (Jonung 1984: 366–7, 383; Schuler 1992b: 159, 178–9, 204–8). The same pattern will probably occur in Russia if it establishes a currency board and adopts the other reforms that we propose.

THE MONEY SUPPLY PROCESS IN A CENTRAL BANKING SYSTEM

A typical currency board cannot administer a discretionary monetary policy because a fixed exchange rate with the reserve currency and a fixed reserve ratio of 100 per cent or slightly more foreign reserves allow it no discretion. The currency board does not alter the exchange rate (except perhaps in emergencies, about which see chapter 6), nor does it actively control the monetary base or regulate commercial banks. Its influence on real economic activity is passive: it provides a sound currency for economic agents to use as they wish. The stated purpose of a typical central bank, in contrast, is to stabilize the price level and real economic activity by controlling such instruments of monetary policy as the monetary base, reserve requirements, and interest rates charged by commercial banks. Unlike a typical currency board, a typical central bank can administer a discretionary monetary policy, and unlike a typical commercial bank, its decisions are not necessarily guided by considerations of economic profit and loss. A typical central bank is bound neither by strict rules concerning its behaviour nor by the discipline of profit and loss.

To reiterate, a central bank is a monetary authority that has discretionary monopoly control of the supply of the reserves of commercial banks, and usually also a monopoly of the supply of notes and coins. A typical central bank performs other functions besides supplying reserves of commercial banks plus its notes and coins in circulation (which are the components of the monetary base in a typical central banking system). A typical central bank regulates commercial banks, acts as their lender of last resort, gives economic advice to the government, and perhaps helps to operate the payments system. Those functions are secondary to its role in supplying the monetary base, though. Usually, only the Central Bank controls the monetary base, whereas other government bodies can and often do perform the secondary functions. For example, in the United States, only the Federal Reserve System supplies Fed funds (deposit reserves of commercial banks) and notes, but it shares regulatory powers with the Treasury Department, powers as a lender of last resort with government deposit insurance agencies,[56] duties as an economic advisor with several other government bodies, and the operation of the payments system with private organizations. The discussion that follows omits consideration of the secondary functions of a typical central bank and concentrates on how a typical central bank supplies the monetary base, and how its actions affect economic activity.

In a typical currency board system, the starting point in the sequence of events in the example of an increase in the money supply (Figure 4.1) was a decrease in the demand for imported goods in the currency board country or an increase in foreign demand for the currency board country's goods. Changes in demand for goods originate in the market, as a result of changes in people's desires. In a typical central banking system, in contrast, the starting point can be a decision by the central bank to increase the monetary base; perhaps it does so to finance deficit spending by the government. That is *not* a decision that originates in the market.

Diagrammatically, the simplified sequence of events for an unexpected increase in the monetary base in a typical central banking system is as in Figure 4.3. We consider only the case of an unexpected increase, to avoid complications of the type emphasized by the 'rational expectations' school of economists. The discussion of the money supply process here assumes that the central bank maintains a floating exchange rate. A floating exchange rate allows the greatest discretionary control of the monetary base, and hence differs most from the fixed exchange rate maintained by a typical currency board. Since a pegged exchange rate maintained by a typical central bank tends not to persist, periodic devaluations of a pegged rate offer almost as much long-run discretionary power to increase the nominal monetary base as would exist if the central bank operated a floating exchange rate. As has been mentioned, the Central Bank of Russia currently maintains a controlled floating exchange rate.

To show more clearly the contrast with a typical currency board system, assume that there are no lags: nominal prices adjust very quickly, leaving real prices unchanged. The only effect of the central bank's action is that the domestic currency depreciates against foreign currency. If instead, more realistically, some nominal prices are 'sticky', the central bank's action has real effects on the economy. In the sequence in Figure 4.3, the likely effect of the central bank's action is that the real exchange rate will depreciate, that is, prices of nontraded goods will decrease compared to the prices of traded goods. That will cause a temporary increase in exports, because nominal wages and prices will take some time to increase in response to the depreciation of the exchange rate. In the meantime, real wages and prices will be lower than before. (If the nominal exchange rate were pegged rather than floating, the likely immediate effect of the central bank's action

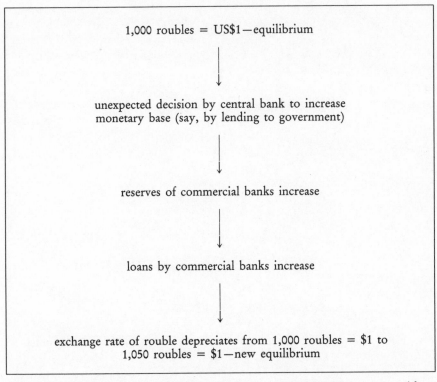

1,000 roubles = US$1—equilibrium

unexpected decision by central bank to increase
monetary base (say, by lending to government)

reserves of commercial banks increase

loans by commercial banks increase

exchange rate of rouble depreciates from 1,000 roubles = $1 to
1,050 roubles = $1—new equilibrium

Figure 4.3 Simplified money supply increase in a central banking system with a
floating exchange rate

would be the opposite: the real exchange rate would temporarily appreciate,
causing a decrease in exports. Eventually, though, a typical central bank
would probably devalue the currency for reasons mentioned in chapter 2,
and the monetary system would then attain a new, though probably transitory, equilibrium.)

The sequence of events for an unexpected *decrease* in the monetary base
in a typical central banking system with a floating exchange rate is as in
Figure 4.4. Again, the exposition omits consideration of expectations and
lags, and assumes that nominal prices adjust very quickly, leaving real
prices unchanged. The only effect of the central bank's action is that the
domestic currency appreciates against foreign currency. If instead, more
realistically, some nominal prices are 'sticky', the likely effect of the central
bank's action is that the real exchange rate will appreciate, that is, prices
of nontraded goods will increase compared to prices of traded goods. That
will cause a temporary decrease in exports, because nominal wages and
prices will take some time to decrease in response to the depreciation of
the exchange rate. In the meantime, real wages and prices will be higher

71

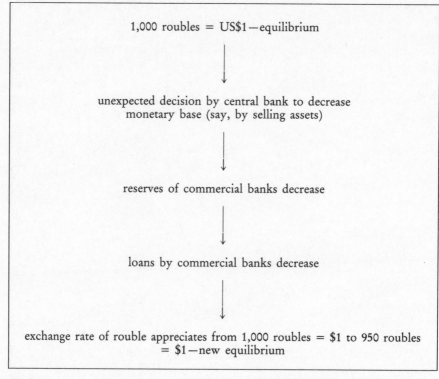

1,000 roubles = US$1 — equilibrium

↓

unexpected decision by central bank to decrease
monetary base (say, by selling assets)

↓

reserves of commercial banks decrease

↓

loans by commercial banks decrease

↓

exchange rate of rouble appreciates from 1,000 roubles = $1 to 950 roubles
= $1 — new equilibrium

Figure 4.4 Simplified money supply decrease in a central banking system with a
floating exchange rate

than before. (If the nominal exchange rate were pegged rather than floating, the likely immediate effect of the central bank's action would be the opposite: the real exchange rate would temporarily depreciate, causing an increase in exports. Eventually, though, the real exchange rate would appreciate and the monetary system would then attain a new, though probably transitory, equilibrium.)

CENTRAL BANKS THAT MIMIC CURRENCY BOARDS

Argentina and Estonia

We have now completed an extensive comparison, begun in chapter 1, of the characteristics of a typical currency board and those of a typical central bank. The results of the comparison enable us to clarify a confusion that has recently developed. Some central banks that mimic certain features of currency boards, such as the current monetary systems of Argentina and

Estonia, have mistakenly been classified as currency boards (Bennett 1992; Hansson and Sachs 1992: 1; IMF 1992g: 52–3; Schwartz 1992b: 17). Although these monetary systems have had some initial success, we believe that in the long run, they will behave more like typical central banks than like typical currency boards, because they lack important features of a typical currency board.

The Argentine convertibility law (Law 23.298), which took effect on 1 April 1991, requires the Banco Central de la República Argentina to maintain an exchange rate of 10,000 Argentine australes (now redenominated as one peso) per US dollar, and to hold 'freely usable reserves in gold and foreign currencies' equal to at least 100 per cent of the monetary base. The Banco Central may count a limited amount of Argentine government bonds payable in dollars (Bonex) as foreign reserves; however, it holds excess foreign reserves greater than the amount of the Bonex bonds (BCRA 1992: Cuadros III.3–4).

Unlike a typical currency board system, the Argentine monetary system has limited convertibility. Permission from the Banco Central is required for certain current-account transactions, although currently permission is merely a formality. The executive branch of the government has the power to impose capital controls by decree, forbidding foreign investments from being converted into foreign currency for up to three years (IMF 1992f: 20–1). Furthermore, institutional protection for the exchange rate and for the reserve ratio is weak. The Banco Central cannot devalue the peso at its own discretion, but it can do so with the permission of the legislature, which it could probably obtain easily. Argentina's long history of failed currency reforms has created anxiety that the peso will be devalued by the time that the current finance minister, who conceived the convertibility law, leaves office. Finally, the Banco Central remains a lender of last resort to commercial banks. If a large commercial bank fails, the Banco Central's role as a lender of last resort may conflict with its promise to hold foreign reserves of 100 per cent of the monetary base.

Argentine interest rates are evidence of the imperfect credibility of the link of the peso to the US dollar, and of the perception that the exchange rate of the peso is pegged rather than fixed. The peso has experienced the typical difficulties of a pegged exchange rate (described in chapter 2). An attack on the peso by currency speculators began on 11 November 1992. For the first time since the convertibility law was passed, the Banco Central intervened in the foreign-exchange market, selling dollars and buying pesos with its excess foreign reserves. The Banco Central also ceased lending to banks that wished to borrow pesos to buy dollars (Nash 1992). In reaction to the attack on the peso, interest rates on short-term peso deposits increased from 15 per cent a year to 85 per cent a year, whereas interest rates on short-term dollar deposits in Argentina remained at 7 per cent. Yields on the long-term peso bonds of the Banco Central (Bics) increased to 25 per cent a year from 20 per cent a year, whereas yields on long-term dollar bonds (Bonex) remained at 12.5 per cent.[57] The dollar deposits and bonds are subject to the same political risk and taxes as the peso deposits and bonds, so the higher peso interest rates must reflect exchange risk that the peso will be devalued. The speculative attack on the peso left the difference between peso and dollar interest rates larger than before, aggravating the difficulty of maintaining the pegged exchange rate of the peso.[58]

The Estonian monetary reform of 20–2 June 1992 replaced the rouble in Estonia with a new currency, the Estonian kroon. The kroon is pegged to the German mark at a central rate of 8 kroons per mark. The exchange rate of the kroon is allowed to fluctuate up to 3 per cent from the central rate. The Bank of Estonia charges no commission fee for exchanges of marks into kroons or the reverse (Law on the Security of the Estonian Kroon). Residents of Estonia who had registered with the government (90 per cent of the population) were allowed to convert up to 1,500 roubles (approximately $12) of rouble notes into kroons at 10 roubles per kroon, a rate close to the prevailing interbank rate of 75 roubles per mark. Enterprises and banks were allowed to convert limited amounts of rouble notes into kroons at the same rate. Most rouble wages, prices, and debts, including household savings deposits, were also converted into kroons at 10 roubles per kroon. Rouble notes and coins exceeding 1,500 roubles were allowed to be exchanged for kroons at 50 roubles per kroon until 1 July, after which the conversion ended. Deposits exceeding 50,000 roubles made after 1 May were temporarily blocked to prevent large-scale conversions of roubles into kroons by nonresidents. During the reform, residents of Estonia converted 2.2 billion roubles of notes, which was almost all of the estimated rouble notes in circulation in Estonia. Household savings deposits were converted into kroons at 10 roubles per kroon, but not all enterprise deposits were converted at that rate. The distinction between the cash and noncash financial circuits was eliminated. The kroon is now the only legal tender currency in Estonia. Like the German mark, it has a floating exchange rate against the rouble (Eesti Pank 1992a; Estonia 1992; Hansson and Sachs 1992).

The Bank of Estonia (Eesti Pank), the central bank, is required to hold gold and foreign-currency assets equal to 100 per cent of the monetary base, like the Argentine central bank. Soon after the currency reform its foreign reserves exceeded 100 per cent. Much of the foreign reserves came from payments made by Western central banks in compensation for gold held by them for the previous Bank of Estonia, but given to the occupation Soviet government in the 1950s. Other foreign reserves came from hoards of foreign notes that Estonians voluntarily exchanged for kroons (Bennett 1992: 3, 16–18).

As in Argentina, in Estonia institutional protection for the exchange rate and for the reserve ratio is weak. The Bank of Estonia cannot devalue the kroon by itself, but the legislature can authorize the Bank of Estonia to devalue the kroon. Advisors to the Estonian government on the monetary reform have characterized the exchange rate as a 'peg' (Sachs and Lipton 1992: 34) rather than a fixed rate, and the governor of the Bank of Estonia has warned that he would have to devalue the kroon if the Estonian parliament approved a high minimum wage (FBIS 1992q).

Unlike Argentina, Estonia does not have a long history of failed currency reforms during its existence as an independent country. As in Argentina, though, a potential conflict exists between the requirement that the 'currency department' of the Bank of Estonia hold foreign reserves equal to 100 per cent of the monetary base and the obligation of the 'banking department' to be a lender of last resort to commercial banks. The banking department is only supposed to lend reserves not needed by the currency department. So far, it has acted as promised, despite the failure of three large Estonian commercial banks on 17 November 1992. The failures resulted from problems unrelated to the monetary reform of June 1992 (FBIS 1992v, w).

The kroon is fully convertible for current-account transactions. Since the beginning of 1993 it has also been convertible for most capital-account transactions. Officials of the Bank of Estonia have told us that many of the capital controls that previously existed were merely a formality. Foreign currency earned by Estonians must be converted into kroons, however (Eesti Pank 1992b). Perceived risk of devaluation, the risk of commercial bank failures, and the inexperience of the legal system in handling bankruptcies, are among the factors that have resulted in interest rates on short-term loans of 50–60 per cent a year, compared with a prime lending rate of 11 per cent in Germany, Estonia's reserve country. Interest rates on short-term deposits are as high as 30 per cent a year (Bennett 1992: 7, 10, 21). Inflation is also much higher in Estonia than in Germany, for reasons explained later in this section.

Early in 1992, before the Estonian monetary reform, we wrote a short book entitled *Monetary Reform for a Free Estonia* (Hanke *et al.* 1992b), also published in an Estonian translation (Hanke *et al.* 1992a). The book explained how to establish a currency board as the issuer of a parallel currency to the rouble. It also included some remarks on converting a central bank into a currency board. Our proposal would have made the Swedish krona the reserve currency, because we envisioned that Sweden would give Estonia the foreign reserves to establish the currency board, perhaps as a gift rather than a loan. We proposed that the exchange rate between the kroon and the krona be truly fixed and that the currency board not be a lender of last resort to commercial banks. The krona was not our first choice as a reserve currency; the German mark would have been better, because it is the most stable and most widely used European currency. It was doubtful that the Swedish government would have granted reserves to a mark-based currency board, however. Interest rates in the krona were as high as 500 per cent in September 1992, when the Bank of Sweden was trying to defend the pegged exchange rate of the krona with the European Currency Unit (ecu). The Bank of Sweden ultimately abandoned the peg, and the krona is now a floating currency. Except during the brief period of speculative pressure on the pegged exchange rate of the krona, though, nominal krona interest rates have been much lower than nominal kroon interest rates.

The idea of a currency board had a significant effect on the Estonian government. It also had an effect on the IMF, which previously had been advising the Estonian government not to introduce a new currency for one or two years until certain 'preconditions' of monetary reform were achieved (Hansson and Sachs 1992: 2; compare Odling-Smee 1992b).

To protect the proposed Estonian currency board from political pressure to convert it into a central bank, we suggested that it operate according to a strict constitution; that it be legally independent from the Estonian government; that it hold its reserves in Stockholm, out of reach of the Estonian government; and that the Swedish government appoint non-Estonian directors to the currency board, who would have veto power over the Estonian directors. The actual Estonian monetary reform included none of those features. The Bank of Estonia holds 100 per cent foreign reserves, like a currency board, but unlike a currency board it is not well protected from political pressure to devalue the kroon, it maintains a pegged rather than a fixed exchange rate, and it does not yet allow full convertibility of the kroon into the reserve currency, the German mark.

Furthermore, the rate the Estonian government used for converting roubles into kroons was questionable. Our earlier book mainly explained how the kroon could be introduced as a parallel currency, but it also explained how to conduct a currency conversion, as Estonia did. For the case of a currency conversion, the book emphasized the importance of using unrestricted exchange rates as a guide for setting a fixed exchange rate with a reserve currency. Before Estonia's monetary reform, Estonia had Soviet-style controls on foreign exchange, not an unrestricted foreign-exchange market. The interbank exchange rate of the rouble at the time reflected even more extensive foreign-exchange controls than those that exist today for the rouble. The exchange rate of 10 roubles per kroon used in the monetary reform made Estonian wages and the prices of traded goods grossly undervalued compared to wages and prices in Germany. Consequently, Estonia has had much higher inflation than Germany since the reform as Estonian wages and prices catch up to market-clearing levels (FBIS 1992r, t). The catch-up period may create political pressure for continuing inflation if wage and price increases achieve such momentum that they temporarily overshoot market-clearing levels, causing the real exchange rate to become overvalued; the Estonian government may respond by devaluing the kroon.

We wish success for the present Argentine and Estonian monetary systems. We think, however, that their prospects for success in the long run would be enhanced if they became orthodox currency board systems.

Other Cases

Besides the monetary systems of Argentina and Estonia, some other monetary systems have also mistakenly been classified as currency board systems. Among them are the monetary systems of Singapore and Brunei. (We ourselves have in the past called Singapore and Brunei unorthodox or modified currency board systems.) The monetary authorities of Singapore and Brunei hold 100 per cent foreign reserves against the monetary base, but hold a basket of currencies rather than a single currency and have maintained no fixed exchange rate with a reserve currency since 1973. In practice, the Singapore and Brunei dollars appreciate gradually against the US dollar (Lee 1986: 85–91, 150–65). Therefore, despite the historical roots of the present Singapore and Brunei systems in the currency board system, and despite the existence of a body called the Singapore Currency Board (which is in effect the note-issuing branch of the Monetary Authority of Singapore), it seems best to classify them as central banking systems that mimic the 100 per cent foreign reserve feature of the currency board system.

Other central banking systems sometimes mistaken for currency board systems hold 100 per cent reserves only against some liabilities.[59] A central bank required to hold 100 per cent foreign reserves against notes and coins in circulation, but not against deposits, is not a currency board. To illustrate the difference, compare Figures 4.5 and 4.6, which are balance sheets with hypothetical numbers. Recall that in a balance sheet, by definition, assets = liabilities + net worth. For simplicity, assume that net worth is zero. Unlike the usual practice in this book, for the moment assume that the currency board, like a minority of past currency boards, accepts deposits from commercial banks. Assuming that the currency board accepts deposits makes comparison of the balance sheets simpler. The currency board holds 100 per cent foreign reserves against its deposits and against its notes and coins in circulation. For a given amount of total liabilities, the foreign reserves of the currency board are the same whether the liabilities are held as notes and coins or as deposits. The currency board holds 100 per cent foreign reserves against all liabilities, no matter what form the liabilities take. The reasons that most currency boards have issued notes and coins only, and have not accepted deposits, originate from historical peculiarities, not from inherent differences in notes and coins versus deposits as liabilities.

Assets		Liabilities	
Foreign securities	150	Notes and coins	150
Domestic securities	600	Deposits of commercial banks	600
		Net worth	0
TOTAL	750	TOTAL	750

Figure 4.5 Simplified central bank balance sheet

Assets		Liabilities	
Foreign securities	750	Notes and coins	150
		Deposits of commercial banks	600
		Net worth	0
TOTAL	750	TOTAL	750

Figure 4.6 Simplified currency board balance sheet

The foreign securities (foreign reserves) of the central bank in Figure 4.5 are equal to its notes and coins in circulation, and its total securities (foreign and domestic) are equal to its notes and coins in circulation plus the deposits of commercial banks with it. That does not make the central bank a currency board, however. The liabilities of the central bank, like those of a currency board that accepts deposits, include deposits of commercial banks as well as notes and coins in circulation. The different types of liabilities are interchangeable: for instance, a one-rouble deposit at the central bank or the currency board can be converted into a one-rouble note issued by the central bank or the currency board, respectively.

For the purpose of the example, what matters is not the ratio of foreign securities to notes and coins, but the ratio of foreign securities to *all* liabilities. To illustrate the point, suppose that all deposits at the central bank of Figure 4.5 and the currency board of Figure 4.6 are converted into notes and coins. The total liabilities of the central bank and the currency board will remain unchanged at 750 roubles. The central bank will have 150 roubles of foreign securities and 750 roubles of notes and coins in circulation, making a reserve ratio of 20 per cent. The currency board, in contrast, will have 750 roubles of foreign securities and 750 roubles of notes and coins in circulation, making a reserve ratio of 100 per cent. To become a currency board, the central bank of Figure 4.5 would have to increase its foreign securities to 750 roubles and sell its domestic securities, or maintain its foreign securities at 150 roubles and cease to accept deposits from commercial banks.

In a currency board system, only the liabilities of the currency board must be backed 100 per cent by foreign reserves. Few currency board countries have imposed reserve requirements on commercial banks. Commercial banks in currency board systems have often held reserves as low as a few per cent of deposits; contrary to a misconception (Congdon 1985: 95), it is not necessary for them to hold 100 per cent foreign reserves. Nor is the currency board system like the Chicago Plan proposed by economists at the University of Chicago during the 1930s (Simons 1934: 18, 25–6), which would require commercial banks to hold 100 per cent reserves in domestic government securities. Nor is a currency board system like proposals for gold warehouse banking, which would forbid commercial banks to invest in interest-earning assets (Rothbard 1962).

Contrary to another misconception, the monetary system of France's former African colonies is not a currency board system. Most of the former colonies have a common currency, the CFA franc. They are organized into two groups, each with its own multinational central bank. The central banks are required to hold French franc reserves equal to at least 20 per cent of their total liabilities, rather than 100 per cent like currency boards (Neurrisse 1987: 150). They must also deposit at least 65 per cent of their foreign reserves with the Bank of France, which pays interest on the deposits and supervises the CFA franc zone. Unlike a typical currency board, the CFA central banks hold domestic securities, and their exchange rates are perceived as pegged rather than fixed to the French franc, as shown by occasional attacks on the CFA franc by currency speculators in response to rumours of devaluation (Boughton 1992: 35; Piot 1992). Furthermore, the CFA franc has capital controls (IMF 1992e: 570–75).

We have emphasized the lack of institutional protection for currency board-type rules in central banking systems that mimic features of the currency board system. Many currency boards, especially in British colonies, have also lacked formal legal protection from changes in their operating rules. They have had much informal protection, though. Most have been managed by British or British-trained civil servants who absorbed a long tradition of financial rectitude. Most British colonial currency boards have had fixed exchange rates with the pound sterling, and the British government would have fired colonial officials who tried to devalue colonial currency against sterling. Argentina and Estonia are not colonies, nor do they have long traditions of financial rectitude. For them, or for Russia, the lack of informal protection makes it all the more important to establish formal legal protection such as our earlier book suggested for an Estonian currency board, and such as chapter 6 and Appendix A of this book suggest for a Russian currency board. A central bank that mimics currency board-type rules is unlikely to obey the rules for long, because the rules tend not to be strictly enforced; hence the central bank will tend to have low credibility.

A BRIEF HISTORY AND ASSESSMENT OF CURRENCY BOARDS

It is now time to summarize briefly the historical record of currency boards and indicate the extent to which it supports the case for a currency board in Russia. The summary is based on a synthesis of many studies.[60]

Approximately seventy countries have had currency boards; Appendix C lists them. The first currency board was established in 1849 in the British Indian Ocean colony of Mauritius. Currency boards spread slowly until approximately 1900, when a few other British colonies and Argentina, an independent country, established them. After 1900, currency boards became the monetary arrangement of choice for British colonies and for some independent developing countries. They reached their greatest extent in the 1950s, when much of Africa, the Caribbean, and South Asia had currency boards.

Two currency boards have existed in Eastern Europe: one in North Russia and one in Danzig. The North Russian currency board operated in the region around Archangel and Murmansk in 1918 and 1919, and had a London office until 1920. It issued a fully convertible currency with a fixed exchange rate with the pound sterling. It lasted until the Bolsheviks conquered the region and replaced the North Russian rouble with the inconvertible Soviet rouble (see chapter 9). From 1922 to 1923 the free city of Danzig (now the Polish city of Gdansk) had a currency board, which also maintained a fixed exchange rate with sterling. In 1923 Danzig established a central bank on the advice of the League of Nations. The later record of the central bank was undistinguished. Both East European currency boards were successful in maintaining full convertibility during their brief lives. The North Russian currency board maintained full convertibility in the midst of a civil war; the Danzig currency board maintained full convertibility despite a deep depression and hyperinflation in Germany, Danzig's main trading partner (Hanke and Schuler 1990).

Currency board systems have typically been successful in encouraging foreign investment. With currency boards, many countries have taken the decisive step from primitive monetary conditions to modern monetary systems that include sophisticated banking and foreign-exchange services. Inflation in currency board systems has typically been low, which has encouraged the use of modern currency in transactions. Economic growth has typically been satisfactory, and in some cases spectacular. Trade in export goods that have remained characteristic of some countries originated during the years of the currency board system. Export of cocoa and peanuts in West Africa, rubber and tin in Malaysia, and textiles and financial services in Hong Kong all developed under currency boards.

Currency board systems have typically been stable. All currency boards have successfully maintained fixed exchange rates and full convertibility into their reserve currencies, although in the 1970s some changed from sterling to more stable reserve currencies (see Appendix C).[61] Even during the Great Depression, all currency boards then existing maintained fixed exchange rates and full convertibility, unlike almost all central banks then existing. The oldest remaining currency board, in the Falkland Islands, has maintained a fixed exchange rate of Falklands £1 per £1 sterling since it opened in 1899. Currency boards have also helped some countries to recover quickly from the economic effects of wartime occupation. During the Second World War, Hong Kong, Malaya, and the Philippines, which had currency boards, were occupied by the Japanese army. The Japanese army issued occupation currencies to replace currency board notes, and imposed a command economy similar in many ways to the Soviet economy. Much as Russians hold foreign notes today, the inhabitants of the occupied territories continued to hold currency board notes during the war. The foreign reserves of the currency boards were kept safe in the reserve countries, Britain and the United States. The occupation currencies experienced extreme inflation and became almost worthless. After the war, Britain re-established rule over Hong Kong and Malaya, and the United States re-established rule over the Philippines. The British and American authorities re-opened the local offices of the currency boards quickly as part of an overall economic strategy of replacing wartime command economies with the market economies that had existed before the war. The currency boards resumed full convertibility into their reserve currencies from the day they re-opened (King 1957: 23, 109).

Failures by commercial banks have been minor in currency board systems. Fixed exchange rates with a reserve currency have encouraged foreign commercial banks, especially those based in the reserve country, to establish branches. Their multinational branch networks have enabled them to diversify risk. Domestic banks have had to be strong to survive competition from the foreign banks. Only some small commercial banks have failed in currency board systems, and the losses they have inflicted on depositors have been tiny.[62]

The full convertibility inherent in the currency board system has resulted in capital flight from some currency board systems during periods of economic or political uncertainty. However, capital flight in currency board systems seems to have been small compared to capital flight in central banking systems where the threat of foreign-exchange controls has existed. Currency board systems have experienced severe shocks to their real exchange rates, but so have central banking systems. Central banking appears on average to have been no more successful than the currency board system in alleviating shocks to real exchange rates or other real prices in the economy, although no systematic study of evidence on the subject exists. An important element encouraging economic growth in currency board systems has been that full convertibility has encouraged foreign investors to take advantage of opportunities for profit during economic downturns. Foreign investment has helped to alleviate shocks to real exchange rates and other real prices in currency board systems.

Despite the economic success of currency board systems, national governments converted most currency boards into central banks in the late 1950s and the 1960s. Some governments were influenced by theoretical arguments that a central bank could promote economic growth better than a currency board. The arguments seemed compelling at the time, but now appear wrong; the most important ones are considered in chapter 8. More important than theoretical arguments against the currency board system were political factors. Newly independent countries established central banks because of the association of the currency board system with colonial rule, and because older, more established countries had central banks. A central bank was a symbol of independence, like a national flag. Politicians in some newly independent countries may also have understood the political advantages of politicized central banks.

The results of central banking in former currency board systems have been lacklustre. On average, inflation has been higher and economic growth has been lower in central banking systems than in the currency board systems they replaced, lower than in their former reserve countries, and lower than in the remaining currency board systems (Schuler 1992b: 202–3). Most central banks that have replaced currency boards have restricted the convertibility of their currencies.[63]

Orthodox currency boards exist today in Hong Kong, Gibraltar, the Cayman Islands, the Falkland Islands, and the Faroe Islands. A modified currency board system with capital controls exists in Bermuda. Hong Kong is the most populous and economically diversified of the currency board systems, with 5.8 million inhabitants. Although less populous than many countries, Hong Kong is an economic giant: its 1991 GDP was $81 billion, more than the GDP of any East European country (Hong Kong 1992: 30). Hong Kong's economic success is well known. It has been among the world's most rapidly growing economies despite its lack of natural resources; moreover, it has had relatively low inflation. Statistics on the other remaining currency board systems are more difficult to find, because they are in small, rather obscure countries. As the list of currency board episodes in Appendix C indicates, however, some large areas have had currency boards in the past. Several British colonial currency boards were joint currency boards that served three or more colonies apiece.

Overall, then, the historical record of currency boards and currency board systems has been good, as measured according to several of the most important criteria that economists use. The characteristics described in chapter 1 as typical of a currency board really have been typical. The actual performance of currency boards has been close to the ideal they have been established to strive for, namely, to maintain full convertibility into a reserve currency at a fixed exchange rate according to strict rules of procedure. Historical experience supports the claim that a currency board in Russia, if established according to similarly strict rules in the manner described in the next two chapters, has a high probability of success.

5

HOW TO ESTABLISH A CURRENCY BOARD IN RUSSIA

The proposed Russian currency board can be established by converting the Central Bank of Russia into a currency board or by making the currency board the issuer of a parallel currency to the Central Bank rouble. Both approaches have been used by past currency boards. This chapter explains both approaches step by step.

HOW TO CONVERT THE CENTRAL BANK OF RUSSIA INTO A CURRENCY BOARD

If the Russian government wishes to convert the Central Bank of Russia into a currency board, how should the government proceed? Experience with currency boards in places as diverse as Palestine, Danzig, and the Philippines indicates that administratively, converting a central bank into a currency board system is simple. (Politically, it may be more difficult; the next section considers that problem.) The steps for conversion are as follows.

1. **Delegate to other bodies all functions of the Central Bank of Russia other than supplying the monetary base.** For instance, the Ministry of Finance can regulate commercial banks and give advice to the president on monetary affairs. Commercial banks can operate the payments system and provide mutual deposit insurance protection. Chapters 7 and 8 return to these points.

2. **Allow a brief period of clean, unrestricted floating exchange rates for the rouble.** The real exchange rate between the reserve currency and the rouble must be appropriate. An overvalued real exchange rate will price Russian exports out of world markets, while an undervalued real exchange rate will make imports expensive, preventing Russians from buying foreign machinery and other goods needed for modernizing the Russian economy. The best indication of the appropriate real exchange rate is the unrestricted nominal market rate, which reflects supply and

84

demand. Accordingly, the first step in fixing an exchange rate for the rouble is to allow the exchange rate to float for a brief period. Unlike the current controlled float of the rouble, the float proposed here will be unrestricted. No limits will exist on exchanging roubles for foreign currency at market-determined floating exchange rates. Official restrictions on conversion of noncash roubles to cash roubles, however, will continue until the government eliminates the distinction between the cash and noncash financial circuits. In the meantime, the government should not restrict unofficial conversions of noncash roubles to cash roubles at floating exchange rates. Reform to eliminate the distinction between the cash and noncash financial circuits can occur before or at the same time as the currency board is established. Chapter 7 discusses further the elimination of the distinction between the cash and noncash financial circuits.

When the Russian government allows the rouble to float without restrictions, it should announce its choice of reserve currency (discussed later) and the date it will fix the exchange rate. The reason for making the announcement is to reduce uncertainty that otherwise may tend to undervalue the rouble as a store of value. A period not exceeding 90 days should be sufficient to indicate approximately the appropriate exchange rate. The float should be a clean one reflecting market forces only, rather than a dirty float reflecting intervention by the Central Bank of Russia. To ensure a clean float, all existing foreign-exchange regulations, such as the regulation requiring 50 per cent of foreign-currency earnings to be converted into roubles, should be abolished.

3. Make the actions of the Central Bank of Russia transparent and predictable. During the period of unrestricted floating, the actions of the Central Bank of Russia should be transparent and predictable, so that they cause no destabilizing random surprises to exchange rates. The Central Bank should be required to disseminate weekly or even daily reports of its activities and its balance sheet. At present, the Central Bank delays reporting its activities and its balance sheet for months. Another way of making the actions of the Central Bank more transparent and predictable is to require it to increase its foreign reserves by 100 per cent of any increase in the monetary base that occurs after the government announces the monetary reform.

4. Convert some required reserves of commercial banks (deposits at the Central Bank of Russia) into currency board notes and coins or into foreign securities, whichever the commercial banks prefer. Cancel remaining reserves. With this step, the deposit liabilities of the Central Bank of Russia will cease to exist. As has been mentioned, the Central Bank of Russia currently imposes a reserve requirement of 20 per cent on commercial banks. Not all deposits of commercial banks at the Central

Bank will necessarily be converted into currency board notes and coins or into foreign securities. 'Excess' reserves will be cancelled (confiscated) to avoid creating inflation. A later section in this chapter discusses what quantity of reserves commercial banks will probably need and what proportion of reserves is excess.

5. Establish a fixed exchange rate with the reserve currency. After the deposit liabilities of the Central Bank of Russia cease to exist, all that will remain are its issues of notes and coins in circulation and its net worth, on the liability side of the balance sheet, and its foreign reserves and miscellaneous holdings such as its offices, on the asset side. Its other assets and liabilities will have been distributed to commercial banks or the government, or will have been cancelled. To convert what remains of the Central Bank of Russia into a currency board, the Russian government must now establish a fixed exchange rate with the reserve currency chosen in step 2. Simultaneously, the government must ensure that reserve assets for currency board notes and coins in circulation equal 100 per cent.

When the date to establish the fixed exchange rate arrives, the Russian government should set the rate somewhere within the range of recent market rates. Setting exchange rates is an art rather than a science; if uncertainty exists about an appropriate nominal exchange rate, it is best to err on the side of an apparent slight real undervaluation rather than a slight real overvaluation compared to the range of recent market rates, so as to be certain that the exchange rate does not price Russian exports out of world markets. It is better to start with an exchange rate that results in competitively priced exports than with an exchange rate that results in overpriced exports. However, a current-account deficit is acceptable if offset by increased foreign investment. As Hong Kong's experience in returning to the currency board system in 1983 illustrates, a range of freedom exists in setting an exchange rate (see Greenwood 1983b). As long as the new rate is credible and not deliberately undervalued or overvalued grossly, the economy will quickly tend to make the minor adjustments necessary to accommodate the new exchange rate.

An alternative way of setting the exchange rate is to set it immediately, without a period of floating, at an estimate of the market-clearing rate or at a deliberately undervalued rate. That method seems disadvantageous because it makes no attempt to gather information from the market.[64]

Some economists distrust the ability of a float, even a clean float, to indicate approximately the appropriate exchange rate. They would prefer to use statistical constructs for setting the exchange rate (Williamson 1992: 43–4). But there is no reason to think that using statistical constructs to set the exchange rate would be any more successful than using statistical constructs to centrally plan other economic activities. Such measurements often have no direct connection to supply and demand. The defects of statistical constructs for determining the exchange rate are examined in more detail later in this chapter.

6. Ensure that foreign reserves equal 100 per cent of rouble notes and coins in circulation. The currency board should begin with foreign reserves equal to 100 per cent of its notes and coins in circulation. (If the currency board accepts deposits, foreign reserves should equal 100 per cent of notes and coins in circulation plus deposits.) Allowing the currency board to operate with a lower reserve ratio may create possibilities for the board to administer a discretionary monetary policy.

Later sections in this chapter describe how to calculate the quantity of initial foreign reserves necessary and how to obtain the reserves.

7. Transfer the remaining assets and liabilities of the Central Bank of Russia to the Russian currency board and open the currency board for business. At the moment that the Russian government fixes the exchange rate with the reserve currency, the currency board will replace the Central Bank of Russia as the issuer of rouble notes and coins and will assume all remaining assets and liabilities of the Central Bank. The Central Bank of Russia will cease to exist.

We envision all the steps being completed within 120 days of the decision to establish a currency board, though they could take as little as 30 days. Historical experience has been that monetary reform is usually most successful at encouraging economic recovery when enacted quickly (see Yeager *et al.* 1981: 42–3).

THE ALTERNATIVE: A PARALLEL CURRENCY APPROACH

Attempts to convert the Central Bank of Russia into a currency board may encounter political opposition. The Central Bank and state enterprises dependent on it for subsidized loans have considerable political power and may oppose monetary reform, although their political power will tend to diminish as extreme inflation diminishes their ability to obtain subsidies. Converting the Central Bank into a currency board will suddenly deprive state enterprises and the government of access to inflationary finance, causing them hardship as they adjust to hard budget constraints. Is there a way to bypass the potential political obstacles posed by entrenched political interests and to ease the transition from extreme inflation to low inflation?

Yes, there is. Establishing the currency board as the issuer of a parallel currency may do so. A parallel currency approach has been successful in Russia before in this century (see chapter 9).

To reiterate, a parallel currency is one that circulates extensively along-side another currency. The parallel currency can have a fixed, pegged, or floating exchange rate with the other currency, and can circulate legally or illegally.

Parallel currencies have been common historically. Many countries have had parallel circulation of gold and silver or silver and copper coins (bimet-allism). Some have also had parallel circulation of, say, gold notes and deposits with silver notes and deposits (Schuler 1992a: 14, 20–2). Today, parallel currencies are common in many border regions; for example, the US dollar and the Canadian dollar both circulate along the US–Canadian border, although the US dollar predominates in the United States and the Canadian dollar predominates in Canada. Gasoline stations, stores, and commercial banks near the border accept both currencies, as they are legally allowed to do. The exchange rate between the US dollar and the Canadian dollar is floating, though in the past it has also been fixed or pegged.

Parallel currencies are also common in countries with extreme inflation and inconvertible currencies, such as Russia. The US dollar and other relatively stable foreign currencies are illegally used by the public in prefer-ence to the domestic currency. This is called currency substitution or dollarization.[65] In Russia today, the dollar and the German mark are the most widely used parallel currencies. Their market exchange rates float against each other and against the market exchange rate of the rouble.

Parallel currencies have a long history, then, and are part of the experi-ence of many Russians today. What will be new to readers is the expla-nation here of how a currency board issuing a parallel currency can reform the Russian monetary system.[66] In the system of parallel currencies pro-posed here, the currency board rouble will circulate alongside the Central Bank rouble as an alternative, officially approved domestic currency. Russia will therefore have two competing domestic currencies. Competition from the currency board will either tend to force the Central Bank to provide a rouble of comparably high quality to the currency board rouble, or cause the Central Bank to wither away as Russians cease to use Central Bank roubles.[67]

Some Western economists have criticized proposals for legalizing a paral-lel currency in Russia (Cooper 1991a: 131–2, 1991b: 312–14; Nuti 1991: 54–5; Williamson 1991b: 402–4). Their criticisms do not apply to a cur-rency board as a parallel issuer, though. The main criticism of legalizing a parallel currency is that it would accelerate inflation in the Central Bank rouble. The Central Bank rouble continues to be used mainly because it has the support of the Russian government, in the form of forced tender laws, which make its use compulsory. Granting equal legal status to the currency board rouble would supposedly reduce the incentive for holding Central Bank roubles. Accordingly, some people would cease holding central bank roubles and instead would hold currency board roubles. As demand for Central Bank roubles diminished, inflation in the Central Bank rouble would increase (the velocity of the central bank rouble would increase) unless the Central Bank reduced the monetary base of the Central Bank rouble. For political reasons, reducing the monetary base would be difficult. Inflation in the Central Bank rouble would therefore accelerate, causing a self-reinforcing cycle of further reductions in demand for the Central Bank rouble. Ultimately the cycle would end in hyperinflation in the Central Bank rouble, which would deprive the government of seigniorage from the Central Bank rouble. Hyperinflation would also deepen the recent decline of the Russian economy.

The criticism is flawed. It assumes that Russians currently use the Central Bank rouble as their only currency. In reality, Russia already has a parallel currency – the US dollar – and many parallel stores of value besides. Many Russians already hold foreign notes at home and some have foreign-currency deposits abroad. Enterprises hoard materials such as bricks as stores of value; consumers hoard durable consumer goods such as vodka. Therefore, the choice in Russia today is not between a situation with a single currency and a situation with a parallel currency, but between two situations with parallel currencies. The only question that remains to be decided is whether a parallel currency will circulate illegally alongside the central bank rouble, as the US dollar now does, or legally, as the currency board rouble will in this proposal.

It is not certain that the existence of a parallel currency board rouble will reduce demand for the Central Bank rouble, even if the Central Bank continues to increase the monetary base of the Central Bank rouble as rapidly as before. In many cases, legalizing a parallel currency has had the consequences that critics fear, but in one particularly relevant case, the Soviet monetary reform of the 1920s, a new parallel, domestically issued currency temporarily increased demand for the previously existing currency. Before the new currency – the chervonets – was introduced, people who wished to exchange the previously existing currency – the sovznak – for a more stable currency had to do so by buying foreign currency illegally. Black markets in foreign currency existed only in a few cities. Once people had acquired foreign currency, they were cautious about spending it for fear of being unable to acquire more foreign currency easily and for fear of being persecuted by government officials. Foreign currency thus was used mainly as a store of value, and the Soviet Union still lacked an adequate, legal medium of exchange. The chervonets filled the void as a medium of exchange for large transactions, although sovznaks continued to be used for small transactions because issuance of chervonets notes was at first limited to large denominations. The chervonets also competed with foreign currency and gold as a store of value and a unit of account. Because the chervonets and the sovznak in combination fulfilled all the three functions of money relatively well, and because people could legally exchange sovznaks for chervonets at market rates at any time, demand for chervonets created increased demand for sovznaks. Receiving payment in sovznaks became less of a disadvantage than before, because people could easily exchange sovznaks for chervonets in numerous places throughout the Soviet Union. The sovznak and the chervonets in combination reclaimed the three functions of money from foreign currency and czarist gold coins. Inflation in the sovznak later increased, but the cause was the government's insistence on printing ever-increasing quantities of sovznaks, not the existence of the chervonets (see chapter 9; Auerbach, *et al.* 1992: 19–23; Rostowski 1992: 95–6; Rostowski and Shapiro 1992: 17, 29).

Suppose, however, that unlike the Soviet monetary reform of the 1920s, the existence of the currency board rouble reduces demand for Central Bank roubles, as critics of a parallel currency argue it will. The good domestic currency will tend to displace the bad one in circulation, as happened with the North Russia currency board in 1918 and 1919 and with the Soviet monetary reform of the 1920s. Inflation in the Central Bank rouble will increase and seigniorage from the Central Bank rouble will cease. But the currency board rouble will enable the Russian government to recapture some of that seigniorage as well as seigniorage now lost to the US Federal Reserve System and the German Bundesbank, and even to the makers of bricks and vodka. More important, the currency board rouble will greatly reduce the economic inefficiency that extreme inflation causes. By using the currency board rouble, Russians will be able to avoid the disturbances to economic activity that the Central Bank rouble now causes because it is an unsatisfactory medium of exchange, store of value, and unit of account (Auerbach *et al.* 1992: 11–18; Rostowski 1992: 94–101).

Another criticism of legalizing a parallel currency pertains to credibility. The credibility of the parallel currency would be low if it too were issued by the Central Bank of Russia or the Ministry of Finance, as some Russian economists have envisioned (Kazmin and Tsimailo 1991). There would be no reason to trust the new parallel currency, because it would be subject to the same political pressure as the existing currency. The low credibility of such a parallel currency would have the result that the parallel currency would not stop inflation at a low cost to the economy.

A parallel currency issued by a currency board, however, will be more credible than one issued by the Central Bank of Russia or the Ministry of Finance. The North Russian currency board, for example, was completely credible even though the continued existence of the North Russian government was doubtful. The credibility of the proposed Russian currency board will emanate from the characteristics of a typical currency board and from some additional features suggested in the next chapter.

Unlike critics of legalizing a parallel currency in Russia, we are little concerned with the fate of the Central Bank rouble in a parallel currency approach. If the Central Bank of Russia withers away as an issuer of currency, fine; it will cease to have an effect on the Russian economy, and the economy will benefit. The Central Bank's remaining functions can be assigned to other government bodies, privatized, or abolished (see chapter 7). If competition from the currency board induces the Central Bank to change its behaviour and the Central Bank rouble continues to exist as a less inflationary currency than it is now, that is also fine. In either case, Russia will have at least one sound domestic currency. A sound domestic currency will help the Russian economy to revive, as it did after the currency reform of the 1920s.

Competition between the Central Bank rouble and the currency board rouble will be greatest if both currencies are allowed by law to serve identical functions. If the currency board rouble is not at first allowed equal legal tender status with the Central Bank rouble, or if currency board rouble notes and coins are limited to large denominations, the competition will be unequal and demand for the Central Bank rouble will be more than it otherwise would be. To reap the full advantages of the currency board rouble as a parallel currency, the Russian government should not limit competition of the currency board rouble with the Central Bank rouble.

HOW TO ESTABLISH THE CURRENCY BOARD AS THE ISSUER OF A PARALLEL CURRENCY

The currency board can be established as the issuer of a parallel currency according to the following steps, which should take no more than 60 days. The North Russian currency board described in chapter 9 was established just eleven weeks after it was first proposed, despite civil war and reliance on less rapid transportation and communications than exist today.

1. **Obtain initial foreign reserves for the Russian currency board.** The next two sections describe how to calculate the quantity of initial foreign reserves necessary for the currency board and how to obtain the reserves.

2. **Make the currency board rouble legal tender for payment of taxes and private debts.** The currency board rouble should be made a legally permissible currency in which to pay taxes and private debts. However, that the currency board rouble should not be forced tender for private debts, that is, Russians should be allowed to make contracts and payments in the Central Bank rouble or other currencies if both parties to a contract or payment wish to do so.

3. **Issue currency board roubles equal to the initial foreign**

reserves.   The currency board will have 100 per cent foreign reserves from the beginning. It will issue no more currency board roubles than the value of its foreign reserves.

4. Put the currency board roubles into circulation, preferably by a distribution to every resident of Russia according to a well-defined plan.   The nominal exchange rate between the reserve currency and the currency board rouble can be anything, so long as the real amount of currency board roubles does not exceed the foreign reserves of the currency board. Suppose that the reserve currency is the US dollar and that the currency board has $1.5 billion of foreign reserves. The currency board will issue 1.5 billion roubles if the exchange rate is one currency board rouble per dollar, or 150 billion roubles if the exchange rate is 100 currency board roubles per dollar. In either case, the amount of currency board roubles issued equals $1.5 billion. An exchange rate of one to one seems best, because it will make conversions easiest to calculate.

The currency board will now inaugurate the parallel currency system by distributing currency board roubles representing up to $1.5 billion. The actual distribution can be designed in various ways. The easiest method is to give every resident of Russia an equal amount of currency board notes and coins as a one-time gift. Since Russia has approximately 150 million inhabitants, $1.5 billion is equal to approximately $10 per person. To a West European or an American, $10 is a small amount of money, but to an average Russian it is a substantial amount. The currency can also be given on a per household basis, or according to various scales: for example, the equivalent of $15 for the first person in each household, $10 for each additional adult, and $5 for each child.

To prevent fraud, the Russian government can take precautions similar to those that it and other governments use to prevent voting fraud. Russians who receive their distribution of currency board roubles can have their identity documents stamped or their fingers dipped in indelible ink. The distribution of currency board roubles should occur simultaneously throughout Russia over a short period.

Another way currency board roubles could enter circulation is through government spending. In that case, the initial reserves of the currency board would be like a loan to the Russian government rather than a loan to individual Russians. Allowing the government to spend currency board roubles into circulation would temporarily reduce its budget deficit, but would also create temptation for corrupt initial distribution of currency board roubles to favoured persons. Giving every resident of Russia some currency board roubles seems preferable because it would be popular and would avoid resentment, common with existing regulations, that the government favours an elite with access to convertible currency.

5. Allow the currency board rouble to circulate as a parallel currency to the Central Bank rouble, at an exchange rate determined by market forces. After the previous steps have been taken, the currency board rouble will circulate alongside the Central Bank rouble. Nobody will be forced to use currency board roubles. Much of the Russian economy will use the currency board rouble as its main medium of exchange, store of value, and unit of account because the currency board rouble will be more stable than the Central Bank rouble. It will be a matter for individual enterprises and persons to decide whether they now wish to pay and accept currency board roubles or Central Bank roubles. Commercial banks will also have to decide whether to allow depositors to convert existing deposits in Central Bank roubles into currency board roubles.

This proposal assumes that there will be an unrestricted market in exchange, so that Russians can exchange any amount of Central Bank roubles for currency board roubles or the reverse at the market rate. Hence it will be no disadvantage, in terms of the function of either type of rouble as a medium of exchange, to be paid in one type of rouble or the other.

The Central Bank of Russia will have to make its rouble sufficiently sound to withstand competition from the currency board rouble or it will wither away in importance as an issuer of currency. We suggest that when the real value of Central Bank rouble notes and coins diminishes to less than 10 per cent of all domestic currency in circulation, the Central Bank of Russia should be abolished. By then the political forces supporting the Central Bank should be weak.

If currency board roubles are introduced by distributing them to the Russian public rather by than giving them to the Russian government, the government will for a time continue to make payments in Central Bank roubles, because it will have no currency board roubles. If the government wishes to receive currency board roubles in tax payments, it must ensure that accounting rules do not favour Central Bank roubles. For example, suppose a taxpayer is assessed for 100,000 Central Bank roubles of taxes on 31 December, which he must pay by 31 January. Suppose also that one currency board rouble, whose real value remains stable, equals 1,000 Central Bank roubles on 31 December, but 2,000 Central Bank roubles on 31 January. If the taxpayer has a choice of paying with either type of rouble, he will pay in currency board roubles only if he can use the exchange rate of 31 January. If he must use the exchange rate of 31 December, his real taxes are twice as much if he pays in currency board roubles rather than Central Bank roubles. In that case, he will pay in Central Bank roubles and the government will receive no currency board roubles.

If the government uses both currencies in payment for a while, and if the Central Bank rouble continues to depreciate, the government will need to devise rules about what combination of currencies it uses. A simple rule is for small payments to consist only of Central Bank roubles, and large payments to consist only of currency board roubles. The size of payments considered 'large' can decrease to zero as the government accumulates more currency board roubles. Persons receiving payments from the government will experience little disadvantage from being paid in Central Bank rouble notes rather than currency board rouble notes, if the government adjusts its payments to the market exchange rate of the Central Bank rouble against the currency board rouble.[68] An unrestricted market will exist for exchanging the two types of roubles, so people will be able to exchange their Central Bank roubles immediately if they wish.

HOW TO CALCULATE THE INITIAL FOREIGN RESERVES FOR THE CURRENCY BOARD

What quantity of initial foreign reserves will the Russian currency board need? The answer partly depends on how the board is established. If the Central Bank of Russia is converted into a currency board, the entire rouble monetary base (except 'excess' reserves discussed later) will require 100 per cent foreign reserves as backing. If the currency board is the issuer of a parallel currency, the initial foreign reserves can be smaller.

Suppose first that the Central Bank of Russia is converted into a currency board. The foreign reserves that the currency board system needs will depend on the size of the monetary base and the exchange rate with the reserve currency. It will also depend on whether the currency board assumes responsibility for all rouble notes and coins in circulation, including those circulating in other former Soviet republics. If the currency board assumes responsibility only for rouble notes and coins circulating in Russia, the foreign reserves it needs will be correspondingly less.

The monetary base in Russia comprises rouble notes and coins in circulation (whether held by commercial banks or the public) and deposits of commercial banks at the Central Bank of Russia. Rouble notes and coins in circulation should be backed 100 per cent by foreign reserves in the currency board system. As was explained earlier in this chapter, not all rouble reserves of commercial banks need be converted into currency board notes and coins or foreign securities, although those that are should be backed 100 per cent by foreign reserves. Currently, commercial banks cannot use their required reserves, for example by reducing their reserves from 25 per cent to 18 per cent, to pay debts they owe to other banks. Their usable reserves are their reserves beyond 20 per cent, so a commercial bank with 25 per cent reserves has usable reserves of only 5 per cent of the public's deposits with it.

In the currency board system, the Russian government should impose no reserve requirements. Commercial banks should determine their own reserve ratios according to their judgments of what is prudent (see chapter 7), as has been the case in most past currency board systems. In modern banking systems with no reserve requirements, commercial banks have usually held reserves of only a few per cent of deposits. The primitive condition of banking technology in Russia will at first make it necessary for Russian commercial banks to maintain higher reserve ratios than banks in modern banking systems with no legal reserve requirements. To provide Russian commercial banks with reserves that are more than adequate, suppose that commercial banks in Russia need reserves of 10 per cent of deposits. (These are reserves that they will have after being restructured, if necessary, according to procedures specified in chapter 7.) The actual ratio to be used if the Russian government adopts this approach will require a more detailed study, for which there is not enough space here.

Since according to this proposal no reserve requirement for commercial banks will exist in the Russian currency board system, all the reserves of commercial banks remaining after monetary reform will be usable reserves. However, allowing all current reserves of commercial banks to become usable reserves in the currency board system may risk causing renewed inflation, because half or more of current reserves may be excess, not needed by the banks to ensure convertibility of their deposits into currency board notes and coins. The excess reserves would become the basis for an increase in bank loans and hence an increase in prices of domestic goods similar to that indicated in Figure 4.1. The Russian economy would eventually achieve a new set of higher, market-clearing prices, but in the meantime inflation would have undesirable effects.

If the Central Bank of Russia is converted into a currency board, the quantity of initial foreign reserves necessary for the currency board system is the sum of rouble notes and coins in circulation plus 10 per cent of rouble deposits, divided by the exchange rate of roubles per unit of reserve currency. Deciding what exchange rate to use in the calculation is difficult because no legal unrestricted market for roubles exists. However, as a first approximation, the interbank exchange rate of the rouble seems the most appropriate rate to use for calculating the foreign-currency value of the rouble. The interbank rate, though a controlled rate, is the nearest thing Russia has to an unrestricted market rate. On the one hand, in an unrestricted market the rouble might be worth even less, because restrictions hinder people from selling roubles, not from buying roubles. On the other hand, announcing that a currency board will be established will increase the credibility of the rouble and hence the demand for roubles. It is difficult to assess the strength of those opposing factors of demand for roubles. For the time being, suppose that they balance, so that the unrestricted market exchange rate equals the interbank rate.

We are now ready to calculate the initial foreign reserves necessary if the Central Bank is converted into a currency board. In December 1992, the most recent month for which complete statistics were available when we wrote this (because the Central Bank of Russia does not publish timely statistics), cash outside banks[69] was approximately 1,650 billion roubles, rouble deposits were 1,314 billion roubles, and the interbank exchange rate was 414.50 roubles per US dollar. Foreign reserves of 100 per cent for cash outside banks would therefore be 100 per cent of 1,650 billion roubles divided by 414.50 roubles per dollar, or approximately $3.9 billion. Foreign reserves of 10 per cent for rouble deposits are 10 per cent of no more than 5,450 billion roubles divided by 414.50 roubles per dollar, or approximately $1.3 billion. According to this calculation, then, the foreign reserves necessary for a currency board system are approximately $5.2 billion.[70]

Officials of the Central Bank of Russia and some economists have argued that the interbank exchange rate grossly undervalues the rouble. They prefer to use statistical estimates or more judgmental estimates to determine what the exchange rate of the rouble should be. In September 1992, when the interbank exchange rate of the rouble exceeded 200 roubles per US dollar, the chairman of the Central Bank estimated that the purchasing power parity of the rouble was 15–27 roubles per dollar, and indicated that he would prefer to set the exchange rate of the rouble at that rate, or perhaps at 60 roubles per dollar to encourage exports (FBIS 1992f). Use of the fundamental equilibrium exchange rate, an alternative method for determining the exchange rate, has been advocated as a possible basis for setting the exchange rate of the rouble by Stanley Fischer (1992: 93) and perhaps by the World Bank (1992b: 30). And apparently using a more judgmental estimate to determine the exchange rate that the rouble should have, John Williamson, a prominent critic of establishing currency boards in the former Soviet Union, has calculated that initial foreign reserves of $50 billion to $100 billion would be necessary to establish currency boards throughout the former Soviet Union (Havrylyshyn and Williamson 1991: 40; Williamson 1992: 27). A currency board for Russia alone would therefore need initial foreign reserves of $30 billion to $60 billion, according to Williamson.

The details of the statistical or judgmental estimates are not important for this discussion. The important thing is that according to all of these estimates, the initial foreign reserves that a Russian currency board system needs are much larger than our calculation states. We therefore must explain why the interbank exchange rate of the rouble is better than the statistical or judgmental estimates as an approximation to the unrestricted market exchange rate.

The defect of the statistical or judgmental estimates is that they treat the rouble as a mere medium of exchange, and neglect the function of money as a store of value. Credibility has no place in the statistical or judgmental estimates, whereas in market exchange rates, credibility is a crucial consideration. It is the rouble's loss of all credibility and its displacement by goods and foreign currency as stores of value that have caused its market value, both in the controlled interbank market and in the unofficial market, to diverge so much from the statistical or judgmental estimates of its value. Using the statistical or judgmental estimates to set the exchange rate presumes that the rouble is as credible as a fully convertible foreign currency. If the Central Bank of Russia remains the issuer of the rouble, however, the rouble is unlikely to be credible for the foreseeable future, and setting the exchange rate at the levels suggested by the statistical or judgmental estimates would grossly overvalue the rouble, causing further flight of capital from Russia.[71]

Nevertheless, suppose that the statistical or judgmental estimates of the exchange rate of the rouble are valid for calculating the initial foreign reserves the currency board will need. Suppose also that the impending conversion of the Central Bank into a currency board increases the credibility of the rouble so much that during the brief period of floating exchange rates (step 2 of converting the Central Bank into a currency board), the exchange rate of the rouble appreciates from the interbank rate to a much higher level, and the initial foreign reserves necessary for the currency board system increase from the $5.2 billion of our calculation to the $30 billion of Williamson's calculation. The next section explains how the Russian government can obtain even such a large quantity of initial foreign reserves.

Before doing so, though, let us calculate the initial foreign reserves that the currency board system will need if the currency board is established as the issuer of a parallel currency rather than if the Central Bank of Russia is converted into a currency board. The answer is that no determinate quantity of initial foreign reserves is necessary, because the currency board will not provide backing for the monetary base of the Central Bank rouble. All notes and coins of the currency board in circulation must be backed 100 per cent by foreign reserves, but the currency board can begin with whatever initial quantity of foreign reserves it obtains. The initial quantity of foreign reserves should be sufficient to indicate to the Russian people that the currency board is a substantial institution. Initial foreign reserves of $1.5 billion should be adequate. If the currency board can obtain larger initial reserves, so much the better. Notice that in the parallel currency approach, commercial banks are given none of the initial foreign reserves. If they wish to offer deposits in currency board roubles, they need to acquire currency board rouble notes and coins or reserve-currency assets as reserves.

HOW TO OBTAIN THE INITIAL FOREIGN RESERVES FOR THE CURRENCY BOARD

Once the quantity of initial foreign reserves the Russian currency board needs has been calculated, how can the currency board obtain the reserves? The calculations of the previous section were that the necessary foreign reserves will be $5.2 billion if the Central Bank of Russia is converted into a currency board, or $1.5 billion if the currency board is established as the issuer of a parallel currency. In the conversion approach, the net amount of foreign reserves that the currency board will need will be the gross amount minus existing foreign reserves. The existing foreign reserves of the Central Bank of Russia seem to be only a few hundred million dollars, so the net amount of initial foreign reserves the currency board will need will probably be almost the same as the gross amount. In the parallel currency approach, the net amount of initial foreign reserves that the currency board will need will equal the gross amount, because the Central Bank of Russia will continue to exist and the currency board will obtain no reserves from the Central Bank.

In either approach, the currency board will need additional foreign reserves to provide backing. Foreign reserves can be obtained from several sources. The Russian government can lease or sell state property for fully convertible foreign currency. Equivalently, if the Central Bank is converted into a currency board, the government can lease or sell state property for roubles and not reissue the roubles. (That would be like the process described in Figure 4.4, which decreases the monetary base and the overall supply of money.) A similar technique was used in Slovenia to privatize apartments and to establish the Slovenian tolar as a new currency to replace the Yugoslav dinar. To buy apartments, Slovenes had to pay tolars, and to obtain tolars, they had to exchange foreign currency, such as German marks and Austrian schillings, for tolars. The combined privatization and currency reform brought foreign currency into the Slovenian central bank (Pleskovic and Sachs 1992).

Another possible source of reserves is a loan from the IMF. As was explained in chapter 3, the American government has authorized the IMF to use the recent increase in the American quota at the IMF to establish currency boards, if the IMF approves. To keep the Russian currency board 'pure', its constitution should forbid it from accepting loans other than a loan for its initial foreign reserves.

If the Russian currency board borrows from the IMF, the currency board will eventually have to repay the loan. Even if the currency board has no other initial reserves than the loan from the IMF, it should have no difficulty repaying the loan within 15–20 years. Because the currency board will issue a sound currency, Russians will tend to exchange the foreign notes that they now hold, and hold currency board notes and coins instead. Because the currency board will help the Russian economy to revive, the overall demand for domestic currency will increase. Consequently, the note and coin circulation of the Russian currency board will increase from its initial level, its foreign reserves will increase accordingly, and the seigniorage from the foreign reserves will increase. Based on historical and current international comparisons of the relationship between income and circulation of notes and coins,[72] the note and coin circulation of the Russian currency board will probably be at least $9 billion within three years after the currency board opens. If net seigniorage of the currency board is 4 per cent of its note and coin circulation, a conservative estimate, the currency board should be able to repay at least $360 million a year to the IMF.

Once the currency board opens, the self-adjusting nature of the money supply process in a currency board system will enable the money supply to accommodate changes in demand for money (see chapter 4 and Appendix B). Experience indicates that the currency board system has not hindered rapid increases in the money supply that have been justified by economic growth. Foreign investment has enabled the money supply in currency board systems to increase consistently despite decades of current-account deficits.

Before ending this discussion of how to obtain the initial foreign reserves of the currency board, it is worth considering a point mentioned in the previous section. It applies only to the conversion approach, not to the parallel currency approach. Suppose that the impending conversion of the Central Bank of Russia into a currency board increases the credibility of the rouble so much that during the brief period of floating exchange rates (step 2 of the proposal), the exchange rate of the rouble appreciates compared to the previous interbank rate, and the foreign reserves necessary for the currency board system therefore exceed the $5.2 billion of our calculation.

In that case, the very success of the monetary reform will enable the Russian government to acquire the necessary additional reserves. The appreciation in the exchange rate of the rouble will reflect increased confidence in the Russian economy. Increased confidence will increase the capitalized value (present value) of assets in Russia, including state property. The value added to Russian assets by the monetary reform will enable the government to lease or sell state property for more than it would have received before it announced the reform. The reform will also increase Russia's tax base by increasing GDP, expressed in dollars, from its 1992 level of $75 billion ($500 per person, approximately the same per person as in Sri Lanka) to perhaps $150 billion ($1,000 per person, approximately two-thirds the level per person in Poland). If the Russian government could collect 25 per cent of the difference between a $75 billion tax base and a $150 billion tax base, it would gain $18.75 billion. Increased confidence in the Russian economy should enable the Russian government to obtain even a large quantity of initial foreign reserves for the currency board by taxation or by borrowing. The government should be able to resume foreign borrowing because the revival of the economy should make it credit-worthy again.[73]

HOW TO CHOOSE A RESERVE CURRENCY FOR THE CURRENCY BOARD

What reserve currency should the currency board choose? Any of the likely choices is more stable and credible than the Central Bank rouble is at present. The most likely choices are the US dollar and the German mark; less likely choices are the European Currency Unit (ecu) and gold.

The US dollar is probably the most appropriate reserve currency. The dollar is the most widely used currency in international trade and finance, including that of Russia. Russia's main exports, such as oil, natural gas, timber and minerals, are predominantly priced in dollars on world markets. The dollar also has the advantage that it already is the most widely used unofficial parallel currency and a popular unit of account in Russia. Choosing the dollar would involve less change of habits than choosing any other reserve currency. Historically, the dollar has had low inflation, high credibility, full convertibility, and low real interest rates. It has a high likelihood of continuing its exceptionally good historical performance.

The German mark is another possible reserve currency. It circulates as an unofficial parallel currency in parts of Russia and it is the dominant currency of Western Europe, Russia's largest trading partner and largest potential source of new foreign investment. Several West European currencies are pegged to the mark. Choosing the mark as the reserve currency would eliminate exchange risk with more of Western Europe than choosing any other reserve currency, promoting trade and foreign investment from the mark zone. Since 1948, when the immediate predecessor to the German Bundesbank was founded, the mark has had low inflation and high credibility. The mark has an even higher likelihood than the dollar of continuing its exceptionally good historical performance, because the Bundesbank has more political independence from the government than the US Federal Reserve System. The main disadvantage of the mark is that the Bundesbank is currently keeping real interest rates high, as a result of German government policies towards the former East Germany.

The European Currency Unit (ecu), a composite of the mark and other currencies in the European Monetary System, has been suggested as a reserve currency for currency boards in Eastern Europe (Schmieding 1992: 137–44; Selgin 1992a). The ecu was intended to replace existing national currencies in the European Monetary System in the late 1990s. Recent difficulties in the European Monetary System have delayed movement towards currency unification in Western Europe, perhaps indefinitely, and have caused the market in ecu bonds to shrink. A currency board with substantial assets that used the ecu as its reserve currency would therefore probably have to hold securities in each currency that is part of the ecu basket, which would complicate the task of administering the currency board. Furthermore, the ecu is unfamiliar as a medium of exchange, store of value, and unit of account to the Russian people, because no ecu notes exist and because little of Russia's foreign trade is conducted in ecus.

A basket of foreign currencies does not seem advantageous as the reserve currency for the Russian currency board.[74] A basket is less transparent to the public than a single reserve currency, and thus may not as quickly achieve high credibility for the currency board. A basket also imposes greater costs on the currency board in terms of management time and transaction fees. A basket does not eliminate exchange risk with any single reserve currency; it sacrifices greater potential variability of exchange rates with each component of the basket for lower variability with the whole basket. If Russians are allowed to hold foreign-currency deposits, those who desire the benefits of lower variability with a basket of currencies can create their own baskets by holding a combination of currencies or by trading currency futures and options, as people do in Hong Kong.

If no foreign currency seems satisfactory, another possible reserve currency is gold.[75] The currency board need not hold much actual gold; it can make interest-bearing gold loans instead. A well-organized market for gold loans exists in London; loan rates are published daily in the *Financial Times*. Gold loans typically earn 3–4 per cent interest a year. To enable the currency board to exchange amounts worth less than the smallest convenient amount of gold (say, one troy ounce), the board could be allowed to accept and pay US dollars for small amounts. That would be a slight complication compared to a currency board based on the US dollar or the German mark, which would use only one currency. The main disadvantage of gold is that no other country adheres to the gold standard, so using gold would not eliminate exchange risk with any country. Therefore gold does not seem to be the most appropriate reserve currency.

We have considered the implications for Russia of choosing various reserve currrencies. It is also worth considering the implications for the reserve country. If the US dollar is the reserve currency, the demand for dollar notes in Russia will probably decrease because people will exchange dollar notes for currency board rouble notes and coins. On the other hand, the role of the dollar as the reserve currency will create demand by Russian commercial banks, either directly or through correspondent banks in the United States, for Fed funds (deposits of commercial banks at the US Federal Reserve System) as a means of settling payments. Dollar notes and coins and Fed funds are the components of the dollar monetary base. The net effect of a currency board rouble on demand for the dollar monetary base is thus unclear if the dollar is the reserve currency. Similar remarks apply if the German mark is the reserve currency. In any case, the Russian economy is now small compared to the American and German economies, so the initial effect of a Russian currency board choosing the dollar or the mark as the reserve currency will be correspondingly small. If gold or the ecu is the reserve asset, though, demand for gold or ecu bonds will clearly increase, since Russians hold little gold or ecu bonds now. The gold and ecu loan markets are small enough that the initial actions of the Russian currency board may affect them significantly.

Linking the currency board rouble to a foreign currency will not subject Russia to foreign political domination (see chapter 8). Rather, linking the rouble to an appropriate foreign currency will restore an element of Russian national pride by giving Russia a currency as sound as the reserve currency.

The next chapter suggests what the currency board should do if the reserve currency becomes unstable.

6

HOW TO OPERATE AND PROTECT A CURRENCY BOARD IN RUSSIA

HOW TO OPERATE THE CURRENCY BOARD

A typical currency board is simple to operate. Past currency boards have usually had staffs of ten or fewer people, although they have not covered as huge a territory or served as large a population as will the proposed Russian currency board. Past currency boards have achieved economies by contracting clerical and investment functions to outside parties; the proposed Russian currency board can do likewise. The extreme simplicity of a currency board is one of the advantages of the currency board system. As has been mentioned, apart from its other problems, the Central Bank of Russia lacks staff with the technical skill to administer monetary policy competently in an emerging market economy, or even to perform the more mundane task of operating the payments system efficiently.

The main administrative details of operating the Russian currency board will be as follows.[76]

Constitution

Appendix A contains a model currency board law that distills features of past currency board constitutions into a form that should enable the Russian currency board to operate efficiently.

Exchange policy

The Russian currency board will exchange its notes and coins on demand at a fixed rate into or from the reserve currency at the board's offices or agencies. People who have reserve currency will be able to exchange it for currency board notes and coins at the fixed rate, and people who have currency board notes and coins will be able to exchange them for reserve

103

currency at the fixed rate. To hold a large supply of reserve-currency notes would reduce the profits of the currency board, because the board would be unable to invest those funds in interest-bearing securities. Hence, the currency board should try to encourage a 'wholesale' currency exchange business with commercial banks and use electronic funds transfer extensively for payment and acceptance of reserve-currency securities.

Clientele

Although the currency board should encourage a wholesale currency exchange business with commercial banks, the Russian public should also be allowed to deal directly with the currency board. Some British colonial currency boards dealt only with banks, as a way of reducing their need for staff (Greaves 1953: 13). It seems unnecessary and unjust to discriminate against the public in this way. Most people will exchange currency through commercial banks in any case, as the West African Currency Board discovered when it changed from dealing with commercial banks only to dealing with the public as well. Giving the public the choice of dealing directly with the currency board will place a low limit on the commission fees that commercial banks charge for exchanging currency board currency for reserve currency. That will tend to tighten the link between the currency board rouble and the reserve currency, which will make arbitrage between Russia and the reserve country more efficient.

Lower and upper limits to exchanges

To reduce their handling costs, many currency boards have imposed minimum exchange amounts. Small British colonial currency boards such as those of Jamaica or Barbados required a minimum of £1,000; larger ones such as the West African Currency Board required a minimum of £10,000 (Greaves 1953: 13).

To strengthen confidence in the Russian currency board, the board should impose no minimum exchange amount. The Russian public will then know that the currency board is always ready to convert any amount of currency board roubles into reserve currency. There will also, of course, be no upper limit to the amount of reserve currency or of its own notes and coins in circulation that the currency board accepts for exchange. No past currency board except the modified currency board of Bermuda has ever had an upper limit to exchanges, because an upper limit restricts the full convertibility into the reserve currency that is the purpose of the currency board system.

Commission fees

Some currency boards have charged commission fees of ⅛ per cent to 1 per cent per transaction; the North Russian currency board, for instance, charged a fee of 1 per cent. Other currency boards have charged lower commission fees for large transactions than for small ones. The Russian currency board should charge no commission fees for exchanges. The social benefits of not charging fees greatly exceed the pecuniary benefits to the currency board of charging fees. Commission fees would loosen the link to the reserve currency, especially for short-term capital movements, because they would impose high costs relative to the benefits of arbitrage. A few currency boards, most notably the East African Currency Board towards the end of its existence, have deliberately manipulated their commission fees to influence capital movements (Kratz 1966: 246–7). But a currency board is intended to eliminate exchange risk with the reserve currency, so it is pointless to erect barriers to exchange into and from the reserve currency. Besides, commission fees would bring little income to the Russian currency board; it will in any case earn most of its income from interest on its foreign assets.

Exchanges by the Russian currency board should be exempt from taxation, to prevent the Russian government from attempting to tax the currency board out of existence. The currency board should also be exempt from other legal barriers that might hinder exchanges by it.

Offices

The Russian currency board should have its main office in Moscow and a few branch offices or agencies in other large cities of Russia. The main office will do most of the business, because Moscow is the financial centre of Russia. The main role of the branch offices or agencies will storing and distributing notes and coins. The currency board should perhaps own or rent a street-level office in Moscow, as a visible symbol to the Russian public of its existence, but it need not have actual branches. Instead, one or more commercial banks can be the board's agent outside Moscow, as the Bank of British West Africa was for the West African Currency Board. The Russian currency board should also have an office abroad, in the reserve country or in a safe-haven financial centre such as Switzerland. The office abroad will provide a back-up location for redeeming notes and coins should the Russian government threaten to harass the Russian offices of the currency board.

Management

The Russian currency board should have a small board of directors to supervise the board's staff. Past currency boards have had three to eight directors. The powers of the board of directors and of the staff will be limited; unlike their counterparts in central banks, they will have no discretionary control of the monetary base. To protect the board of directors from political pressure to convert the currency board into a central bank, directors should have staggered terms. Also, some directors should be foreigners, appointed by Western commercial banks, or perhaps by the IMF if the IMF lends some of the initial foreign reserves of the currency board. The next section returns to this proposal.

Staff

The staff of the Russian currency board will perform two functions: exchanging currency board rouble notes and coins for reserve currency, or the reverse, and investing the assets of the currency board in low-risk securities denominated in and payable in the reserve currency. The exchange work will require only a small number of bank tellers. The investment work will require some expert financial traders, but since the currency board will follow rather routine, conservative investment practices, its investment expenses should be smaller than those of commercial banks with portfolios of similar size. The assets of the Russian currency board should be held at suitable institutions abroad, for example with one or more large Western commercial banks or central banks.

Past currency boards have had small staffs. The West African Currency Board, which served Nigeria, the Gold Coast (Ghana), Sierra Leone, the Gambia, Cameroons, and Togoland, had only one full-time employee at its London headquarters (Loynes 1962: 18). It and other currency boards contracted their exchange and investment work to commercial banks or other agents. The Russian currency board can do the same if that is more efficient than hiring its own staff.

Reserve ratio

The Russian currency board will begin with foreign reserves equal to 100 per cent of its notes and coins in circulation. In addition, like most past currency boards, the Russian currency board should accumulate a reserve fund to ensure that its foreign reserves are never less than 100 per cent, even if its assets lose part of their market value (for example, if interest rates increase, reducing the principal of fixed-rate securities). Many currency boards have accumulated a reserve fund of 10 per cent of notes and coins in circulation (Clauson 1944: 9). They have usually paid all net seigniorage into the reserve fund until the reserve fund is full. They have paid all additional net seigniorage to their governments. These rules leave no opportunity for discretionary monetary policy when the foreign reserves of the currency board are between 100 per cent and 110 per cent. The Russian currency board should adopt similar rules.

Composition of reserves

The Russian currency board should hold its foreign reserves in low-risk assets payable in the reserve currency only. Most of its foreign reserves will be low-risk, interest-earning securities. It can also hold some foreign reserves in interest-bearing deposits at reputable commercial banks in the reserve country, or in reserve-currency notes or noninterest-earning deposits at the central bank of the reserve country. As much as possible, the currency board should avoid holding assets that earn no interest.

The currency board should not hold assets denominated in Central Bank or currency board roubles, because that would open the way to central banking-type operations. Specifically, the currency board would be able to increase or decrease the domestic monetary base by changing its holdings of domestic securities, as a central bank does by means described in chapter 4. Allowing holdings of domestic assets was one of the steps that led the East African and Southern Rhodesia currency boards, among others, towards becoming central banks (Newlyn and Rowan 1954: 67–9; Kratz 1966: 236–41). It is desirable to specify in the constitution or by-laws of the Russian currency board what types of assets it may hold.

Besides opening the way for central banking, holding domestic assets can be risky, as the experience of the North Russian currency board shows. The North Russian currency board held 25 per cent of its reserves in North Russian government bonds. When the Red Army captured North Russia, the North Russian government defaulted on the bonds. The British government, the main holder of currency board notes, lost approximately 15.5 million roubles as a result (see chapter 9).

Limiting the Russian currency board to assets payable in the reserve currency need not limit the currency board to securities issued in the reserve country. Many governments and companies issue securities denominated in foreign currency in Eurocurrency (offshore) markets. Branches of French banks in London issue bonds for US dollars, for example, and the Russian currency board can buy such bonds if the dollar is the reserve currency. To prevent the currency board from becoming entangled in the politics of Russian government finance, though, the currency board should be forbidden to hold Russian government securities or securities issued by Russian state enterprises, no matter in what currency they are payable.

Maturity of reserves

It may be desirable for the constitution or by-laws of the Russian currency board to limit the maturity of the assets it holds to, say, ten years. Long-term bonds with fixed interest rates fluctuate widely in value as interest rates change, although they may offer higher average returns than short-term assets. Some British colonial currency boards that invested in long-term pound sterling bonds suffered large losses when sterling interest rates rose sharply in the 1950s. Their foreign reserves exceeded 100 per cent even so, because they had accumulated reserve funds, typically equal to 10 per cent of notes and coins in circulation.

British colonial currency boards often divided their foreign reserves into a 'liquid reserve' and an 'investment reserve'. The liquid reserve consisted of securities payable in less than two years, and was typically 30 per cent of total reserves. The investment reserve consisted of securities payable in more than two years, and was the rest of total reserves. The investment reserve was equal to the public's estimated minimum, 'hard-core' demand for currency board notes and coins (Clauson 1944: 8–11). The liquid reserve of the Russian currency board should probably exceed 30 per cent initially, but later the board should be able to hold an increasing proportion of assets in the higher-yielding investment reserve as Russia's economic situation improves.

Expenses

Judging from the experience of past currency boards, average expenses of the Russian currency board should be no more than 1 per cent of total assets, and may be as low as ½ per cent. (In comparison, the Central Bank of Russia charges other former Soviet republics that use rouble notes a fee of 1 per cent to cover the costs of printing and transporting the notes [IMF 1992a: 25 n. 6].) The largest expense will be printing notes and minting coins. Salaries will probably be the next largest expense. Rent, utilities, and remaining costs will probably be small. The cost of transporting notes and coins will be more than for most past currency boards because Russia is so huge.

The notes issued by the currency board should be printed abroad, not in Russia as the notes of the Central Bank of Russia are. Printing the notes abroad will prevent the Russian government from seizing the printing presses and overturning the currency board system by printing notes unbacked by foreign reserves. The cost of printing notes will be higher than it would be if they were printed in Russia, but the extra expense is worthwhile as a type of insurance. The notes should also be of higher quality than existing rouble notes, which are too easily counterfeited. The cost of printing notes in the West is $26-$45 per thousand, depending on what design features the notes have (Berreby 1992; see also Shapiro 1993).

Seigniorage

Unlike securities and many bank deposits, notes and coins pay no interest. Hence, notes and coins are like an interest-free loan from people who hold them to the issuer. The Russian currency board will earn *gross* seigniorage equal to interest from its holdings of reserve-currency securities. Its *net* seigniorage (profit) will be the gross seigniorage minus the expense of putting and maintaining notes and coins in circulation. In addition, if notes and coins are destroyed, the net worth of the currency board will increase, because its liabilities will decrease but its assets will not.[77]

Suppose that the reserve currency of the Russian currency board is the US dollar. In the currency board system, the only difference between using currency board rouble notes and coins instead of dollar notes and coins is that the Russian currency board rather than the US Federal Reserve System will capture the net seigniorage. The Russian currency board can earn significant net seigniorage. A portfolio of long-term and short-term securities should earn an average return of at least 5 per cent a year. The expenses of the currency board should not exceed 1 per cent a year, and may be as low as ½ per cent a year. Net seigniorage, then, will probably be at least 4 per cent a year of the average circulation of the currency board's notes and coins in circulation.[78] In the previous chapter it was stated that the note and coin circulation of the currency board will probably equal at least US$9 billion within three years after the currency board opens. Net annual seigniorage of 4 per cent of $9 billion is $360 million.

HOW TO PROTECT THE CURRENCY BOARD

Despite the economic success of the currency board system earlier in this century, currency boards exist today only in a few countries. Currency boards elsewhere were converted into central banks because governments were influenced by incorrect economic criticisms of the currency board system, the desire to establish central banks as symbols of national independence, and an understanding of the political advantages of politicized central banks. As has been mentioned, many currency boards have relied on informal protection rather than formal legal protection from changes in their operating rules. The experience of most such currency boards, and of central banking in Russia, strongly suggests that the proposed Russian currency board should have strong legal protection from being converted into a central bank.[79] Anxiety that the monetary constitution embodied in the Russian currency board might be subverted would reduce the willingness of foreigners to invest in Russia, diminishing one of the main advantages of the currency board system. Therefore, this section proposes ways of strengthening the Russian currency board as a monetary constitution. The proposals can be summarized as *credibility*, *commitment*, and *competition*. They are complementary; any can be implemented separately or with the others. They will tend to make the Russian currency board even better than a typical currency board.

The Russian currency board can strengthen its credibility by protecting itself from potential pressure from the Russian government. Previous chapters explained how the various features of a typical currency board make credible its commitment to a fixed exchange rate. Since any human institution, no matter how rule-bound, is administered by people and can be changed by people, the model currency board constitution of Appendix A includes a provision that a majority of the board of directors be foreigners. That will help prevent the Russian government from bending the rules of the currency board. The foreign directors should be appointed by Western commercial banks, or perhaps by the IMF if the IMF lends some of the initial foreign reserves of the currency board. The directors appointed by the IMF should not be IMF officials or officials of IMF member governments, because their decisions may too easily be influenced by political considerations.[80] Precedents exist for such an arrangement. For example, only three of the eight directors of the Libyan Currency Board of the 1950s were Libyan; the rest were British, French, Italian, and Egyptian, and were chosen by their respective governments (Blowers and McLeod 1952: 453). To reduce the political influence of the Russian government on the Russian directors of the currency board, the Russian directors could be required not to be government officials and could be appointed by a trade association of privately owned banks rather than by the Russian government.

Another way to strengthen the credibility of the Russian currency board is for it to hold its assets in a safe-haven country such as Switzerland. The currency board should be incorporated in the safe-haven country. The currency board will then be a nonprofit, nongovernmental institution independent of the Russian government, although the permission of the Russian government will of course be necessary for the currency board to operate in Russia. The Burmese and Jordanian currency boards, among others, approached but did not quite achieve this degree of protection from political pressure by their governments; their headquarters remained in London even after Burma and Jordan became independent.

Yet another way to strengthen the credibility of the Russian currency board is for its notes to contain a statement that they are convertible into the reserve currency at a fixed rate at the board's offices in Russia and abroad. Whether or not notes and coins issued by the currency board contain an explicit statement of convertibility, they should be considered a type of contract promising a fixed exchange rate, unlike notes and coins issued by a typical central bank. Holders of notes and coins should have the right to sue the currency board for breach of contract in the very unlikely event that it fails to redeem its notes and coins at the fixed exchange rate on demand.

The Russian currency board can commit itself to buy and sell forward exchange at the fixed rate with the reserve currency. Some currency boards, such as that of Hong Kong, have offered three- and six-month forward exchange contracts as a way of increasing the liquidity of their foreign-exchange markets. When the forward market becomes well established, the currency board can leave it to commercial banks and cease dealing in forward exchange.

The currency board should cease dealing in forward exchange if the reserve currency approaches the inflation limits discussed in the next section, so as to avoid incurring losses from changing the reserve currency.

The Russian currency board can be subjected to competition to induce it to maintain high-quality service. Russians should be allowed to make contracts, payments, and deposits in any currency they wish. In particular, reserve-currency notes should be allowed to circulate alongside the notes of the currency board, as has been the case in many currency board systems based on the pound sterling. However, use of reserve-currency notes in Russia will probably be small, for reasons explained in the next section. (Notice that as a party to contracts and payments, the Russian government need not accept the reserve currency for tax payments; it can insist on payment in currency board rouble notes and deposits.) Foreigners should be allowed to hold deposits in currency board roubles.

To subject the Russian currency board to even more intense competition, solvent privately owned commercial banks in Russia could be allowed to issue notes and coins to compete with the notes and coins issued by the currency board (and the Central Bank, if it continues to exist). Like currency board notes, some bank notes would no doubt be convertible into the reserve currency at the fixed exchange rate. Hence, currency board notes and bank notes would be like different brands of traveller's cheques circulating alongside one another. Other bank notes might be convertible into other reserve currencies; for example, some bank notes might be convertible into Japanese yen while other bank notes and the notes of the currency board were convertible into US dollars. Whatever the case, what brands of notes and coins were most widely used would depend on what brands best satisfied the needs of consumers. The currency board would have no responsibility to ensure the convertibility of notes and coins issued by commercial banks, just as it has no responsibility for ensuring the convertibility of their deposits into its notes and coins or into the reserve currency. The Russian public should be warned that it would use at its own risk notes and coins issued by commercial banks.

Competition between currency board notes and bank notes has existed before. In British Caribbean colonies, commercial banks issued convertible notes subject to no reserve requirements. Bank notes competed with currency board notes until the 1950s, when local governments outlawed bank note issue to monopolize seigniorage (Sayers 1952: 428, 437). In Hong Kong today, the currency board itself issues no notes; rather, it holds the 100 per cent reserves in US dollar assets that the two (soon to be three) note-issuing banks deposit against their issues of Hong Kong dollar notes, plus a reserve fund of 5 per cent (Freris 1991: 188). If solvent commercial banks in Russia are allowed to issue notes and coins, their notes and coins should be subject to no reserve requirement. Commercial banks that promise convertibility of their notes and coins into some reserve currency at a fixed exchange rate should of course be strictly required to fulfil their promise.

If commercial banks were permitted to issue notes, their notes might eventually dominate the market. We suggest (following Dowd 1992b) that if the Russian currency board's market share of domestic notes in circulation were to diminish below 10 per cent, the board should be closed. The 100 per cent foreign reserves of the currency board would enable it to pay without difficulty all holders of its notes and coins. The provision to close the currency board should not become effective until five years after commercial banks begin issuing notes, so as to provide a steadying influence during a period that might see some ill-fated experiments before competitive note issue settles into a stable pattern.

As one of many competitive issuers of notes and coins, the Russian currency board would earn less seigniorage than it would earn as a monopoly issuer. The seigniorage that the currency board would lose would tend not to accrue to note-issuing commercial banks, however, but to consumers, in a dissipation of producers' profits that is typical of competitive markets. There would be no need to worry if competitive note issue reduced the seigniorage of the currency board. Unlike the current situation, in which Russians use parallel foreign currencies and create seigniorage for foreign central banks, in a system of competitive note issue Russians would use parallel domestic currencies and the seigniorage would remain within Russia, either as benefits to consumers (consumer's surplus) or as profits of commercial banks in Russia and profits of the Russian currency board. Anyway, for the Russian government, the main financial benefit of the currency board system, especially in the long run, will not be seigniorage, as it currently is with central banking in Russia, but the increase in real taxes that will be possible as extreme inflation ends and the Russian economy revives.

If allowing competitive note issue by commercial banks were not politically feasible at first, the Russian government could introduce a limited degree of competition by offering two or more franchises to operate competing currency boards. The franchises could be awarded by open bidding and the winning bidders could be required to provide a minimum level of service specified in the franchise contracts. The franchised currency boards would in that case be privately owned and operated, but subject to a degree of government regulation, as are utilities in other countries. (Incidentally, extensive historical experience indicates that issue of notes has never been a natural monopoly [Schuler 1992a: 15–16]. Hence multiple franchises would be second best to unrestricted competitive issue of currencies.)

HOW TO CHANGE THE RESERVE CURRENCY, IF NECESSARY

Besides lacking protection from being converted into central banks, past currency boards have had one other defect: they have lacked well-defined rules for untying their own currency from an unstable reserve currency. Most currency board currencies were linked to the pound sterling, which was stable for more than a century until the Second World War. When the currency boards were established, confidence in sterling was so great that nobody considered the possibility that sterling would become unstable. After the Second World War, though, sterling did become unstable. British colonial currency boards devalued their currencies with sterling against gold and the US dollar in 1949, 1967, and 1972. Devaluation hurt them by increasing the cost of many foreign goods that they needed for their economic development, such as the food that Hong Kong imported from China. Hong Kong, Singapore, Brunei, and the East Caribbean Currency Board, as well as some countries with central banks, changed from sterling to the more stable US dollar as their reserve currency in the 1970s (Yeager 1976: 445, 459–68).

Changing the reserve currency is beneficial if the existing reserve currency becomes quite unstable, because otherwise the currency board system suffers the monetary problems afflicting the reserve country. (However, freedom to make contracts and payments in other currencies offers some escape from the problem.) If the Russian currency board has the power to change the reserve currency, though, the procedure should be carefully specified in its constitution and should be enacted by the currency board itself, rather than being a somewhat arbitrary government decision as was the case with the currency boards that changed reserve currencies in the 1970s.

We suggest that the Russian currency board should not be allowed to change the reserve currency unless annualized inflation in the consumer price index of the reserve country exceeds the range −5 per cent to 20 per cent for more than two years, or −10 per cent to 40 per cent for more than six months. These are inflation rates that historically have caused substantial economic disruption if exceeded.[81] If inflation in the reserve country exceeds the specified range, the Russian currency board should be

113

allowed to devalue or revalue its currency in terms of the reserve currency by no more than the amount of the inflation rate in the reserve country for the period just specified (two years or six months). Alternatively, the currency board should be allowed to choose a new, more stable reserve currency and set a new fixed exchange rate at the rate then prevailing between that currency and the original reserve currency. (If gold is the reserve currency, Russia itself will be considered the reserve country.)

It may also be desirable for the constitution of the Russian currency board to contain a similar provision allowing the currency board to reset the exchange rate with the reserve currency if the reserve currency appreciates or depreciates very rapidly against a basket of foreign currencies representing other countries important in Russia's foreign trade. These provisions may appear to open a loophole for destabilizing speculation, as often occurs with a pegged exchange rate, but they do not. Destabilizing speculation occurs when the commitment to an exchange rate is uncertain. The commitment of the Russian currency board to maintaining the existing exchange rate would be certain, provided that the reserve currency remains within the predetermined range of inflation or appreciation. Outside the range, the commitment of the currency board to changing the exchange rate or the reserve currency would be certain; hence no uncertainty would exist about the behaviour of the currency board, although uncertainty might exist about the behaviour of the reserve currency. In any case, speculation would not reduce the foreign reserves of the currency board to less than 100 per cent of its notes and coins in circulation.

We offer the foregoing guidelines for changing the reserve currency as suggestions, which are more experimental than the other operating rules we have discussed. The general point we wish to emphasize is that it is better to respond to instability in the reserve currency by having well-defined rules, known in advance to the public, than to respond in the improvised, even capricious ways that some currency boards and governments have done.[82]

7

THE CURRENCY BOARD AND REFORM OF THE RUSSIAN MONETARY SYSTEM

The unsound condition of the rouble is a consequence of many problems of the Russian monetary system. The government budget has a huge deficit; enterprise arrears increase the difficulty of knowing the true financial condition of state enterprises; the commercial banking system is inadequate for mobilizing and allocating savings and is potentially unstable; the payments system is inefficient; and the government is in default on Russia's foreign debt. The source of most of these problems is soft budget constraints, which persist because the Central Bank of Russia is a lender of last resort to the Russian government and state enterprises. The inflation that the Central Bank causes by financing soft budget constraints worsens the problems of the Russian economy.

A currency board will tend to impose a hard budget constraint on the Russian government; that will tend to make the government impose hard budget constraints on state enterprises, including state commercial banks. Hard budget constraints will encourage economic growth by tending to shift resources from less valuable to more valuable uses. However, hard budget constraints will also cause some transitional difficulties for the Russian economy, because the economy is accustomed to soft budget constraints.

This chapter sketches the most important consequences of the currency board system for other aspects of the Russian monetary system – the government budget, state enterprises, commercial banks, and so on. Its structure resembles that of chapter 3, which described the main features of the Russian monetary system at present. This chapter does not pretend to propose solutions for all the problems of the Russian monetary system and the Russian economy. However, this chapter does show that most of the problems of the Russian monetary system result from the soft budget constraints permitted by the Central Bank of Russia and by the other effects of the Central Bank on the monetary system. By tending to impose hard budget constraints and by reforming some other aspects of the monetary system, the Russian currency board will provide a framework within which Russian politicians, managers of state enterprises, commercial bankers, entrepreneurs, and workers can solve the problems of the Russian monetary system in a way that will be beneficial for the Russian economy. This chapter describes the framework. Readers who desire a more detailed, sector-by-sector description of the economic reforms that will be necessary can begin by consulting the recent World Bank report on reforming the Russian economy (World Bank 1992b), although, as we have said, we do not agree with all of its recommendations.

THE GOVERNMENT BUDGET

The budget deficit of the Russian government is a large proportion of GDP (5–30 per cent, depending on the method of calculation) because the government has a soft budget constraint. The Central Bank of Russia is a lender of last resort to the government: it finances by means of inflation whatever government spending cannot be financed by other taxes or by noninflationary borrowing. By tending to impose a hard budget constraint on the Russian government, the proposed Russian currency board will tend to force the government to balance the budget, or to finance the budget deficit by noninflationary borrowing.

Balancing the budget without inflationary finance may seem politically unrealistic for Russia at present. But other countries, and Russia itself in the 1920s (see chapter 9) have been able to balance their government budgets after periods of large deficits and extreme inflation. With appropriate changes that are politically realistic, the Russian government of today can also balance its budget.

Using currency board roubles will, by itself, eliminate almost all of the loss in real revenue that the government now suffers because of extreme inflation between the time taxes are assessed and collected (the Olivera-Tanzi effect). In addition, some changes of policy can be made that are politically realistic and can reduce the government budget deficit substantially. In particular, the government can increase its revenue substantially by a more sensible policy on energy prices, especially the price of oil. Production of oil in Russia has been decreasing since 1989. It decreased 13.5 per cent in 1992, and the minister of energy has warned that it may decrease 15 per cent in 1993 (World Bank 1992b: 176, 306; FBIS 1993d; Freeland 1993). The Russian government limits the domestic price of oil to a fraction of the world price. The precise figure changes as inflation erodes the effect of increases in the rouble price of oil, but in early 1993 the domestic price of oil was perhaps 30 per cent of the world price. The Russian government has promised the IMF and the World Bank to allow the domestic price of oil to increase to the world price by the end of 1993, although the government now appears unlikely to fulfil the promise. Production of oil and government revenue from oil export taxes have decreased steeply because it is more profitable for producers to keep oil in the ground than to pump it (Uchitelle 1992a; see also Wallich 1992: 106).[83] (Exported oil is subject to a tax equal to the difference between the domestic price and the world price.) Assuming that the world price of oil stays the same, oil producers in Russia can earn a real return of 300 per cent or more by waiting until the domestic price increases to the world price. If exporters pump oil now and deposit the proceeds in foreign currency, they earn a real return in the low double digits at most.

To encourage production of oil, the Russian government should deregulate the price of oil. If it wishes to reduce the effect on consumers of increases in the price of oil, it should subsidize them directly from the government budget. It has been estimated that liberalizing the price of oil would increase government revenue from oil export taxes by $4 billion to $25 billion (Kumar and Osband 1991), which at the current exchange rate for the rouble is more than the government budget deficit. Deregulating rather than merely liberalizing the price of oil would increase production and government revenue from oil export taxes even further, and would help to reduce the corruption that now exists in the Russian oil industry (Boulton 1992b) and tends to exist whenever governments impose price controls.

Another way for the Russian government to increase its revenue is to lease or sell state property to Russians or foreign investors for convertible foreign currency. The type of property easiest to lease or sell is probably mineral rights. Selling mineral rights for convertible foreign currency – or, equivalently, for currency board roubles – could produce substantial revenue. Despite obstacles, notably claims of ownership by lower levels of government, the Russian government has offered some oil and gas fields for lease (Lloyd 1992).

Other possibilities exist for increasing government revenue and reducing spending.[84] Obviously, there will be intense political debate about which possibilities should be chosen. We will not enter the debate here. The most important feature of the debate will be not so much its specific outcome, but its occurrence within the framework of hard budget constraints that the currency board will tend to impose, and the consequent noninflationary character of Russian government finance. However, should it seem desirable for the government to continue to collect revenue from extreme inflation for a time, a parallel currency approach may enable the transition to a new regime of taxation and spending to be more gradual than it would be if the Central Bank is converted into a currency board. Like liberalizing rather than deregulating oil prices, it may reduce the shock of a sudden transition to a new set of rules.

Some emerging market economies in Eastern Europe have recently had a 'fiscal honeymoon' after making market-oriented economic reforms. During the honeymoon, the government budget briefly turns from deficit to surplus, then back to deficit (Schmieding 1992: 55–8). The deficit returns because a stabilization crisis occurs and tax revenue decreases, or because political pressure for government spending increases as the political unity that made reforms possible fades. Instead of ending, the fiscal honeymoon will tend to persist in a Russian currency board system, because the currency board will not finance spending by the Russian government. Credible monetary reform by means of a currency board will make noninflationary finance easier by reviving economic activity, which will increase both tax revenue and the government's ability to borrow compared to the present.

ENTERPRISE ARREARS AND ENTERPRISE RESTRUCTURING

In a full-fledged market economy, credit granted by enterprises to one another (commercial credit) is substantial, but typically causes no problems to the economy as a whole because the enterprises have hard budget constraints. They have no access to central banks as lenders of last resort, so they grant credit only to firms that seem financially sound. In a full-fledged market economy, unrepaid commercial credit inflicts losses on its creditors alone and does not result in an inflationary rescue financed by the central bank. In Russia, in contrast, unrepaid enterprise credit causes inflation because state enterprises have soft budget constraints: the enterprises correctly anticipate that the government or the Central Bank of Russia will ultimately finance their unpaid debts.

The Russian currency board will not be a lender of last resort to the Russian government or to state enterprises. The hard budget constraint that the currency board will tend to impose on the government will tend to make the government impose hard budget constraints on state enterprises. Hard budget constraints will result in *de facto* bankruptcy for state enterprises that do not pay their debts, even if the official bankruptcy law is loosely enforced. The possibility of *de facto* bankruptcy of debtors will tend to make state enterprises more careful about granting credit. New enterprise arrears will therefore tend to be small.

There remains the question of how to settle existing arrears of state enterprises. In the parallel currency approach, inflation in the Central Bank rouble will probably reduce the real value of enterprise arrears almost to zero. In the conversion approach, though, substantial enterprise arrears may remain. One way to reduce them is to establish a clearinghouse to settle enterprise debts. Net bad debts (debts remaining unpaid after settlement) can be paid by giving creditor state enterprises assets from debtor state enterprises or perhaps by giving them non-negotiable government bonds. A more radical approach is to cancel (write off) all arrears of state enterprises. On a consolidated basis, all credits within the state sector of the economy are balanced by liabilities within the state sector, so net credit

118

of the state sector to itself is zero. The dangers of cancelling enterprise arrears are that cancellation may deprive some net creditor state enterprises of all their working capital, in effect bankrupting them; also, debtor state enterprises may expect the government to finance their debts in the future, creating problems of moral hazard (Ickes and Ryterman 1992: 31–8; Sachs and Lipton 1992: 49–52; Whitlock 1992: 36). The problem of enterprise arrears is complex, and a more detailed discussion of it is beyond the scope of this book. Whatever method the Russian government uses to settle existing enterprise arrears, though, a hard budget constraint will tend to prevent the government from financing new debts of state enterprises to the extent that it currently does.

Ultimately, for the Russian economy to achieve sustained growth, state enterprises that continue to accumulate debts and that are unlikely to become profitable must be restructured or closed (World Bank 1992b: 81, 105). This includes state enterprises that accumulate large new arrears after existing arrears are settled. The government need not close all unprofitable state enterprises; there may be some that can become profitable soon. It should close the worst money-losers, though, such as 'value-subtracting' enterprises whose outputs are worth less than the value of the materials they use. It is estimated that almost 8 per cent of industrial enterprises in Russia are 'value subtractors' and that 35 per cent of industrial production in Russia is unprofitable, that is, the goods produced are worth less than the value of materials plus the labour and capital used (Senik-Leygonie and Hughes 1992).[85]

The restructuring and closing of unprofitable state enterprises will benefit the Russian economy by shifting resources from less valuable to more valuable uses. As with the government budget, there will be intense political debate about which possibilities for restructuring and closure should be chosen. Again, we will not enter the debate here. The most important feature of the debate will be not so much its specific outcome, but its occurrence within the framework of hard budget constraints that the currency board will tend to impose.

Although soft budget constraints are the main cause of enterprise arrears, conditions in the payments system are also a cause. To reduce the incentive that state enterprises now have to grant enterprise credit as a way of evading the value-added and profits taxes collected through the payments system, the Russian government can use a combination of lower tax rates and more vigorous efforts to tax payments made outside the payments system. In other words, the tax base should be broader, including payments inside and outside the banking system, and tax rates should be low and uniform. Reform of the payments system, which is discussed later in this chapter, can eliminate lengthy delays in receiving payments as a cause of enterprise arrears.

119

COMPETITION AND REGULATION IN COMMERCIAL BANKING

The Russian banking system is at present inadequate for mobilizing and allocating savings to encourage economic growth. Russian commercial banks are small, unsophisticated, and unstable by world standards. Competition among them is limited because the banking sector is still in effect socialized. Therefore, the most promising strategy for rapidly developing an efficient, modern, stable banking system in Russia is to encourage extensive branch banking by reputable foreign commercial banks.

By providing a sound currency, the Russian currency board will tend to attract foreign investment, foreign banks, and foreign banking skill on a large scale. A sound currency will enable commercial banks to operate in conditions conducive to long-term stability, and will encourage Russians to save by holding interest-earning deposits in currency board roubles rather than by holding noninterest-earning foreign notes.

Foreign commercial banks will be credible institutions for deposits in currency board roubles. Many Russian commercial banks lack such credibility. Foreign banks will bring new techniques and expertise now lacking in the Russian commercial banking system. They will also provide services for exchanging currency board roubles for foreign currency. Foreign commercial banks will provide easy access to foreign investment, especially from the reserve country. Past currency board systems have had few bank failures because they have had sound currencies and strong commercial banks, including branches of large, stable foreign commercial banks. By providing stability, efficiency, and modern services, competition from foreign commercial banks has held domestic commercial banks to high standards in currency board systems. Where taxes and political risk have been low, competition from foreign commercial banks has also kept interest rates in currency board systems close to interest rates in their reserve countries. The average quality of commercial banks in currency board systems has been high (Schuler 1992b: 190–6).

Foreign commercial banks should be allowed to establish full branches anywhere in Russia, to offer the same services as Russian commercial banks, and to buy or be bought by Russian commercial banks.[86] There should be no requirement that the Russian subsidiaries of foreign commercial banks have any local ownership.

Developing countries usually restrict the operations of foreign commercial banks to protect domestic commercial banks from competition. Such restrictions tend to hinder economic growth. An active presence of foreign banks is a sign that foreigners think that a country is an attractive place to invest and to trade with. Where foreign commercial banks are most numerous and least restricted, it is easiest for local depositors and borrowers to obtain the most competitive interest rates, and commercial banks contribute most to economic growth. Competition from foreign commercial banks may hurt some existing Russian commercial banks, but it will benefit Russian consumers, and the Russian economy as a whole, by increasing opportunities to lend and borrow.

The Russian government should reduce existing special regulations on commercial banks and other financial institutions. In fact, we recommend a much smaller set of special regulations than now exists in Russia and most other countries. Many economists emphasize that vigorous government regulation is necessary to prevent financial institutions from taking risks that endanger the stability of the monetary system (Fry 1988: 300–1, 316–19; IMF *et al.* 1991, 2: 120–4; McKinnon 1991: 143, 147–8; World Bank 1992b: 113). We think that they mis-state the benefits of regulation. The important thing is not merely to regulate, but to make regulation consistent for risks and rewards. If commercial banks are allowed to reap the rewards of extensive freedom in their activities, they should also bear exclusive responsibility for their mistakes. Socializing risks creates problems of moral hazard; socializing rewards destroys the incentive to work efficiently; therefore the most consistent and beneficial policy is to privatize both risks and rewards. Experience suggests that banking systems are usually strongest and most efficient when they are least subject to intrusive special regulations (Cameron 1972: 3–25; Fry 1988: 419–41; Schuler 1992a: 19–27).

We see no need for special banking regulations, or a special government office that supervises banks, provided that Russia adopts and strictly enforces generally accepted Western accounting standards and ordinary laws against fraud and embezzlement that apply to commerce generally in developed market economies. (That does not imply that banking *law* is unnecessary, only that most banking *regulation* is unnecessary.) We can think of only two special banking regulations that may be desirable in Russia. One is to require commercial banks to publish monthly or more frequent financial statements, attested by the bank managers. Periodically, independent accounting firms should audit the statements. The statements should identify large borrowers and large holdings of stock by the banks, to disclose potential instances of favouritism in lending. The other special regulation is to impose jail sentences on managers of state commercial banks who make grossly negligent mistakes, if bureaucratic imperatives prevent other effective incentive programmes from being devised before the banks are privatized. Imposing jail sentences has worked well to encourage prudent behaviour among managers of state commercial banks in Taiwan (Fry and Nuti 1992: 37, citing Patrick 1990: 34).

One existing type of banking regulation that should be abolished is reserve requirements, which are a tax on commercial banking activity. They harm lenders and borrowers by increasing the spread between deposit interest rates and loan interest rates that commercial banks must charge to make a profit.[87] Currently, commercial banks other than the Savings Bank must hold noninterest-earning reserves of 20 per cent of deposits with the Central Bank of Russia. All commercial banks must pay fees of 3 per cent of gross income to the Central Bank for deposit and other insurance, and pay standard business taxes of 30 per cent of net income. The burden of taxes and the risks of compensating for extreme and variable inflation have the result that to earn adequate profits, commercial banks in Russia must maintain interest rate spreads of 100 per cent or more (see World Bank 1992b: 113). That compares with spreads of 2–4 per cent in developed countries (see IMF 1992f: 48). Russia needs to reduce the spread between deposit interest rates and loan interest rates to encourage savings to return to the domestic financial system; therefore, reserve requirements seem counterproductive. Determination of the reserves of nonstate commercial banks can be left to the banks' judgment of what is prudent, since no central bank will exist to induce moral hazard behaviour by them. Reserves of state commercial banks can also be left largely to the banks' judgment of what is prudent, but it would be wise for the Russian government to protect its investment in them by using experienced Western bankers as monitors until state commercial banks become more experienced in profit-oriented banking. The inability of the Russian currency board to act as a lender of last resort to commercial banks will tend to make them appropriately cautious in their judgments about what amount of reserves is prudent.

Another type of banking regulation that should be abolished is restrictions on the types of activities banks may engage in. Russia should follow the Western trend towards allowing banks to own and be owned by companies that engage in other types of business.[88] There is no need to separate commercial banking activity, such as mortgage lending, from investment banking activity, such as owning stock in private or public enterprises. In the United States, market forces are blurring the legally mandated separation of commercial banking and investment banking; this suggests that the separation is not efficient. The German system of 'universal' banking, which combines commercial banking and investment banking, is admirably stable and seems to be a more appropriate model for Russia than the American commercial banking system. Problems of collecting information and monitoring the performance of firms are severe in Russia now. Allowing banks to own stock in firms that they lend to will improve their ability to monitor firms (Corbett and Mayer 1991: 56, 66–8).[89]

Some readers may agree that extensive special regulations for commercial banks are unnecessary, yet be uneasy with the absence of a central bank as a lender of last resort in the currency board system. Our analysis of the Russian commercial banking system is that the existence of the Central Bank of Russia as a lender of last resort has, in fact, caused the main problems that currently afflict the system, and that solving the problems permanently requires abolishing the lender of last resort as it exists in a central banking system. The next chapter explains how commercial banks can remain liquid by means other than using a central bank as a lender of last resort.

RESTRUCTURING OF BANKRUPT COMMERCIAL BANKS

Many Russian commercial banks, especially state commercial banks, have deposit liabilities that exceed the true value of their loans and other assets. They would be bankrupt if not for loans from their lender of last resort, the Central Bank of Russia, and extreme inflation, which has reduced the real value of their liabilities.

The Russian currency board will end extreme inflation and will not be a lender of last resort to commercial banks. Consequently, some existing commercial banks may go bankrupt, so the Russian government should devise procedures for handling failures of commercial banks. Widespread bankruptcy of domestic commercial banks will not be the calamity it would have been a few years ago, because most savings by Russians are now held outside the domestic banking system, in the form of foreign notes and deposits at foreign banks. Furthermore, the currency board system will encourage branching by foreign commercial banks, which will be stable institutions for deposits and payments and will be an alternative to domestic commercial banks.

The Russian government has already declared its intention to corporatize and eventually privatize state commercial banks and, by corporatizing and privatizing state enterprises, to do the same to the commercial banks owned by them. A currency board system will merely tend to force the government to achieve its goal sooner rather than later. The question is how to achieve the goal.

A distinction should be made between deposits at commercial banks existing before the currency board opens and deposits made afterwards. At present, the Russian government explicitly or implicitly guarantees all deposits. In the currency board system, the government should guarantee no new deposits. For the sake of honouring its previous guarantee, though, the government could continue to guarantee old deposits up to the amount they contained just before the currency board opened. The guarantee of old deposits should cease for commercial banks not declared bankrupt within, say, five years after the currency board opens.

There are two ways to equalize the old assets and old liabilities of bankrupt commercial banks: increase the assets or reduce the liabilities of the banks. We oppose reducing the liabilities. The government should not confiscate or freeze deposits of the public and enterprises at bankrupt commercial banks. Doing so would further reduce confidence in existing commercial banks in Russia because it would be reminiscent of arbitrary

Soviet monetary reforms, such as the confiscation of 50- and 100-rouble notes in January 1991 and the freezing of deposits at the Bank for Foreign Economic Affairs in December 1991. Instead, the government should replenish the assets of bankrupt commercial banks by giving the banks equity shares in enterprises that are in default on bank loans, privatization vouchers, or, perhaps less preferably, non-negotiable government bonds equal to the difference between the assets and liabilities of the banks.[90] The government also may restructure or close bankrupt commercial banks after replenishing their assets, for example by selling them to solvent nonstate commercial banks. In the conversion approach to establishing a currency board, privatization vouchers or non-negotiable government bonds should be issued to bankrupt commercial banks only if their excess reserves (as defined in chapter 5) are insufficient to cover their bad loans. In the parallel currency approach, no excess reserves will exist because the currency board will not provide backing for the monetary base of the Central Bank rouble.

The treatment of cash and noncash deposits is discussed later in this chapter.

INTEREST RATES

Even with a sound currency and a strong, competitive commercial banking system, real interest rates will be high in Russia if property rights are insecure. Secure property rights will reduce the risk premium in real interest rates that compensates for political risk. Secure property rights will encourage foreigners and Russians with foreign assets to invest in Russia, which will increase the supply of loans and reduce real interest rates.

The Russian government can create conditions conducive to low real interest rates. One way to do so is to privatize much more urban and agricultural land. The attitude of the Russian parliament about private ownership of land has been indecisive: as of April 1993 it has not passed a law allowing large-scale ownership and resale of land by private parties, although small-scale ownership and resale are allowed (Marnie 1993). Such a law is urgently needed if Russia wishes to become a full-fledged market economy. Private ownership of apartments, shops, and farmland by private parties on a large scale will enable owners to offer property as collateral for bank loans, reducing the cost of default and enabling commercial banks to charge lower rates on loans than otherwise. By creating a widespread new type of collateral, privatizing land will mobilize investment. Allowing foreigners to own land on the same basis as Russians will encourage foreign investment. In the long run, most investment in the Russian economy will have to come from Russians if the economy is to grow rapidly. Especially at first, though, foreign investment can reduce the shock of economic reforms by enabling Russians to increase their consumption now, when it is low, and repay later, when it will be larger if Russia moves further towards a market economy.

Secure property rights include the right of a lender to claim property of a defaulting borrower as compensation. Bankruptcy laws should be strictly enforced. Russia needs more judges trained in bankruptcy law and needs to modify its system of law enforcement to accommodate enforcement activity that did not exist in the centrally planned economy.

The freedom that Russians will have in the currency board system to make contracts, payments, and deposits in any currency will tend to enable them to borrow at the lowest real interest rates consistent with a free market in credit. If Russians fear that the currency board rouble will be devalued against the reserve currency, they can use reserve currency, converting it into currency board roubles only as necessary. The cost of doing so will be exchange fees that are low (for currency exchange through commercial banks) or zero (for currency exchange through the currency board). As people gain confidence in the currency board, they will make more and more loans in currency board roubles and real interest rates in currency board roubles will decrease. If property rights are secure, arbitrage with foreign financial markets, especially those in the reserve country, should soon reduce real interest rates to levels near to those in the reserve country.

THE PAYMENTS SYSTEM

Merely by providing a sound currency, the Russian currency board will somewhat improve the payments system and will tend to impose harder budget constraints. Payments will no longer lose most of their real value in transit between the payer and the recipient. The payments system will need more drastic reform, though, if it is to serve the Russian economy as well as Western payments systems serve their economies. Russian commercial banks that do not go bankrupt will need to become competitive with the foreign commercial banks that will establish branches in the currency board system. Retaining the current payments system would place Russian commercial banks at a disadvantage to foreign banks, which have much faster, less error-prone payments procedures.

Competition is as desirable in the payments system as in commercial banking. The Central Bank of Russia, which operates the payments system, has discouraged commercial banks from developing competing payments systems that bypass it (Summers 1992: 18). Whether the Central Bank is converted into a currency board or continues to exist for a time as the issuer of a parallel currency, its powers to restrict competing payments systems should be abolished. The operation of the Central Bank's payments system should be privatized. Given the opportunity to manage the existing payments system as a consortium or to develop competing payments systems, it is likely that Russian commercial banks will respond rapidly, because many changes can be made that would improve the payments system quickly.[91]

It may be advantageous for the Russian currency board to be involved with the ultimate settlement of payments, as some past currency boards have been. Unlike the Central Bank of Russia, the currency board will not have the power to prevent competing payments systems from developing. The currency board may attain a competitive advantage, however, because combining settlement of payments and the currency board's normal exchange business with commercial banks may achieve economies of scale that reduce the cost of operating the payments system. Also, commercial banks may decide that the currency board is the most trustworthy institution for holding their settlement accounts and operating the payments system.

If the Russian currency board decides to become involved in the payments system, it must not guarantee payments for commercial banks that go bankrupt, as do the US Federal Reserve System and some other central banks. Commercial banks should bear the risk of nonpayment, as they do in the payments systems of Switzerland and some other countries (see *Economist* 1992b). For the Russian currency board to guarantee payments would make it a lender of last resort. Another rule of procedure that should guide the currency board is that its involvement in the payments system should be self-supporting, not subsidized from its seigniorage on notes and coins.

An important aspect of the payments system that will need reform is the separation of payments into cash and noncash financial circuits. As was explained in chapter 3, the cash circuit comprises household deposits, notes, and coins; the noncash circuit comprises enterprise deposits. In the parallel currency approach, the separation of the cash and noncash circuits can continue for Central Bank roubles, although commercial banks will be legally obligated to make all deposits in currency board roubles convertible into currency board notes and coins. In the conversion approach, it will be necessary to end the separation, because all domestic-currency deposits will be in currency board roubles, and the currency board system requires cash convertibility for deposits.

An equitable way to end the separation between the cash and noncash financial circuits is to pass a law converting noncash deposit roubles into a smaller amount of cash-convertible deposit roubles. Currently, noncash roubles unofficially trade at a discount to cash roubles because noncash roubles are less useful. Converting noncash roubles into cash rouble deposits at an exchange rate of one to one would be undesirable because it would redistribute wealth from what is now the cash circuit to what is now the noncash circuit. The conversion rate should instead be closer to the unofficial rate prevailing before reform is announced. Noncash deposits can be converted to cash deposits at a rate of, for example, 1.3 noncash deposit roubles per cash deposit rouble. The conversion will not be confiscatory; it will exchange less useful noncash deposits for more useful cash-convertible deposits that are smaller in nominal terms but have approximately equivalent real value. After the conversion, all deposits will have cash convertibility.

If the Russian government uses the conversion approach to establish the Russian currency board, it will be necessary to devise procedures for dealing with existing contracts that specify payment in Central Bank roubles. A strong argument can be made that in long-term contracts, converting Central Bank roubles into currency board roubles at the current market exchange rate would impose unjust burdens on debtors. The details of procedures for dealing with old contracts are beyond the scope of this book, but a possible solution is to allow contracts that specify payment in Central Bank roubles to be renegotiated for the portion that remains to be fulfilled after a fixed exchange rate is established between the currency board rouble and the reserve currency. In the parallel currency approach, in contrast, existing contracts that specify payment in Central Bank roubles can continue to be fulfilled without imposing unjust burdens on debtors. In any case, few long-term contracts will exist (because of extreme inflation), so problems will be minor.

INTERREPUBLICAN EXCHANGE; FOREIGN EXCHANGE

Because the currency board rouble will be fully convertible, there will be no need to continue the bilateral clearing arrangements that now exist between Russia and other former Soviet republics. The Russian government and the Central Bank of Russia can cease their involvement in interrepublican exchange, and leave the task and risk of accepting payment in the currencies of other republics to commercial banks and other market participants. They can also cease their involvement in foreign exchange. The government should abolish foreign-exchange restrictions, including regulations that require 50 per cent of foreign-currency earnings to be exchanged for roubles and special licences for dealing in foreign currency. Commercial banks, especially foreign commercial banks, will offer more extensive and convenient means of conducting interrepublican and foreign exchange than the Central Bank now does.

Many monetary reforms, such as the Estonian reform of July 1992, have restricted foreign-currency deposits (see chapter 4). There will be no need to support the currency board rouble with such restrictions. The currency board rouble should be legal tender for paying taxes and settling debts in Russia; that is, it should be valid if no other currency is specified in a contract. As has been mentioned, though, the currency board rouble should not be a forced tender for private debts; Russians should be allowed to use other currencies, or commodities, as means of payment or units of account if both parties to the transaction agree to do so. Russians should have the freedom to make contracts, payments, and deposits in any currency they wish.

FOREIGN DEBT

The Russian government has taken responsibility for all of the foreign debt of the former Soviet Union, in exchange for ownership of certain former Soviet government assets. The Russian government is in default on most of the foreign debt, which totals $86 billion and is all payable in foreign currency. The currency board system should enable the Russian government to repay more of the debt than it is currently doing. By issuing a sound currency, the Russian currency board will encourage foreign investment, which will tend to increase economic growth and ultimately produce more government revenue than would a monetary system with an unsound currency. Even with a currency board system, it may be necessary for Russia's foreign creditors to forgive some of the debt, but the amount ultimately repaid should be larger than it will be if the Central Bank of Russia continues to make monetary policy.

WAGES AND PRICES

The hard budget constraints, fixed exchange rate with the reserve currency, and full convertibility of the currency board system will all necessitate some adjustment of wages and prices. This section describes how wages and prices will be determined in Russia once the Russian currency board opens.

The currency board will maintain a fixed exchange rate between the currency board rouble and the reserve currency. The fixed rate will be an 'anchor' for nominal wages and prices in currency board roubles (see chapter 4). It is impossible to know in advance the proper wages and prices in the currency board system. Market forces should be allowed to determine wages and prices without hindrance. The currency board rouble will facilitate adjustment of wages and prices because it will be a more stable unit of account than the Central Bank rouble now is. Some market participants will make mistakes in setting wages and prices, causing surpluses or shortages of goods. Arbitrage by other market participants will tend to correct errors in pricing, however. Some surpluses and shortages will continue to occur, as in all market economies, but they will tend to be much less severe than they now are in Russia's emerging, incompletely developed market economy. Divergences of prices across regions in Russia will also tend to diminish because the stability of the currency board rouble as a unit of account will make more exact price calculations possible.

It is important that wages and prices within Russia be flexible after the currency board is established. Flexibility will enable wages and prices eventually to attain market-clearing levels given the fixed exchange rate of the currency board rouble. Privatizing state property will help to make wages and prices more flexible, because the private sector of the Russian economy is more atomistic and has more incentive to adjust quickly than the state sector. The government should not regulate wages and prices in the private sector or in corporatized state enterprises (those with hard budget constraints), except perhaps prices charged by monopoly utilities. In the currency board system, wage and price controls are unnecessary for 'fighting' inflation; the currency board system itself does that, by maintaining a fixed exchange rate with a stable reserve currency.

Let us describe further how wages and prices will be determined in the Russian currency board system. Many wages and prices are currently above or below their market-clearing levels. When translated into currency board roubles, they will also be above or below their market-clearing levels. Adjustment through trial and error will be necessary whatever monetary system Russia has; no simple formula exists for determining the market-clearing relative prices of goods. However, if the currency board is established as the issuer of a parallel currency, the effect on the *general* level of prices will be different than if the Central Bank of Russia is converted into a currency board. In the parallel currency approach, the government will not set an exchange rate that influences the general level of Russian wages and prices compared to foreign wages and prices. Nobody will be forced to use the currency board rouble, and the exchange rate of the currency board rouble with the Central Bank rouble will be determined by market forces. In the parallel currency approach, the role of the government will be passive except insofar as it, like other parties that use the currency board rouble, must convert prices in Central Bank roubles to prices in currency board roubles. The government need not set conversion rates for dealings in the private sector of the Russian economy. In the conversion approach, in contrast, the government will have to set conversion rates.

In either approach to establishing the Russian currency board, there remains the practical question of what rate to use for converting wages and prices from Central Bank roubles to currency board roubles. An obvious solution is to use the market exchange rate of the central bank rouble against the reserve currency as a starting-point for setting prices in currency board roubles. Suppose that a worker receives a salary of 10,000 Central Bank roubles. Suppose also that the market exchange rate is 1,000 Central Bank roubles per US dollar, that the dollar is the reserve currency, and that one currency board rouble equals one dollar. If the worker is now paid currency board roubles, he can initially be paid 10 currency board roubles per month, which is equivalent to his previous salary of 10,000 Central Bank roubles.

Extreme inflation makes rouble prices not indexed to inflation or the exchange rate very cheap, in terms of convertible foreign currency. After the currency board rouble enters circulation, wages and prices in Russia, in terms of currency board roubles and convertible foreign currency, will probably increase significantly because confidence in the future of the Russian economy will increase. That is what usually happens after a successful currency reform. The Russian government should not try to anticipate later success by setting wages and prices in terms of currency board roubles at high levels initially; doing so would only cause unemployment. Nor should the government later try to reduce increases in wages and prices by imposing controls on the private sector.

The fixed exchange rate of the currency board rouble with the reserve currency will set lower and upper limits to wages and prices in Russia. Wages and prices will tend to reflect the value of Russian workers and goods compared to workers and goods abroad, particularly in the reserve country. Wages and prices in Russia will tend to increase at rates comparable to those in the reserve country, plus a premium for increases in the expected productivity of Russian workers, land, and so on (see chapter 4). Especially in the first few years, the increases may be quite large, but they are natural for a rapidly developing economy with a sound currency. Real wages can increase rapidly, as they have in Hong Kong.

A STABILIZATION CRISIS?

High real interest rates and initially inflexible wages inherited from the current economic situation may cause a 'stabilization crisis', a final decline in economic activity that occurs before the economy begins sustained growth with a reformed monetary system. A stabilization crisis does not always happen after an extreme inflation, and may not happen in Russia because production may already be near its lowest point. A parallel currency approach may enable Russia to repeat the experience of the 1920s, when production increased despite hyperinflation in the old currency (see chapter 9).

If a stabilization crisis occurs, little can be done to avoid it. The currency board system can reduce the harmful effects of real shocks to the economy by providing a sound currency and encouraging foreign investment, but it cannot eliminate all real shocks. The Soviet and Russian governments have made many mistakes in economic policy that will affect the Russian economy adversely no matter what monetary system Russia has. In particular, unemployment will increase. But continuing the Central Bank of Russia's recent policy of extreme inflation in an attempt to reduce unemployment will ultimately worsen the real shocks to the Russian economy of the transition from the failed centrally planned economy to a full-fledged, prosperous market economy. The currency board system will minimize difficulty for the Russian economy compared to continuing with extreme inflation or attempting a stabilization of the rouble that lacks credibility. Russia's choice is between a possible temporary decline in production with the currency board system, followed by a rapid recovery, or a probably long period of stagnation with central banking.

If a stabilization crisis occurs, unemployment may afterwards continue to increase even though production is increasing, as hard budget constraints force some state enterprises to fire workers. The Russian government can reduce unemployment by granting limited subsidies to keep workers employed at certain state enterprises. Granting subsidies to those enterprises may be less costly than paying unemployment compensation to workers. Again, there will be intense political debate about this, but we will not enter the debate here. The hard budget constraints that the Russian currency board will tend to impose will tend to limit subsidies.

INDEXATION

In April 1993 the Russian government made laws promising to index to inflation government wages and pensions, and deposits at the Savings Bank. If Russia establishes a currency board, the government should not index anything to inflation in the currency board rouble. Doing so would hinder the adjustments in relative prices that a sound currency is intended to facilitate.

8

OBJECTIONS TO A CURRENCY
BOARD IN RUSSIA

This book has argued that a currency board system can provide a sound currency and a framework within which other problems of the current Russian monetary system can be solved in a way that will be beneficial for the Russian economy. To investigate whether establishing a currency board has disadvantages compared to allowing the Central Bank of Russia to make monetary policy, this chapter considers the main objections to a currency board in Russia.

In the 1950s and 1960s, it was claimed that the currency board system had certain disadvantages compared to central banking. More recent economic theories and historical investigation have refuted or reduced the significance of those objections to the currency board system, but since they continue to be made, and since no widely available refutation exists, this chapter briefly considers them, as well as more recent objections.[92] The objections to the currency board system do not apply with full force to a parallel currency approach. For the sake of argument, though, we will assume that the Central Bank of Russia has been converted into a currency board or that the Central Bank has withered away because nobody uses its currency.

Most of the objections that economists have made to the currency board system, in print and in conversation with us, have been purely theoretical, and have often neglected the historical record of currency board systems, which was summarized in chapter 4. Many of the theoretical objections have had little practical importance for currency board systems and many have also neglected the need to compare monetary institutions systematically. The currency board system and central banking are both integral wholes. Certain of their features imply certain other features; therefore, one should not argue as if the advantages of either system are independent of its disadvantages. For example, the flexibility possible with completely discretionary monetary policy (if flexibility is really attainable) is unavoidably connected with the risk of extreme inflation.

We begin with abstract objections to a currency board in Russia and proceed to more concrete objections based on specific features of Russia's current economic and political situation. The most abstract objection of all, which is that discretionary monetary policy more effectively stabilizes the economy than rule-bound monetary policy, has already been answered in chapter 2.

NO LENDER OF LAST RESORT

Perhaps the most common objection to a currency board system is that it is susceptible to financial panics because it lacks a lender of last resort.[93]

One possible reply is that the government can be a lender of last resort even if no central bank exists. The government can lend to commercial banks; for example, the Hong Kong government has several times paid depositors of insolvent banks from its accumulated budget surpluses (Freris 1991: 38–9). The absence of a central bank merely prevents the government from providing assistance by creating inflation.

A more fundamental reply is that a government-sponsored lender of last resort creates more problems than it solves. As was explained in chapter 1, the Central Bank of Russia and many other central banks are lenders of last resort not only to commercial banks, but to state enterprises and to the government. The substantial arrears that Russian state enterprises have accumulated are an example of the problems of moral hazard caused by the existence of a lender of last resort in Russia. Even if the Central Bank of Russia can be limited to acting as a lender of last resort only to commercial banks, problems of moral hazard will tend to occur because commercial banks will expect that the Central Bank will rescue them when they become illiquid.

Lack of a central bank as a lender of last resort does not seem to have harmed currency board systems. Failures by commercial banks have been minor in currency board systems. No large commercial bank has ever failed in a currency board system, and losses to depositors from the few small commercial banks that have failed have been tiny (Schuler 1992b: 191–3). Since the founding of the first currency board in 1849, there have apparently been no cases in which commercial banks in currency board systems have relied on central banks as lenders of last resort. For example, British overseas commercial banks in currency board systems apparently have never relied on the Bank of England as a lender of last resort. Currency board systems have performed well without lenders of last resort. Therefore, it seems likely that after an initial restructuring of the type described in the previous chapter, commercial banks in the proposed Russian currency board system can become strong, stable, and capable of preserving their liquidity without a government-sponsored lender of last resort.

Two important sources of stability for commercial banks in currency board systems have been interbank lending markets and international branch networks. As the Russian commercial banking system develops, a large interbank lending market is likely to develop. Illiquid banks will borrow from more liquid ones, as they do in the currency board system of Hong Kong and the central banking systems of many other countries. Borrowing need not be limited to the domestic market; commercial banks can also borrow abroad and in Eurocurrency markets. By eliminating exchange risk with the reserve currency, the currency board will facilitate access of commercial banks in Russia to foreign financial markets. The currency board system will also encourage foreign commercial banks to establish branches in Russia, in effect importing access to foreign financial markets. Commercial banks that have international branch networks tend to be able to diversify their risks more than banks with domestic branch networks only, and hence tend to be less susceptible to failure because of localized economic shocks. In the currency board system, Russians will be able to take advantage of the stability of commercial banks with international branch networks by depositing funds with the banks legally in Russia, as some Russians already do illegally abroad.

The risk of financial panics in a currency board system can also be reduced by private, voluntary deposit insurance. Government deposit insurance, whether explicit or implicit, is likely to be a burden to Russian taxpayers. In many countries that have allowed wide freedom to commercial banks, such as Britain and Canada, government deposit insurance did not exist until recently because commercial banks did not desire it. In the United States, where commercial banks are much regulated, government rescues of commercial banks are costing taxpayers tens of billions of dollars, many times the sum that depositors would have lost from a few bank failures. Competition promotes sound banking, and is the best guarantee of safety. If permanent compulsory deposit insurance is thought to be a political necessity, it should be operated by the banks themselves, as are the private, voluntary deposit insurance systems of Switzerland, Germany, and other countries (for a list, see Talley and Mas 1990). Insurance should cover at most, say, 80 per cent of the value of large deposits, so that depositors have an incentive to avoid imprudently managed banks that pay unsustainable high interest rates.

Another way to reduce the risk of financial panics is for commercial banks in Russia to include a 'notice of withdrawal clause' (option clause) in their contracts with depositors. The notice of withdrawal clause would allow a commercial bank to delay for a specified period the requests of depositors to convert deposits into currency board notes and coins. In return, the bank would pay a penalty rate of interest; for example, 3 per cent above the rate prevailing before it exercised the notice of withdrawal clause. Banks would be free to offer a notice of withdrawal clause or not, and depositors would be free to do business with such banks or not. Notice of withdrawal clauses have precedents; for example, they were widespread among savings banks in the United States until perhaps the 1970s.[94]

IS RUSSIA TOO LARGE FOR A CURRENCY BOARD?

Another objection to the currency board system is that it is appropriate for small economies that are open (have much foreign trade), such as Hong Kong, but not for large economies that are closed (have little foreign trade), such as Russia. The objection implies that a crawling peg or a floating exchange rate would encourage greater economic stability than a fixed rate.

We could reply that Russia *is* a small, open economy. Its 1992 GDP, converted into US dollars at the average interbank rate, was $75 billion, compared to $93 billion for Hong Kong (Hong Kong 1992: 11). The Russian economy is, or at least was, open: in 1990, Russia's outward shipments were 17 per cent of GDP and inward shipments were 25 per cent of GDP (IMF 1992c: 6–7; see also World Bank 1992b: 121), which are similar to the ratios of large West European countries. (Admittedly, the openness of the Russian economy is somewhat artificial. Russia has much trade with other former Soviet republics, which is the product of the centrally planned economy, and little trade with the rest of the world. Trade with former Soviet republics decreased in 1992 and will continue to decrease in 1993 [Williamson 1992: 7–9; World Bank 1992b: 120].)

A more serious reply is that terms such as 'large', 'closed', and even 'economy' are vague. Any economic grouping can be made arbitrarily large or small, open or closed, by redrawing its boundaries. For example, Russia can be considered a single, relatively large (or at least populous), somewhat open economy, or a group of much smaller, more open regional economies (western Russia, the Urals, Siberia, the Far East). The only completely, perpetually closed economy is the world. Almost every part of the world trades with the outside, therefore almost every part is to some extent open. Every large economy is composed of smaller economic units. Accordingly, economists have had difficulty devising widely accepted definitions of what constitutes a large, small, open, or closed economy.

Even accepting the terms 'large', 'small', 'open', and 'closed' as meaningful for monetary policy, experience suggests that the objection has no practical significance for the currency board system. Currency boards have been successful in small, open economies such as Hong Kong and large (populous), closed economies such as Nigeria and British East Africa, which initially had little trade with the outside world. Currency boards have opened previously closed economies by providing sound currencies that encouraged trade. Russia will become wealthier if it can trade more easily with the rest of the world. A currency board will help it to do so. The monetary policy of the Central Bank of Russia is an important cause of the low level of trade between Russia and countries outside the former Soviet Union.

FIXED VERSUS FLOATING EXCHANGE RATES

Yet another objection to the currency board system is that a floating exchange rate is best not only for small, open economies, but for almost all countries, whether large or small. A floating exchange rate, whether clean or dirty, supposedly better enables an economy to adjust to shocks in the real exchange rate than does a fixed exchange rate.

We begin by taking the argument on its own terms. We reply that a fixed exchange rate is preferable for Russia today because a credible fixed exchange rate will enforce a durable monetary and fiscal constitution and will cease to be a subject of political contention. In particular, a fixed exchange rate will tend to end soft budget constraints. At present, expectations that the Central Bank of Russia will continue to accommodate soft budget constraints induce a vicious cycle of inflation. A fixed exchange rate maintained by a currency board, on the other hand, will stop inflation because the hard budget constraints that the currency board system tends to impose will induce workers and state enterprises to limit wage and price increases to competitive levels, and will prevent the government from acceding to all wage and price increases by subsidizing all unprofitable state enterprises.

Additionally, a fixed exchange rate will tend to eliminate exchange risk with the reserve currency. If Russia establishes a currency board using, say, the US dollar as its reserve currency, it will join a common currency zone much more populous and wealthy than the now-defunct rouble zone. Trade with countries in the common currency zone will be easier than it would be with a floating exchange rate because the fixed exchange rate will tend to eliminate exchange risk in the prices of goods. Russians and other people in the common currency zone will be able to make more exact price calculations for internationally traded goods. That will tend to enhance economic efficiency by making the lowest-cost producers within the common currency zone those with the greatest natural advantages, not those temporarily benefiting from the extreme fluctuations in real exchange rates common with a pegged exchange rate, and to some extent with a floating exchange rate.[95] A fixed exchange rate will also enable entrepreneurs to apply to other problems talent that, in a monetary system with a floating exchange rate, they would apply to foreign-currency speculation and hedging. (Exchange risk with currencies outside the common currency zone will remain, though, so some wealth and talent will continue to be applied to foreign-exchange speculation.)

Eliminating exchange risk will encourage foreign investment in Russia, particularly from other countries within the common currency zone. Investors will know with certainty what exchange rate they will receive in terms of the reserve currency should they wish to repatriate profits. A fixed exchange rate will also enable Russia to 'piggyback' on the financial markets of other countries in the common currency zone. Entrepreneurs in Russia will be able to use as points of reference the highly liquid, well-established markets elsewhere in the zone. Entering financial markets elsewhere in the zone will become easier. Financial markets in the West offer facilities for interest-rate hedging, foreign-exchange swaps, and other transactions that will not be available on a similar scale in Russia for years. Easy access to large foreign financial markets, with no exchange risk, will tend to increase the growth of the Russian economy.

A deeper reply than the foregoing to objections to a fixed exchange rate is that debate about 'fixed' versus floating exchange rates usually assumes that the monetary authority is a central bank. For that reason, advocates of floating exchange rates (for example, Friedman 1988 [1953]: 8–10) correctly contend that the exchange rate maintained by a central bank cannot be truly fixed, merely pegged. Unlike a typical central bank, though, a typical currency board can maintain a truly fixed exchange rate.[96]

Debate about 'fixed' (in reality, pegged) versus floating exchange rates also usually assumes that everybody in a country uses the same currency. In currency board systems, though, foreign-currency deposits, particularly reserve-currency deposits, have been common. In Hong Kong, foreign-currency deposits exceed Hong Kong dollar deposits (Hong Kong 1992: 34; Jao 1992), and deposits in Japanese yen (a currency that floats against the Hong Kong dollar) are common. (As has been mentioned, despite the existence of extensive foreign-currency deposits, almost everyone in Hong Kong uses Hong Kong dollar notes and coins rather than foreign notes and coins.) Allowing Russians to hold foreign-currency deposits inside or outside Russia in the currency board system will enable them to choose the mixture of fixed and floating currencies most suitable for them. A Russian enterprise that trades with Japan may wish to hold Japanese yen. If the currency board rouble floats with respect to the yen, holding yen will enable the enterprise to protect itself against currency risk to some degree, which will tend to improve its profitability.

Allowing Russians to hold deposits in foreign currency also offers a solution to economists' longstanding, inconclusive arguments about optimum currency areas, that is, the extent to which it is beneficial that a country should have one currency or multiple currencies, and fixed exchange rates or floating rates (Mundell 1961; Fenton and Murray 1992; Kawai 1992).[97] Allowing Russians to hold deposits in foreign currency will enable them to take advantage of any benefits of floating currencies by holding deposits in currencies that float against the currency board rouble. Competition among currencies, as among other goods, is the proper way to determine optimum areas of service (see White 1989b).[98]

137

DEFLATION

Another objection to a currency board is that it is deflationary in a growing economy. If one makes certain stringent theoretical assumptions (enumerated in Appendix B), an increase in the demand for currency board notes and coins requires a current-account surplus to produce additional foreign reserves as backing. As an economy with a currency board grows, then, it must achieve continual current-account surpluses for the supply of currency board notes and coins to increase as quickly as the demand. Continual surpluses are unlikely, implying that in periods of balance or deficit in the current account, the supply of notes and coins will increase more slowly than the demand, resulting in deflation. Deflation would not occur if the notes and coins were liabilities of a typical central bank, which could increase the supply of notes and coins without acquiring additional foreign reserves.[99]

We reply that theoretical assumptions are so stringent that they rarely or never apply to actual currency board systems. A developing country experiencing healthy economic growth, such as most countries with currency boards have been, typically has a capital-account surplus (foreign investment) that exceeds its current-account deficit. Furthermore, the international branch networks typical of commercial banks in a currency board system reduce the demand for reserves in the currency board country compared to what it would otherwise be. Commercial banks can pool reserves between the reserve country and the currency board country. For example, ignoring the effect of differences in reserve requirements, the overall reserve position of a commercial bank with branches in Hong Kong and the United States does not change if customers of the bank in Hong Kong write Hong Kong dollar cheques to customers of the bank in the United States, which the American customers then exchange for US dollars. The effect is the same as if customers of the bank in San Francisco write cheques to customers of the bank in Los Angeles. Similarly, considering commercial banks as a group, if all have branches in the currency board country and the reserve country, their combined reserves do not change when people in one country make payments to people in the other country.

There has apparently been only one case of deflation in a currency board system caused by an increase in demand for notes and coins. It occurred in Hong Kong in early 1984. A few months before, Hong Kong had reintroduced the currency board system. During the Chinese New Year, the demand for notes increased because it is customary to give gifts of money. The increased demand for notes affected commercial bank reserves and interest rates in Hong Kong for two weeks, after which they returned to their previous levels. During subsequent Chinese New Years, commercial banks in Hong Kong have held more reserves than at other times of the year, and interest rates have been affected little (Selgin 1988a: 19).

Historical experience strongly suggests that the danger of deflation in a typical currency board system is small compared to the danger of inflation in a typical central banking system.[100]

THE INFLATION TAX

A somewhat related objection to a currency board is that it deprives a country of the opportunity to impose an inflation tax of its own choosing. A currency board will supposedly deprive the Russian government of revenue precisely when the government most needs revenue. As a corollary, one may argue that at any time, a country has the sovereign right to change the rules governing its currency.

We reply that the restraint on inflation that a currency board tends to impose is an advantage rather than a disadvantage. Russia is now suffering from the effects of a high inflation tax, which have been disastrous. Most Russians would prefer a monetary system that drastically reduces the inflation tax, as shown by the increasing use of convertible foreign currency and barter in Russia.

We also reply that if the Russian government establishes the Russian currency board as the issuer of a parallel currency, the government can continue for a time to impose an inflation tax of its own choosing by means of the Central Bank rouble, as the Soviet government did with the sovznak from 1922 to 1924. In the long term, though, the parallel Central Bank rouble may vanish from circulation, so the objection reappears. A more fundamental reply, then, is that a currency board does not try to earn the most seigniorage possible, but to earn an amount of seigniorage consistent with maintaining a sound currency. The seigniorage produced by extreme inflation is large in the short term, then tends to decrease steeply. Abundant experience shows that seigniorage from extreme inflation is not a reliable source of tax revenue in the long term. Moreover, extreme inflation hinders economic growth and reduces the revenue that can be generated from other taxes.

THE COST OF RESERVES

Still another objection to a currency board is that requiring the currency board to hold 100 per cent foreign reserves deprives the economy of real resources that are available in a central banking system, because a typical central bank holds much less than 100 per cent foreign reserves. Economists who investigated this topic in the 1950s claimed that 30–50 per cent of the reserves of currency boards were surplus, since there was a hard core of notes and coins that people would never return to the boards for conversion into the reserve currency. (The hard core corresponded to the 'investment reserve' of the currency boards [see chapter 6].) Surplus reserves are costly, because they could be used to buy imports, thus increasing the real goods available in the economy.

We reply that the surplus foreign reserves may not be as large as was claimed (Birnbaum 1957). But even if they are, consider their cost. Once spent, they are gone, and earn no interest. Foreign reserves held by a currency board, in contrast, earn interest because the currency board invests them. The stream of future interest payments has a capitalized (present-value) equivalent. The cost of surplus reserves is the difference between the value of the goods they could buy now and the capitalized equivalent of the interest that they will earn if invested. Alternatively, it is possible to calculate the risk-adjusted interest that the surplus foreign reserves would earn if lent domestically, and to compare it with the risk-adjusted interest from foreign assets. Only if domestic interest rates are significantly higher than foreign interest rates for *similarly* risky investments is a currency board more costly than central banking in the narrow sense of the cost of holding reserves.

Critics of the currency board system have often failed to consider that in many currency board systems, the reason that real domestic interest rates have been higher than real rates in the reserve countries is that higher rates have reflected higher political risk, higher risk of default by borrowers because of different property rights, and higher operating costs for commercial banks. After adjusting for those factors, the rates of return from domestic investments and foreign investments have been much closer to equality (Schuler 1992b: 193–5).

As Appendix C shows, some currency boards have held domestic securities as part of their assets, partly because they sought a higher return on assets, unadjusted for risk. The Russian currency board should not hold domestic assets, such as Russian government bonds.[101] Holding domestic assets would risk involving the currency board in Russian politics, for example by purchasing or not purchasing certain types of domestic securities for political reasons. The more domestic assets the currency board held, the more it would be subject to political risk and political pressure from the Russian government. Another reason that the Russian currency board should not hold domestic assets is that 100 per cent foreign reserves is a 'natural' ratio that is easy to agree about. If the ratio is 90 per cent, there will be political pressure to decrease the ratio to 80 per cent, then to 70 per cent, and so on, as with a few past currency boards. Minimum gold or foreign-exchange reserve ratios imposed on central banks have tended to be reduced whenever governments have deemed it advisable in the name of temporary expediency. The US Federal Reserve System, for instance, was originally required to hold a gold reserve ratio of 40 per cent of its notes in circulation; today the ratio is zero. A 100 per cent ratio for foreign reserves has a psychological appeal shared by no other ratio.

COLONIALISM

Other objections to a currency board have been made that are more specific to Russia. One objection is that the currency board system will create a colonial relationship between Russia and the reserve country. For example, if the reserve currency is the US dollar, Russia will supposedly be subject to American political and economic domination.

We reply that the currency board system by itself creates no colonial relationship. Historically, most currency boards have existed in British colonies, but currency boards have also existed in independent countries, including Argentina, Ireland, and Jordan. The effect of a currency board is not to create a colonial relationship, but to achieve more credibility than a domestic central bank can. That is why the Hong Kong dollar is linked to the US dollar, even though Hong Kong is a British colony. The Bank of England perhaps has more credibility than a Hong Kong central bank would have, but the US Federal Reserve System has more credibility still.

More generally, a fixed exchange rate, or even a pegged exchange rate, tends to create close economic relationships between countries adhering to fixed or pegged rates, yet no colonial relationship need be implied. The gold standard did not make Britain and France colonies of South Africa and Russia, two of the main gold-producing countries, nor do the pegged exchange rates of the European Monetary System make France a colony of Germany.

As for the possibility that the currency board itself could somehow become a tool of colonialism, chapter 6 proposed ways to protect the currency board from interference by foreigners and the Russian government alike. It proposed a role for foreigners as directors of the currency board to prevent the Russian government from appointing a majority of directors intent on converting the currency board into a central bank. The proposal that a majority of the directors of the currency board should be foreigners may seem to be an insult to Russian national pride, because it imposes an external restraint on the Russian monetary system. But restraints are typically necessary for a monetary constitution to be success-ful, and external restraints are especially desirable for a country that has a history of lack of self-restraint in monetary policy.

Anyway, Russia's current monetary system is not now an object of national pride; Russians shun the rouble in preference to convertible foreign currency. If the Central Bank of Russia continues its current policies, the result will be the unofficial but almost complete dollarization of the Russian economy, which is already in progress. It is difficult to imagine a more colonialist type of monetary relationship than unofficial yet pervasive dollarization, which signals the inability of the domestic government to provide a currency that people wish to hold. A currency board will tend to reverse the dollarization of the Russian economy and restore an element of national pride by providing Russia with something it has not had in the lifetime of most Russians: a sound domestic currency.

IS RUSSIA A QUAGMIRE?

Another objection to a currency board in Russia is that if the IMF helps Russia to establish a currency board, it implicitly accepts responsibility for the future of the Russian economy – a commitment that it should not undertake.

In reply, we emphasize again that lending the initial foreign reserves for the Russian currency board will not obligate the IMF to make further loans to the Russian government or the Russian currency board. The constitution of the currency board should explicitly recognize that the initial foreign reserves, if obtained from the IMF, are a one-time loan, never to be repeated. In contrast, if the IMF continues to help the Central Bank of Russia in trying to devise and administer an economic stabilization scheme that is difficult to implement and likely to fail if implemented fully, a risk exists that Russia will need foreign aid for a long time.[102] Furthermore, a failed stabilization will discredit the IMF. Establishing a currency board is the most likely path to a successful stabilization.

MISCELLANEOUS QUESTIONS

There are some other important questions (not really objections) that people have asked about establishing a currency board in Russia. The previous chapter discussed two of them: how to set a 'correct' exchange rate between the currency board rouble and the reserve currency, and whether a stabilization crisis would occur with a currency board. Now for the other questions.

One question is whether the currency board system implies any particular border controls. We reply that the full convertibility characteristic of the currency board system implies unlimited freedom to import or export currency and capital. Proper controls can be enforced to ensure that people pay taxes or that money acquired in criminal activity is detected. As the experience of Hong Kong shows, such controls need not hinder ordinary financial transactions.

Another question is whether the currency board system will inadvertently strengthen the Russian mafia. We reply that to the extent the currency board affects the mafia, it will weaken the mafia slightly. Some of the mafia's revenue comes from finding ways to evade restrictions on foreign exchange imposed by the central bank. By eliminating the restrictions, a currency board will eliminate gains from evading them. As for the mafia's other activities, they are the concern of the police, not of the currency board.

Still another question is what would happen to the Russian currency board in the worst case imaginable. The worst case for the currency board that we can imagine is that the Russian public converts all currency board roubles into reserve currency. We reply that even in that case, little would happen. The 100 per cent foreign reserves of the currency board would ensure that it could meet all demands to convert currency board rouble notes and coins. Instead of having currency board notes and coins, Russians would have reserve currency.[103] If the exchange rate between the currency board rouble and the reserve currency were one to one, as was suggested in chapter 5, it would not even be necessary for shops to recalculate prices in reserve currency for the benefit of persons spending reserve currency. Deposits at commercial banks would also be unaffected.

Even in the worst case, then, the currency board could not disturb the Russian economy. But the worst case will not happen. Conversion of currency board roubles into reserve currency will begin a sequence of events whose simplest version is sketched in Figure 4.2. The chain of events is self-correcting, leading to new market-clearing levels of the nominal money supply, prices, and incomes. Furthermore, the necessity that payments to the Russian government be made in currency board roubles will create a hard core of demand for currency board roubles, which will limit the amount of currency board notes and coins that Russians convert even in the worst case.

OTHER ALTERNATIVES TO CENTRAL BANKING

This book has continually compared the currency board system to central banking as possibilities for the Russian monetary system. Other possibilities exist, so this section briefly compares them to the currency board system as alternatives to central banking.

One alternative is dollarization (currency substitution), which would at minimum grant the US dollar or another foreign currency equal legal status to the Central Bank rouble, and at maximum replace the rouble with the foreign currency as the sole official currency. With full dollarization, the Central Bank of Russia would cease to exist, and the US Federal Reserve System would in effect become Russia's central bank, though it would have no obligation to be a lender of last resort to Russian commercial banks. Dollar notes, coins, and deposits would replace rouble notes, coins, and deposits. Dollarization would achieve a truly fixed exchange rate because it would eliminate the power of the Russian government and the Central Bank of Russia to alter the exchange rate. Russia would become an offshore part of the US dollar zone, like Puerto Rico or Panama.

Compared to the currency board system, dollarization has two main disadvantages. The economic disadvantage is that dollarization would send all seigniorage from notes and coins in Russia to the US Federal Reserve

System. If, as has been mentioned, the Russian currency board will probably earn $360 million per year or more of net seigniorage, that would be the yearly cost of dollarization to the Russian economy. (To be precise, it would be the 'flow cost' [Fischer 1982: 301–5]. Russians have already incurred most of the 'stock cost' of acquiring dollars initially because they already hold many dollars as a store of value.) Admittedly, the Russian government could make an agreement with the American government to share seigniorage from dollarization, but that seems unlikely. No such agreement now exists between the United States and any other country. Historically, the multicolonial currency boards listed in Appendix C seem to have been the only examples of long-lasting harmonious agreement to share seigniorage (for an example, see King 1957: 46–8), except for a few agreements between very small countries and much more populous ones with central banks.

The political disadvantage of dollarization is that the Russian government strongly opposes it. Government officials, including the president, have expressed dissatisfaction about the increasing use of foreign currencies as unofficial parallel currencies in Russia (Lloyd and Volkov 1992). Full dollarization of the Russian economy, although it would be beneficial, is unlikely because the Russian government is unlikely to allow a monetary system with no domestically issued currency. The consequence would instead probably be a Latin American-style, incompletely dollarized economy whose efficiency would be hindered by the legally mandated use of the unstable, inconvertible Central Bank rouble. A currency board offers a solution to this political problem because it will provide Russia with a sound domestically issued currency, whose notes and coins will have pictures of famous Russians, words in Russian, and other signs of Russian identity.

We have proposed that reserve-currency notes and coins should be allowed to circulate alongside the notes and coins of the currency board. If so, can currency board rouble notes displace the foreign notes that Russians now hold? Yes, they can. The Russian government will use only the currency board rouble (and the Central Bank rouble if the Central Bank exists as a parallel issuer), not foreign currency. Use of the currency board rouble by the government will not force Russians to use currency board roubles except in the brief period between, say, receiving currency board roubles in payment of wages from the government and exchanging them for foreign currency. However, the government's use of the currency board rouble will create demand for the currency board rouble in preference to foreign currency, just as the government's use of the Central Bank rouble currently creates demand for the Central Bank rouble. If the US dollar is the reserve currency, some dollar notes and coins will circulate, but currency board notes and coins will predominate in Russia. The relationship between the currency board rouble and the reserve currency will probably be similar to the relationship between the US dollar and the Hong Kong dollar. It is legal to use US dollar notes and coins in Hong Kong, but almost nobody does: Hong Kong dollar notes and coins predominate.

Besides dollarization, another alternative to central banking is free banking without a currency board (Anderson 1992). Free banking is a system of parallel currencies in which banks issue competing brands of notes.[104] In the 1800s and early 1900s approximately sixty countries, although not Russia, had free banking. Where least hindered by regulations, free banking was typically stable, credible, and orderly (Schuler 1992a). As has been mentioned, sometimes currency boards issued notes alongside bank-issued notes. Free banking is compatible with a currency board. However, free banking without a currency board as one of the issuers seems less advantageous for Russia than free banking with a currency board. Free banking is less well understood than the currency board system even by specialists in money and banking, much less by policymakers and the general public. No free banking system remains today as a living example for policymakers and the Russian public, whereas several currency board systems remain. Also, although free banking without a currency board would eventually result in the notes and coins of stable commercial banks dominating the market, an unruly period of bank failures might occur first, as it has in other free banking systems that lacked effective enforcement of commercial banks' promises to provide convertibility of their notes and coins at a fixed rate on demand (Schuler 1992a: 29, 35). (If commercial banks were to issue new floating currencies, the new currencies would probably not survive competition from currencies with fixed exchange rates to foreign currencies or to commodities [Selgin 1992b: 11–12].) The existence of a currency board will ensure that at least one brand of notes and coins is unquestionably sound during the transition of the Russian banking system to a form more appropriate for a market economy. Finally, the Russian government desires a role in issuing notes and coins. A currency board allows it a limited role, whereas free banking without a currency board would allow it no role.

Our remarks on the political feasibility of dollarization and free banking without a currency board do not mean that we oppose them. On the contrary, either would be better than the current Russian monetary system. However, the currency board system has political as well as economic features that make a currency board more advantageous for Russia today than dollarization or free banking without a currency board.

Other objections can be made and other questions can be asked about the currency board system. We think, however, that we have answered the main objections and questions, and we will answer some of the minor ones in a forthcoming book (Hanke and Schuler forthcoming).

9

TWO SUCCESSFUL RUSSIAN MONETARY REFORMS

Because the currency board system and the parallel currency approach to monetary reform are unfamiliar to most people, it is worth describing how they have worked in practice in Russia. A parallel currency approach to monetary reform has been tried in Russia twice before in this century, once using a currency board.

THE NORTH RUSSIAN CURRENCY BOARD, 1918–20

A little-known currency board existed during the Russian civil war. It was established by the White Guard (anti-Bolshevik) government of the region around Archangel and Murmansk, in cooperation with its ally the British government. The North Russian currency board is interesting both because it worked well in difficult conditions and because it was the idea of the most influential economist of the century, John Maynard Keynes.[105]

A series of accidents and blunders entangled the First World War Allies in the Russian civil war on the side of the White Guard. They supported the White government headquartered in Archangel, which was one of many White governments throughout Russia. Allied troops, which began landing in North Russia in June 1918, soon were a force of approximately 10,000 men. One of the urgent needs of the force was a convenient means to pay for local services. Currency in North Russia was diverse: czarist, Kerensky, Bolshevik, and local White notes all circulated. Russia as a whole had more than 2,000 separate issuers of roubles. All were floating, depreciating currencies; the rouble had not been fully convertible into gold at a pegged exchange rate since the beginning of the First World War. The roubles of some issuers depreciated faster than those of others, but almost all types of roubles experienced high inflation because of the policies of their issuers. The Russian State Bank branch at Archangel was among the issuers: it declared itself independent of the Petrograd (St Petersburg) head office and issued its own notes as the State Bank of Northern Russia. Because so many different types of currency with different degrees of

146

acceptability were in use, the method by which the Allies paid for local goods and services was confused (FO 1918a: 102).[106]

The British War Office sent to North Russia an official, Dominick Spring-Rice, to advise the Allied force on finance and methods of payment. In a memorandum of 3 July 1918, he suggested to London that 'the task of providing currency for local needs should, if possible, fall on the local authority', perhaps in combination with a loan to the North Russian government in pounds sterling (FO 1918b: 249–50). On 9 July, the British general in Murmansk asked the British government to print notes for British military use at Murmansk (Spring-Rice 1919: 282).

John Maynard Keynes, who was then a British Treasury official responsible for war finance, became involved in establishing a North Russian currency in August. Both Spring-Rice (1919: 284) and Foreign Office records (FO 1919b: 22) acknowledge that Keynes formulated the details of the currency issue scheme. Indeed, Keynes wrote two notes on the subject (FO 1918a: 52–5, 62–4; published in Hanke and Schuler 1991a: 60–3).

On 11 September 1918, the British commissioner in Archangel received a telegram outlining Keynes's scheme. The North Russian government officially announced the note issue scheme on 11 November. Its essential elements were as follows (Spring-Rice 1919: 286).

The North Russian government established an agency called the National Emission Caisse (North Russia). ('Emission Caisse' is French for 'note issue office'.) The Emission Caisse was to be an organ of any successor (White) government to the North Russian government. The president of the Emission Caisse for the first six months was a British banker, Ernest M. Harvey.

The Emission Caisse issued notes for 1–500 roubles and was also allowed to issue small-change coins or notes. It exchanged its roubles for sterling at a fixed rate of 40 roubles per £1 by issuing cheques on banks abroad, mainly in London. The Emission Caisse also accepted US dollars and French francs at their exchange rates against sterling. Anyone wishing to buy Emission Caisse notes had to do so with foreign currency. The North Russian government guaranteed the notes with its whole property. More important, the note issue of the Emission Caisse was backed with a sterling reserve equal to 75 per cent of its notes in circulation. The sterling reserve was provided by a loan from the British government to the North Russian government. The sterling reserve was deposited at the Bank of England, and was the Emission Caisse's inviolable property, so it could not become the property of the Bolsheviks should the North Russian government be defeated. Unlike an orthodox currency board, which holds 100 per cent foreign reserves, the Emission Caisse was allowed to buy North Russian government bonds equal to 25 per cent of its notes in circulation. The purchase of North Russian government bonds was a concession to the financial demands of the North Russian government.

The Emission Caisse was expected to make profits because its deposit at the Bank of England and its holdings of North Russian government bonds paid interest, while the notes it issued did not. The Emission Caisse and the government were to share net seigniorage equally until the Emission Caisse accumulated a reserve fund of 10 per cent of its note and coin circulation. Any further net seigniorage was to be remitted to the government (FO 1918a: 343–7, 529–31).

The Emission Caisse was modelled after the West African Currency Board, which had been established for Britain's colonies in that region in 1912. Keynes was familiar with the West African Currency Board and with the somewhat similar Indian currency authority (Keynes 1971 [1913]; 1983 [1913]). (The West African Currency Board held 100 per cent foreign reserves, but the Indian currency authority held some Indian government bonds.) Keynes also fully appreciated the advantages of the currency board system for the colonies: it allowed local governments to issue at low cost a currency as good as sterling, while enabling them to capture the seigniorage that would have accrued to the Bank of England had its notes been used instead.

The British government bought 100 million roubles of notes from the Emission Caisse to provide the initial sterling reserves of the Emission Caisse. The notes entered circulation in Archangel (the headquarters of the Emission Caisse) and Murmansk by British military payments to the local population. The Emission Caisse opened for business on 28 November 1918 (FO 1918a: 527).

The British commissioner in Archangel estimated that as of mid-October 1918, approximately 600 million roubles of all types were in circulation in North Russia (FO 1918a: 89), which had a population of approximately 600,000. When the new Emission Caisse roubles were introduced, British military authorities, who still needed old roubles for some purposes, set the exchange rate at 48 old roubles per 40 Emission Caisse roubles (£1), as the directors of the Emission Caisse and British government officials had proposed. (The pre-war exchange rate had been 9.45 roubles per £1.) The State Bank of Northern Russia tried to maintain the exchange rate at 45 old roubles per 40 Emission Caisse roubles, perhaps because it had issued some of the old rouble notes in circulation. It was unsuccessful, because the supply of old roubles was increasing rapidly as the Bolsheviks and White governments elsewhere inflated rapidly to finance their wartime deficit spending. The rate that the British military offered per 40 Emission Caisse roubles was 48 old roubles in April 1919, 64 in early May, 72 in mid-May, and 80 in late June (FO 1919a: 455; 1919b: 48, 80, 149). The continuing depreciation of old roubles overcame the initial reluctance of many people to use the unfamiliar but stable Emission Caisse rouble. From mid-October 1918 to mid-April 1919, the circulation of old roubles in North Russia decreased from perhaps 600 million to perhaps 300 million (FO 1919a: 478). In real terms, the decrease was even more, since old roubles were depreciating against the Emission Caisse rouble. The note circulation of the Emission Caisse increased from zero in November 1918 to a peak of 52.7 million in July 1919. (This excludes notes held by the British military and not yet spent by it into circulation among the public.) Emission Caisse notes were displacing the old, depreciating roubles from circulation in North Russia. The process would have continued had the North Russian government continued to exist.

However, the Allied intervention in North Russia became more and more unpopular in Allied countries after the end of the First World War in November 1918. The intervention no longer served any purpose related to war against Germany, and it entangled the Allies in a bloody civil war. The British government decided in March 1919 to withdraw its troops from North Russia. The other Allies took similar action. By 27 September 1919, the last Allied troops left North Russia (Rhodes 1988: 121).

The Emission Caisse announced that it would close in Archangel and redeem all of its notes presented to it. The British military command in North Russia still held 55 million roubles of Emission Caisse notes. To prevent them from being captured by the Bolsheviks, the War Office instructed the British military commander to burn the notes. Because the notes were wrapped in bundles, which the weather had made damp, they would not burn. They were dumped at sea (Ironside 1953: 81) and the British military received a book-entry credit for the destroyed notes.

The Emission Caisse officially closed to the public in Archangel on 4 October 1919, despite protests by the North Russian government. It continued to redeem notes collected by the North Russian government and the State Bank of Northern Russia until 15 October (FO 1919b: 492, 498). It then moved to London, where its main business was redeeming the 55 million rouble credit that the British government held. Approximately 13.5 million Emission Caisse roubles remained in circulation among the public. British troops returning from North Russia held a small amount of Emission Caisse roubles, but most of the roubles were still in Russia. The Emission Caisse's president suggested that the North Russian government and a bank that was serving as the Emission Caisse's agent in Norway should be allowed to redeem notes as long as the North Russian government retained control of Archangel. He proposed accordingly that the British government should not redeem all of its rouble credit, so as to provide a reserve against Emission Caisse roubles still in circulation among the public. He argued that 'the assertion of our financial integrity is well worth £300,000. The Northern Rouble is known throughout North Russia and Scandinavia as the English Rouble. . . . It is the only good money seen in Russia since the Bolshevik revolution' (FO 1919b: 507–21).

Without Allied troops, the existence of the North Russian government was precarious. It survived for several months because the Bolsheviks were concentrating their forces elsewhere. When the Red Army attacked North Russia early in 1920, the North Russian army disintegrated. The North Russian government fled on a ship to England on 19 February, and two days later the Red Army entered Archangel. The Emission Caisse remained open in London until 30 April 1920 (FO 1919b: 597). After that date, note redemption ceased. The archives of the British Foreign Office seem to contain no records of the final disposition of the Emission Caisse, but correspondence from the last few months of its existence indicates that most of the 13.5 million Emission Caisse roubles in circulation among the public never were redeemed, inflicting a loss on their holders because the Bolshevik government did not allow Emission Caisse notes to circulate legally. The British government, therefore, suffered a loss of approximately 15.5 million Emission Caisse roubles (£378,500), the difference between the now worthless North Russian government bonds held by the Emission Caisse and the value of notes that were never redeemed.

THE CHERVONETS, 1922–6

The North Russian currency board was established by a government opposed to the Bolsheviks. Another parallel currency, not issued by a currency board, was established by the Bolsheviks themselves, after they had defeated the North Russian government and other hostile forces in the Russian civil war.

The Bolshevik government had continued the policy of the czarist and Kerensky governments of printing money to finance wartime deficit spending. After the Russian civil war ended in 1920, the Bolshevik government continued to print money, relying on seigniorage for 80 per cent of its monetary revenue (Rostowski and Shapiro 1992: 28). (The government budget also included substantial nonmonetary revenue and spending.) Prices increased 1,700 per cent in 1921 and almost 7,400 per cent in 1922. The Soviet rouble was called the sovznak, meaning 'Soviet token', to distinguish it from other roubles such as those issued by the old czarist government and by White Guard governments during the civil war. The supply of sovznaks increased 1,500 per cent in 1921 and more than 11,000 per cent in 1922 (Arnold 1937: 128–9).

Hyperinflation was one characteristic of War Communism, the period during and immediately after the Russian civil war. As was mentioned in chapter 3, War Communism tried to introduce aspects of a moneyless economy by paying wages in barter and distributing goods and services free of charge. By 1921 it was clear that the economic results of War Communism were disastrous. To reverse economic collapse, the government introduced the New Economic Policy, which was proclaimed in

March 1921. As a first step to returning to a monetary economy, the State Bank of the USSR (Gosbank), which had been abolished on 19 January 1920 at the urging of left-wing Bolsheviks, was re-established on 16 November 1921. The State Bank was subordinate to the People's Commissariat of Finance (Narkomfin – later the Ministry of Finance). However, the State Bank was ordered to be a self-financing organization, which allowed it some independence from the Commissariat of Finance (Arnold 1937: 70, 88–9, 119–20).

The State Bank offered deposits partly indexed against inflation, and both it and the government began using the pre-war czarist gold rouble as a unit of account. A partial market economy could not work well without a fairly stable currency, however. In outlying regions of the Soviet Union and even in Moscow, czarist gold coins and foreign currency were displacing the rapidly depreciating sovznak in circulation. The real revenue from additional issues of sovznaks was decreasing, and the purchasing power of notes in circulation was just 32 million pre-war roubles at its lowest point on 1 April 1922, compared to 3.015 billion roubles on 1 August 1914. Because the government relied extensively on inflation to finance the budget deficit, it decided to reform the monetary system by introducing a stable parallel currency rather than by ceasing inflation in the sovznak. The government decided in July 1922 to establish a new unit, the chervonets, which was introduced on 28 November 1922.[107] The name was chosen to suggest stability: the old chervonets had been a gold coin in circulation at the time of Peter the Great. The new chervonets was backed by a minimum of 25 per cent precious metals; however, it did not have a pegged exchange rate with any precious metal. Gold chervonets coins (whose face value was greater than their bullion value) were minted beginning in 1923; the government withdrew them from circulation at the end of the decade. The chervonets was issued by the State Bank, whereas the sovznak was issued by the Commissariat of Finance (Arnold 1937: 91–4, 127–49, 158–9; Brabant 1992: 377).

The chervonets was introduced first in cities. It spread to the countryside rather slowly. The minimum denomination of chervonets notes was high – equal to 10 pre-war roubles – and coins had disappeared from circulation because their value as metal exceeded their face value; consequently, sovznak notes continued to be used for small transactions. Since the countryside was much poorer than the cities, few transactions there were large enough to make use of chervonets notes anyway. The chervonets was not at first made legal tender. Like the initial minimum denomination of 10 pre-war roubles, the lack of legal tender quality for the chervonets preserved some demand for the sovznak, which the government was still issuing in large quantities to pay workers and to buy food from peasants (Arnold 1937: 155, 194).

The chervonets circulated at a floating exchange rate to the sovznak. It soon began to displace the sovznak as a medium of exchange for large purchases. It also displaced as a store of value and unit of account the foreign currency and czarist gold coins that had come into circulation in outlying regions of the Soviet Union. The real supply of chervonets notes increased continuously in the first twelve months of monetary reform. It then reached a plateau of 130 million to 140 million pre-war roubles, where it remained until August 1924, when it began to increase again. Contrary to the experience of other countries that have had hyperinflation, the real domestic supply of notes in the Soviet Union, comprising chervonets and sovznaks, increased during the final stages of hyperinflation. (Hyperinflation only affected the sovznak.) Even the real supply of sovznak notes increased during the first several months of the monetary reform, from 90 million pre-war roubles on 1 December 1922 to 114 million pre-war roubles on 1 April 1923, because inflation decreased. Real government revenue from seigniorage increased in late 1922 and 1923, after having decreased rather steadily since 1917. The chervonets enabled the Soviet Union to avoid the collapse in the real money supply[108] and production that occurred in other European hyperinflations of the time, most notably in Germany (Arnold 1937: 128–9, 186–98, 226–30; Rostowski and Shapiro 1992: 14–17).

As was explained in chapter 5, the apparent reason for the increase in the real supply of sovznaks was that the chervonets filled gaps left by the sovznak. The chervonets displaced the sovznak as a medium of exchange for large transactions and displaced foreign currency and gold as a store of value and a unit of account. The sovznak remained the medium of exchange for small transactions. The chervonets and the sovznak in combination fulfilled all the three functions of money relatively well. Because people could legally exchange sovznaks for chervonets at market rates at any time, demand for chervonets created an increase in demand (a derived demand) for sovznaks. Receiving payment in sovznaks became less of a disadvantage than before, because people could easily exchange sovznaks for chervonets in numerous places throughout the Soviet Union and hence avoid the effects of hyperinflation on large holdings of domestic currency.

Ultimately the sovznak continued to depreciate as the government printed more and more sovznaks. Chervonets became a steadily increasing share of the real money supply. On 5 February 1924 the Commissariat of Finance began to issue 'gold' treasury notes for denominations smaller than one chervonets (ten new-style roubles). They had fixed exchange rates to the chervonets, but had no pegged exchange rate to gold. To prevent the treasury notes from repeating the fate of the sovznak, the maximum circulation of treasury notes was limited to half the circulation of chervonets. A decree of 14 February ordered the Commissariat of Finance to cease issuing sovznaks the next day. A decree of 7 March 1924 fixed an exchange rate of 50,000 sovznaks per chervonets as a prelude to withdrawing the sovznak from circulation. Since two previous changes of denomination of the sovznak had already occurred, the exchange rate between the original, pre–1921 sovznak and the chervonets was 50 billion to one. The Commissariat of Finance and the State Bank ceased accepting sovznaks for payment and exchange on 1 June 1924 (Arnold 1937: 191, 211–18).

The chervonets and the other reforms of the New Economic Policy revived the Soviet economy. From 1921 to 1926 the index of industrial production more than trebled and attained 1913 levels. Agricultural production doubled and exceeded the 1913 level by 18 per cent. The New Economic Policy resulted in a higher rate of growth than the Russian economy has had before or since (Shmelev and Popov 1989: 13). Contrary to the experience of other countries that have had hyperinflation, but have not had legal parallel currencies, rapid growth in the Russian economy began *during* hyperinflation. Production was higher than it would have been without a parallel currency, although the economy did suffer the 'scissors crisis' in 1923. The scissors crisis was an increase in the price of manufactured goods compared to food sold by peasants. It took its name from the appearance of graphs showing price indexes of manufactured goods and food, which over time opened a gap like the blades of scissors. The scissors crisis occurred because industrial state enterprises used their market power to withhold manufactured goods from the market. Peasants selling food had no market power and often had to accept sovznaks in payment, which they then spent as quickly as possible. The spread of the chervonets offered the peasants a more durable store of value than food. Prodded by lack of demand at existing prices and by government actions to reduce their market power, industrial state enterprises eventually decreased the prices of manufactured goods compared to food (Arnold 1937: 171–4, 200–1).

When the chervonets was introduced, the budget of the Soviet government was still in deficit. By relying almost exclusively on the sovznak for inflationary finance and creating some confidence that the chervonets would remain relatively stable, the government was able to make a smooth transition from inflation to noninflationary taxes (including profits from state enterprises) as its main source of revenue. Seigniorage decreased from 46.3 per cent of total government revenue in the fourth quarter of 1922, when the chervonets was introduced, to 9.6 per cent in the fourth quarter of 1923. As the economy revived, aided by the existence of the chervonets, real revenue from taxes increased (Arnold 1937: 236–42; Rostowski and Shapiro 1992: 28).

After the reforms of 1924 to stabilize and then withdraw the sovznak, the State Bank bought and sold chervonets in foreign-exchange markets to keep the exchange rate somewhat close to one chervonets per pound sterling. (Sterling, like most other currencies at the time, was floating against gold.) The chervonets had only limited convertibility, because the State Bank controlled the foreign-currency deposits of state enterprises and the government had an official monopoly of foreign trade. When it became apparent that stabilizing the chervonets at existing levels would require continuing sales of foreign currency by the State Bank, reducing its foreign reserves, the government on 9 July 1926 forbade the export of chervonets, and the chervonets became inconvertible. On 21 March 1928 the government forbade the import of notes, to further extend its control over the currency (Arnold 1937: 262–3).

The inconvertibility of the chervonets was a sign of the government's turn from a partial market economy to socialism. The left wing of the Communist Party, including Stalin and Trotsky, disliked the concessions to free markets embodied in the New Economic Policy. At the end of 1927, the Communist Party congress, under the influence of the left wing, confirmed the policy of collectivizing agriculture and approved the First Five-Year Plan, which took effect in 1928. The Five-Year Plan ended the New Economic Policy. The centrally planned economy needed an inconvertible currency to reduce opportunities for people to bypass the organs of central planning.

A COMPARISON OF THE REFORMS

The Emission Caisse rouble, issued by a currency board as a parallel currency, was credible because it was issued with British assistance and was backed by foreign reserves of 75 per cent on deposit at the Bank of England. The Emission Caisse rouble was fully convertible and never deviated from its fixed exchange rate with sterling. Unlike the currencies issued by other Russian governments at the time, the Emission Caisse rouble was a reliable store of value. Consequently, it tended to displace other roubles from circulation in North Russia. With Emission Caisse roubles, the Allied force was able to buy and sell goods almost as easily as if it had been at home on manoeuvres.

Besides being useful to the Allies, the Emission Caisse would have earned seigniorage for the North Russian government had the government and the Emission Caisse continued to exist. During its short life, the Emission Caisse was unprofitable because of the high cost of printing notes quickly and because its North Russian government bonds became worthless. (Administrative expenses were only 400,000 Emission Caisse roubles.) Had the Emission Caisse continued to exist in North Russia instead of moving to London and ceasing new business, it would have probably earned net seigniorage of approximately 5 million Emission Caisse roubles per year from 1920 onwards. The 7.2 million rouble cost of printing the first batch of notes was an unusual expense. Later issues could have been printed less quickly at lower cost. Furthermore, many of the notes would have remained in circulation for years before wearing out and needing replacement. The North Russian government bonds that the

Emission Caisse purchased at the start of its operations would have been redeemed had the Whites defeated the Bolsheviks. Because the North Russian government ceased to exist, the bond sales became a 'gift' from the British government to the North Russian government. The British government financed the losses that the Emission Caisse incurred from holding North Russian government bonds.

The North Russian currency board suffered only one significant defect: the purchase of North Russian government bonds as reserves for 25 per cent of the note issue. Orthodox policy for a currency board requires 100 per cent reserves in foreign assets only. When the time came to liquidate the Emission Caisse, the worthlessness of the North Russian bonds left it bankrupt. Fortunately for the British government, which held most of the Emission Caisse notes, some notes were in circulation too far away to make redemption in London feasible before the Emission Caisse closed; that reduced losses to the British government.

The chervonets was issued by the State Bank of the USSR as a parallel currency to the sovznak, which was issued by the People's Commissariat of Finance. The chervonets had only moderate credibility, but it was a much more stable and credible currency than the sovznak. It contributed greatly to the revival of the Soviet economy during the period of the New Economic Policy. The chervonets was never fully convertible, and ultimately became inconvertible. It was issued by a central bank, which unlike the North Russian currency board was not well protected from political pressure. Soviet monetary policy was subordinate to the economic and political policy of the Bolsheviks, who correctly viewed a convertible currency as an obstacle to a centrally planned economy. The later policy of the Soviet government rather than the parallel currency approach itself was responsible for the inconvertibility of the chervonets. An interesting aspect of the chervonets is that its existence actually increased demand for sovznaks despite continuing hyperinflation in the sovznak.

10

CONCLUSION

Central banking in its current form in Russia has resulted in an unsound currency, extreme inflation, and economic decline. The Central Bank of Russia has no definite plan for providing a sound currency. Even if reformed, the Central Bank of Russia is unlikely to provide Russia with a sound currency soon. Therefore, we recommend that Russia establish a currency board. The currency board can be established by the Russian government alone, or in collaboration with the IMF if the IMF provides some of the initial foreign reserves. The currency board system, as used in Hong Kong and elsewhere, is a well-proven means of providing a stable, credible, fully convertible currency, and of encouraging rapid economic growth.

A currency board has many advantages for Russia today. It can be established quickly, it will be simple to operate, it will be a credible monetary authority that will issue a stable, fully convertible currency, and it will tend to encourage international trade and investment in Russia. A currency board has advantages for the West as well: it will ensure that the IMF stabilization fund is used to provide a sound currency rather than to earn profits for currency speculators, and it will create an institution that will enable subsequent foreign investment to be most beneficial for the Russian economy. A currency board will solidify the emerging market economy in Russia. Without a currency board, the rapid macroeconomic stabilization and microeconomic restructuring necessary to encourage economic growth may be delayed, and Russia will probably for a long time remain a poor country dependent on foreign aid to maintain even the current low standards of living for its people.

This book has proposed two ways to establish the Russian currency board: by converting the Central Bank of Russia into a currency board, or by establishing the currency board as the issuer of a parallel currency. The conversion approach tends to impose hard budget constraints immediately. The parallel currency approach allows a brief transition period during which budget constraints harden and during which the Russian government can continue to collect some revenue from inflation in the Central Bank rouble. At the same time, the existence of the parallel currency board rouble will enable much of the Russian economy to protect itself from extreme inflation.

The proposal for monetary reform in Russia made in this book is detailed and requires the Russian government to take action on many points. The most important elements of the proposal are that the currency board be established, and that the currency board be protected from political pressure to convert it into a central bank. Appropriate safeguards to protect the currency board can be devised (see chapter 6).

The hard budget constraints that the Russian currency board will tend to impose will create momentum for further reforms of government finance, state commercial banks, and state enterprises. The currency board will best promote economic growth if all the reforms proposed in this book are achieved quickly; however, the proposal is robust enough to survive and help the Russian economy even if political pressure temporarily delays elements of reform other than the currency board itself. The currency board will tend to force other monetary and economic reforms to occur rapidly because it will tend to eliminate the soft budget constraints that perpetuate the current monetary system.

Monetary reform is now the most important step for establishing a market economy that will generate growth and progress for Russia, and a currency board is the most promising means of achieving a durable, beneficial monetary reform.

SUMMARY OF PROPOSALS

Converting the Central Bank of Russia into a currency board (chapter 5)

1 Delegate to other bodies all functions of the Central Bank of Russia other than supplying the monetary base.
2 Allow a brief period of clean, unrestricted floating exchange rates for the rouble.
3 Make the actions of the Central Bank of Russia transparent and predictable.
4 Convert some reserves of commercial banks (deposits at the Central Bank of Russia) into currency board notes and coins or into foreign securities, whichever the commercial banks prefer. Cancel remaining reserves.
5 Establish a fixed exchange rate with the reserve currency.
6 Ensure that foreign reserves equal 100 per cent of rouble notes and coins in circulation.
7 Transfer the remaining assets and liabilities of the Central Bank of Russia to the Russian currency board and open the currency board for business.

Establishing the Russian currency board as the issuer of a parallel currency (chapter 5)

1 Obtain initial foreign reserves for the Russian currency board.
2 Make the currency board rouble legal tender for payment of taxes and private debts.
3 Issue currency board roubles equal to the initial foreign reserves.
4 Put the currency board roubles into circulation, preferably by a distribution to every resident of Russia according to a well-defined plan.
5 Allow the currency board rouble to circulate as a parallel currency to the Central Bank rouble, at an exchange rate determined by market forces.

Other reforms of the Russian monetary system (chapter 7)

- Reform oil pricing, which will substantially increase government revenue.
- Settle arrears of state enterprises, perhaps by means of a clearinghouse.
- Enforce bankruptcy laws more strictly.
- Broaden the tax base by more vigorous tax collection of payments made outside the banking system; make tax rates low and uniform.
- Allow foreign banks to enter the market unrestrictedly.
- Abolish reserve requirements for commercial banks.
- Allow commercial banks to engage in any legal financial or commercial activity.
- Restructure bankrupt state commercial banks by giving them enterprises shares, privatization vouchers, or perhaps non-negotiable government bonds to replenish their assets.
- Commercialize and eventually privatize state commercial banks.
- Transfer responsibility for the payments system from the Central Bank of Russia to another body or bodies; allow alternative payments systems.
- End the separation of the cash and noncash financial circuits by converting noncash deposits to cash-convertible deposits at the market rate of exchange. (Applies only if the Central Bank of Russia is converted into a currency board.)

158

- Devise procedures for dealing with existing contracts that specify payment in Central Bank roubles. (Applies only if the Central Bank of Russia is converted into a currency board.)
- Allow Russians to make contracts, payments, and deposits in any currency.
- Abolish foreign-exchange controls, including forced conversions into roubles.

A comprehensive programme of economic reforms (chapter 1)

1 Reform the monetary system by means of a currency board.
2 Abolish remaining vestiges of central planning, such as central allocation of trade among state enterprises.
3 Abolish remaining price controls and subsidies.
4 Corporatize state enterprises.
5 Privatize much more state property, particularly housing and farmland. Eliminate the system of residence permits, which restricts labour movement.
6 Continue to deregulate trade. (Lower barriers to importing goods will help to prevent domestic monopolies from prevailing.) Abolish export quotas.
7 Reduce tax rates, to encourage entrepreneurial activity.
8 Avoid giving unions or industries special privileges that shield them from competitive market forces.
9 Enact laws that secure rights to private property, assure the enforcement of contracts, and make it easy to establish new businesses.
10 Publicize the economic changes to make the Russian people and foreigners understand the course and probable consequences of reforms.

Note: The currency board system will hasten other economic reforms (see chapter 1).

APPENDIX A

A model constitution for a currency board in Russia

To illustrate the legal foundation necessary for a currency board to work efficiently, this appendix offers a model constitution for a currency board in Russia. The model constitution has many features adapted from the formal and informal constitutions of currency boards in West Africa, Hong Kong, the British Caribbean, Libya, Burma, and elsewhere. It will require minor changes if other former Soviet republics wish to join Russia in establishing the currency board.

CONSTITUTION OF THE RUSSIAN CURRENCY BOARD

1 The Russian Currency Board is hereby created by the Russian government and the International Monetary Fund in joint cooperation. The purpose of the Currency Board is to issue notes, coins, and deposits in currency board roubles, and to maintain them fully convertible at a fixed exchange rate into a reserve currency as specified in paragraph 6.

2 The Currency Board shall have its legal seat in Switzerland.

3 (a) The Currency Board shall be governed by a board of five directors. Three directors shall be non-Russian citizens appointed by the International Monetary Fund. They shall not be employees of the International Monetary Fund or its member governments. Two directors shall be appointed by the government of Russia.

(b) A quorum shall consist of three members of the board of directors, including at least one of the directors chosen by the government of Russia. The board of directors may meet at the board's legal seat; in Moscow; or in such other locations as it designates. Decisions shall be by majority vote, except as specified in paragraph 15.

(c) The first two directors appointed by the Russian government shall serve terms of one and four years. The first three directors appointed by the International Monetary Fund shall serve terms of two, three, and five years. Subsequent directors shall serve terms of five years. Directors may be reappointed once. Should a director resign or die, the appropriate organization as specified in paragraph 3(a) shall choose a successor to complete the remainder of the term.

4 The board of directors shall have the power to hire and fire the Currency Board's staff, and to determine salaries for the staff. The by-laws of the Currency Board shall determine salaries for the directors.

5 The Currency Board shall issue notes and coins denominated in currency board roubles. The notes and coins shall be fully convertible into the reserve currency. The notes shall be printed outside Russia. The Currency Board may accept deposits of the reserve currency.

6 (a) The reserve currency is the foreign currency or the commodity to which the currency board rouble has a fixed exchange rate. Initially, the reserve currency shall be the US dollar and the fixed exchange rate shall be one currency board rouble equals one dollar.

(b) Failure to maintain the fixed exchange rate with the reserve currency shall make the Currency Board subject to legal action for breach of contract according to the laws of Switzerland. This provision does not apply to embezzled, mutilated, or counterfeited notes, coins, and deposits, or to changes of the reserve currency in accord with paragraph 13.

7 The Currency Board shall charge no commission for exchanging currency board roubles for the reserve currency, or the reverse.

8 The Currency Board shall begin business with foreign reserves equal to at least 100 per cent of its notes and coins in circulation and deposits with it. It shall hold its foreign reserves in securities or other forms payable only in the reserve currency. The Currency Board shall not hold securities issued by the national or local governments of Russia, or by enterprises owned by those governments.

9 The Currency Board shall pay all net seigniorage (profits) into a reserve fund until its unborrowed reserves equal 110 per cent of its notes and coins in circulation and deposits. It shall remit to the government of Russia all net seigniorage beyond that necessary to maintain 110 per cent reserves. The distribution of net seigniorage shall occur annually.

10 The head office of the Currency Board shall be in Moscow. The Currency Board may establish branches or appoint agents in other cities of Russia. The Currency Board shall also maintain a branch in Switzerland or in the reserve country.

11 The Currency Board shall publish a financial statement, attested by the directors, quarterly or more often. The statement shall appraise the Currency Board's holdings of securities at their market value.

12 The Currency Board may issue notes and coins in such denominations as it judges to be appropriate.

13 Should the annual change in the consumer price index in the reserve country fall outside the range −5 per cent to 20 per cent for more than

two years, or −10 per cent to 40 per cent for more than six months, within sixty days the Currency Board must either:

(a) devalue (if the change in the index is negative) or revalue (if the change in the index is positive) the currency board rouble in terms of the reserve currency by no more than the change in the index during the period just specified, or

(b) choose a new reserve currency and fix the exchange rate of the currency board rouble to the new currency at the rate then prevailing between the new reserve currency and the former reserve currency.

14 If the Currency Board chooses a new reserve currency in accord with paragraph 13, within one year it must convert all its foreign reserves into assets payable in the new reserve currency.

15 The Currency Board may not be dissolved nor may its assets be transferred to a successor organization except by unanimous vote of the board of directors.

16 Beyond an initial loan of reserves from the International Monetary Fund, the Currency Board may not accept loans or grants of reserves from international agencies or foreign governments.

17 Exchanges by the Currency Board shall be exempt from taxation by the Russian government.

18 Currency board roubles shall be legal tender for paying taxes and settling debts in Russia. However, they shall not be forced tender for contracts between private parties.

APPENDIX B

More about the money supply process in a currency board system

This appendix goes into more detail than chapter 4 to illustrate the connections between the balance of payments and the domestic money supply in a currency board system. It uses balance sheets to supplement the flow diagrams of chapter 4. The flow diagrams (Figures 4.1–4.4) depict sequences of events, whereas here the balance sheets depict conditions at particular stages for the relevant agents in a currency board system.[109] Near the end of the appendix, we progress from a simplified account to a more complicated and realistic account of the money supply process in a currency board system.

Assets	Liabilities
Foreign securities	Notes and coins
	Deposits of commercial banks (optional)
	Net worth

Figure B.1 Simplified currency board balance sheet

Figure B.1 is a simplified balance sheet for a typical currency board. Recall that in a balance sheet, by definition, assets = liabilities + net worth.

Figure B.2 is a simplified balance sheet for a typical commercial bank in a currency board system. Later we will combine the balance sheets of commercial banks into a single balance sheet.

Figure B.3 is a simplified balance sheet for a typical member of the public (meaning anybody in the financial sector except the currency board and commercial banks). Later we will combine the balance sheets of members of the public into a single balance sheet.

Assets	Liabilities
Currency board notes and coins (reserves)	Public's deposits
Loans and investments	Stockholders' equity (net worth)

Figure B.2 Simplified commercial bank balance sheet

Assets	Liabilities
Deposits at commercial banks	Bank loans
Currency board notes and coins	Net worth

Figure B.3 Simplified balance sheet of a member of the public

The money supply is the left-hand (asset) side of the combined balance sheet of members of the public.

Return for a moment to Figure 4.1, the flow diagram in chapter 4 that shows what happens when a current-account surplus occurs in a currency board system. To make the analysis concrete and simple, we make certain assumptions, as follows.

1 Deposits of commercial banks are convertible into currency board notes and coins (cash) at a fixed rate.
2 The currency board is the only domestic issuer of notes and coins.
3 Commercial banks' desired ratio of commercial bank deposits to commercial bank reserves (the deposit-to-reserve ratio) is constant.
4 The public's desired ratio of commercial bank deposits to currency board notes and coins (the deposit-to-cash ratio) is constant.
5 Income and the money supply move in the same direction.
6 There is no international branch banking between the currency board country and the reserve country.
7 Changes in the balance of payments occur only in the current account; the capital account does not change.
8 No binding minimum reserve ratios or other special bank regulations exist.
9 Commercial banks and the public do not hold reserve currency or use the reserve currency in domestic transactions.[110]

To illustrate the relationship between commercial banks and the currency

Currency board		
Assets	*Liabilities*	
Foreign securities 600	Notes and coins	600
	Net worth	0

Commercial banks		
Assets	*Liabilities*	
Currency board notes and coins (reserves) 100	Public's deposits	5000
Loans and investments 4900	Net worth	0

Public		
Assets	*Liabilities*	
Deposits at commercial banks 5000	Bank loans	4900
Currency board notes and coins 500	Net worth	600

Money supply = 5500

Commercial banks' deposit-to-reserve ratio = 5000:100 = 50:1 (equilibrium)

Public's deposit-to-cash ratio = 5000:500 = 10:1 (equilibrium)

Figure B.4 Simplified money supply increase in a currency board system, initial stage

board in the sequence of events, the balance sheets that follow use hypothetical numbers. Let the initial stage be a situation where the current-account balance is zero and the relevant markets clear – an equilibrium. For the sake of simplicity, assume that net worth in the balance sheet of the currency board and stockholders' equity in the balance sheets of commercial banks are zero. Assume further that commercial banks desire a deposit-to-reserve ratio of 50:1, and that the public desires a deposit-to-cash ratio (also known as a deposit-to-currency ratio) of 10:1 (see Figure B.4). The currency of the currency board country is the currency board rouble. Initially, 600 currency board roubles of notes and coins are in circulation. (The numbers in the examples that follow were chosen because they result in convenient whole-number solutions.)

Currency board		
Assets	*Liabilities*	
Foreign securities 612	Notes and coins	612
	Net worth	0

Commercial banks		
Assets	*Liabilities*	
Currency board notes and coins (reserves) 112	Public's deposits	5012
Loans and investments 4900	Net worth	0

Public		
Assets	*Liabilities*	
Deposits at commercial banks 5012	Bank loans	4900
Currency board notes and coins 500	Net worth	612

Money supply = 5512 (increase = 12)
Commercial banks' deposit-to-reserve ratio = 5012:112 = 44.75:1
  (disequilibrium)
Public's deposit-to-cash ratio = 5012:500 = 10.24:1 (disequilibrium)

Figure B.5 Simplified money supply increase in a currency board system, intermediate stage

When a current-account surplus occurs in a currency board system, the money supply process works as in Figure 4.1. The monetary system is initially in equilibrium, and the balance sheets of the currency board, commercial banks, and the public are as in Figure B.4.

Now let there be a current-account surplus of 12 currency board roubles, in the form of foreign currency that the Russian public deposits in commercial banks in Russia. Since, by assumption, commercial banks hold all reserves in the form of currency board notes and coins, the banks exchange the foreign currency for currency board notes and coins. (They exchange the reserve currency at the fixed exchange rate, and other currencies at prevailing market rates.) The assets and liabilities of the currency board become 12 currency board roubles more than in the initial stage, reserves

Currency board		
Assets	*Liabilities*	
Foreign securities 612	Notes and coins	612
	Net worth	0

Commercial banks		
Assets	*Liabilities*	
Currency board notes and coins (reserves) 102	Public's deposits	5100
Loans and investments 4998	Net worth	0

Public		
Assets	*Liabilities*	
Deposits at commercial banks 5100	Bank loans	4998
Currency board notes and coins 510	Net worth	612

Money supply = 5500

Commercial banks' deposit-to-reserve ratio = 5000:100 = 50:1 (equilibrium)

Public's deposit-to-cash ratio = 5000:500 = 10:1 (equilibrium)

Figure B.6 Simplified money supply increase in a currency board system, final stage

of commercial banks become 12 currency board roubles more than in the initial stage, and deposits of the public at commercial banks become 12 currency board roubles more than in the initial stage. Furthermore, the money supply is 12 currency board roubles more than in the initial stage. This is the intermediate stage (Figure B.5).

Notice that commercial banks have a deposit-to-reserve ratio of 44.75:1 in the intermediate stage, which is less than their desired, initial ratio of 50:1. Notice also that the public has a deposit-to-cash ratio of 10.024:1 in the intermediate stage, which is more than its desired, initial ratio of 10:1. Hence the monetary system is in disequilibrium (the relevant markets do not clear). Commercial banks therefore increase their loans, and the public increases its holdings of cash, to restore the ratios of the initial stage. In

Currency board			
Assets		*Liabilities*	
Foreign securities	600	Notes and coins	600
		Net worth	0

Commercial banks			
Assets		*Liabilities*	
Currency board notes and coins (reserves)	100	Public's deposits	5000
Loans and investments	4900	Net worth	0

Public			
Assets		*Liabilities*	
Deposits at commercial banks	5000	Bank loans	4900
Currency board notes and coins	500	Net worth	600

Money supply = 5500
Commercial banks' deposit-to-reserve ratio = 5000:100 = 50:1 (equilibrium)
Public's deposit-to-cash ratio = 5000:500 = 10:1 (equilibrium)

Figure B.7 Simplified money supply decrease in a currency board system, initial stage

the final stage, they do so, achieving a new equilibrium, with the money supply now 110 currency board roubles greater than it was in the initial stage (see Figure B.6).

As the balance sheets illustrate, efforts by commercial banks to reattain their desired deposit-to-reserve ratio, and by the public to reattain its desired deposit-to-cash ratio, increase the money supply. Their efforts cause changes in interest rates, prices, and incomes that move the currency board system to a new equilibrium when a current-account surplus occurs. The foregoing example in a sense collapses the effects of those relationships into the deposit-to-reserve and deposit-to-cash ratios. The currency board responds passively by virtue of its 100 per cent reserve ratio, its fixed exchange rate with the reserve currency, and its inability to change the

Currency board	
Assets	*Liabilities*
Foreign securities 588	Notes and coins 588
	Net worth 0

Commercial banks	
Assets	*Liabilities*
Currency board notes and coins (reserves) 88	Public's deposits 4988
Loans and investment 4900	Net worth 0

Public	
Assets	*Liabilities*
Deposits at commercial banks 4988	Bank loans 4900
Currency board notes and coins 500	Net worth 588

Money supply = 5488 (decrease = 12)

Commercial banks' deposit-to-reserve ratio = 4988:88 = 56.68:1 (disequilibrium)

Public's deposit-to-cash ratio = 5988:500 = 9.976:1 (disequilibrium)

Figure B.8 Simplified money supply decrease in a currency board system, intermediate stage

deposit-to-reserve ratio of commercial banks by imposing reserve requirements on them.

When a current-account *deficit* occurs in a currency board system, the money supply process works as in Figure 4.2. As in the case of a current-account surplus, the monetary system is initially in equilibrium, and the balance sheets of the currency board, commercial banks, and the public are as in Figure B.7, which is the same as Figure B.4.

Now let there be a current-account deficit of 12 currency board roubles. Foreigners only accept payment in foreign currency. By assumption, the currency board holds all the foreign currency in the Russian monetary system. Russians obtain reserve currency by converting 12 currency board

169

Currency board			
Assets		*Liabilities*	
Foreign securities	588	Notes and coins	588
		Net worth	0

Commercial banks			
Assets		*Liabilities*	
Currency board notes and coins (reserves)	98	Public's deposits	4900
Loans and investments	4802	Net worth	0

Public			
Assets		*Liabilities*	
Deposits at commercial banks	4900	Bank loans	4802
Currency board notes and coins	490	Net worth	588

Money supply = 5390 (decrease = 110)

Commercial banks' deposit-to-reserve ratio = 4900:98 = 50:1 (equilibrium)

Public's deposit-to-cash ratio = 4900:490 = 10:1 (equilibrium)

Figure B.9 Simplified money supply decrease in a currency board system, final stage

roubles of deposits at commercial banks into currency board notes and coins, then converting the currency board notes and coins into foreign currency. The assets and liabilities of the currency board become 12 currency board roubles less than in the initial stage, reserves of commercial banks become 12 currency board roubles less than in the initial stage, and deposits of the public at commercial banks become 12 currency board roubles less than in the initial stage. Furthermore, the money supply is 12 currency board roubles less than in the initial stage. This is the intermediate stage (see Figure B.8).

Notice that commercial banks have a deposit-to-reserve ratio of 56.68:1 in the intermediate stage, which is more than their desired, initial ratio of 50:1. Notice also that the public has a deposit-to-cash ratio of 9.976:1 in the intermediate stage, which is less than its desired, initial ratio of 10:1. Hence the monetary system is in disequilibrium. Commercial banks therefore decrease their loans, and the public decreases its holdings of cash, to restore the ratios of the initial stage. In the final stage, they do so, achieving a new equilibrium, with the money supply now 110 currency board roubles less than it was in the initial stage (see Figure B.9).

As in the case of a current-account surplus, efforts by banks to reattain their desired deposit-to-reserve ratio, and by the public to reattain its desired deposit-to-cash ratio, reduce the money supply and move the currency board system to a new equilibrium when a current-account deficit occurs.

We made some simplifying assumptions earlier. If we discard them, the picture becomes too complex to analyse easily. However, the many additional factors that can complicate the analysis should not obscure the important point: market forces determine and limit expansion of the money supply in the currency board system. As long as it is more profitable to invest funds in the currency board country than elsewhere (after making allowances for differences in rates of inflation, exchange risk, political risk, and transactions fees), commercial banks in the currency board system tend to increase their loans. They can do so because foreign investment tends to occur, bringing additional foreign reserves to the currency board system. Eventually commercial banks expand their loans in the currency board system to such an extent that making further loans there is less profitable than investing the funds abroad. At that point, commercial banks hold the supply of loans constant in the currency board system, and the money supply ceases to increase.

If it becomes more profitable to invest funds abroad than in the currency board country, the currency board system loses foreign reserves, commercial banks reduce their loans to preserve their solvency, and the money supply decreases. The role of the currency board in all this is passive: it merely exchanges its notes and coins for the reserve currency in such quantities as the public and commercial banks demand.

APPENDIX C

A list of currency board episodes

Country (current name) [colonial power], year independent	Years	Reserve ratio and assets	Exchange rate, exchange spread
Abu Dhabi [UK], 1971	1966–73	100+% gold and foreign exchange	1 Bahrain dinar = 17s. 6d. stg
Aden and Aden protectorate (part of Yemen) [UK], 1967	1951–72	100%* stg 1942–65; 100+% stg after first 2.5 million dinars 1965–72	20 East African shillings = £1 stg, ±½% 1942–65; 1 South Arabian/ South Yemen dinar = £1 stg, ±¾% 1965–72
Argentina	1902–14, 1927–9	100% gold after first 293 million pesos	1 peso = 0.63870849 g gold, no spread
Bahamas [UK], 1973	1916–74	100+% stg	Bahamas £1 = £1 stg, 1916–66; Bahamas $1 = US$0.98 1966–70; Bahamas $1 = US$1 1970–4
Bahrain [UK], 1971	1965–73	100+% foreign exchange	1 Bahrain dinar = 17s. 6d. stg
Barbados [UK], 1966	1937?–73	100+% stg 1937?–51; 110% stg 1951–73	(Barbados) West Indies $4.80 = £1 stg 1937?–51; West Indies/ East Caribbean $4.80 = £1 stg, +⅜% and −7⁄16% 1940–73
Bermuda [UK]	1915–present	110+% stg 1915–70; 115% US$ 1970–present	Bermuda £1 = £1 stg 1915–70; Bermuda $1 = US$1 1970–present

Country (current name) [colonial power], year independent	Years	Reserve ratio and assets	Exchange rate, exchange spread
British Guiana (Guyana) [UK], 1966	1937–65	100% stg 1937–51; 100% stg + 10% Guiana (West Indies) $ 1951?–65	(Guiana) West Indies $4.80 = £1 stg, ±1% 1937–51; West Indies $4.80 = £1 stg, +⅜% and −⁷⁄₁₆% 1951–65
British Honduras (Belize) [UK], 1981	1894–1981?	67% gold + 33% stg and US$ = 110% 1894–1939; 110% stg and US$ 1939–58; 100% stg after first Belize $350,000–$1 million = 110% 1958–81?	Belize $1 = US$1 1894–1949; Belize $4.00 = £1 stg, 1949–74; Belize $2 = US$1 1974–81?
British Solomon Islands (Solomon Islands) [UK], 1978	1930s?–40s	100+% Australian £ and stg?	Solomon Islands £1 = Australian £1
British Somaliland (part of Somalia) [UK], 1960	1942–61	100% stg*	20 East African shillings = £1 stg, ±½%
Brunei [UK], 1983	1952–73	110% stg 1952–67; 100% gold and foreign exchange 1967–73	Malay $1 = 2s. 4d. stg, ±⅛% 1952–67; Brunei $1 = 2s. 4d. stg 1967–73
Burma [UK], 1948	1947–52	100% stg	15 Burmese rupees = £1 stg, ±⁹⁄₃₂%
Cameroons (part of Cameroon and Nigeria) [UK], 1959	1916–59	110% stg	West African £1 = £1 stg, ±½%
Cayman Islands [UK]	1933–61, 1972–present	100% stg 1933–61; 100% US$ 1972–present	used Jamaican currency to 1972 (see Jamaica); US$1 = Cayman $0.83 1972–present
Ceylon (Sri Lanka) [UK], 1948	1884–1950	33–50% coin + 50–67% stg and rupees = 110% 1884–1917; 110% stg and rupees 1917–50	1 Ceylon rupee = 1 Indian rupee, no spread

173

Country (current name) [colonial power], year independent	Years	Reserve ratio and assets	Exchange rate, exchange spread
Cyprus [UK], 1960	1928–64	110% stg	Cyprus £1 = £1 stg
Danzig (Gdansk, Poland)	1923–4	100% stg	25 gulden = £1 stg
Dubai [UK], 1971	1966–73	100% gold and foreign exchange	1 Qatar/Dubai riyal = 0.16621 g gold
Eritrea [Italy, Ethiopia], 1993	1942–5	100%* stg	20 East African shillings = £1 stg, ±½%
Ethiopia	1942–5	100%* stg	20 East African shillings = £1 stg, ±½%
Falkland Islands [UK]	1899–present	100+% stg	Falkland £1 = £1 stg
Faroe Islands (part of Denmark)	1940–present	100% stg 1940–9; 100% Danish kroner 1949–present	22.40 Faroese kroner = £1 stg, no spread 1940–9; 1 Faroese krone = 1 Danish krone, no spread 1949–present
Fiji [UK], 1970	1913–75	100+% stg	Fiji £1 = £1 stg, 1913–33; Fiji £1.11 = £1 stg 1933–67; Fiji £1 = £1 stg 1967–69; Fiji $2 = £1 stg 1969–75?
Gambia [UK], 1965	1913–71	110% stg 1913–64; 100% foreign exchange 1964–71	West African £1 = £1 stg, ±½% 1913–64; Gambia £1 = £1 stg, ±½%? 1964–71
Gibraltar [UK]	1927–present	100+% stg	Gibraltar £1 = £1 stg
Gold Coast (Ghana) [UK], 1957	1913–58	110% stg	West African £1 = £1, stg, ±½%

Country (current name) [colonial power], year independent	Years	Reserve ratio and assets	Exchange rate, exchange spread
Hong Kong [UK]	1935–41, 1945–74, 1983-present	105% stg 1935–41, 1945–72; 105% US$ 1983-present	managed float, HK$15.36–16.45 = £1 stg 1935–9; HK$16 = £1 stg, +0% and −1.17% 1935–41, 1945–67; HK$14.55 = £1 stg, no spread 1967–72; HK$5.65 = US$1, ±2¼%** 1972–3; HK$5.085 = US$1, ±2¼%** 1973–4; HK$7.80 = US$1, no spread 1983–present
Iraq [UK], 1932	1931–49	100+% stg	1 Iraqi dinar = £1 stg, ±½%?
Ireland [UK], 1921	1928–43	100% stg after first Irish £6 million	Irish £1 = £1 stg, no spread
Italian Somaliland (part of Somalia) [Italy], 1960	1941–59	100%* stg 1941–50; 100% foreign exchange and gold 1950–9	20 East African shillings = £1 stg, ±½% 1941–50; 20 somali = £1 stg 1950–9
Jamaica [UK], 1962	1933–61	100% stg 1933–53?; 70% stg + 30% Jamaican 1953?–61	Jamaican £1 = £1 stg, +7⁄16% and −½%
Kenya [UK], 1963	1897–1966	100%* stg	20 East African shillings = £1 stg, ±½%
Kuwait [UK], 1961	1961–9	min. 50% gold + max. 50% US$ and stg = 100%	1 Kuwaiti dinar = £1 stg

Country (current name) [colonial power], year independent	Years	Reserve ratio and assets	Exchange rate, exchange spread
Leeward Islands (Anguilla, Antigua and Barbuda, St Kitts and Nevis, Montserrat) [UK], not all independent	1935–83	110% stg 1951–64; 70% stg + 30% West Indies $ = 110% 1964–8; 100% stg + some West Indies $ = 110+% 1968–71; 90% stg + 10% East Caribbean $ = 110% 1971–4; 100% foreign exchange + some East Caribbean $ = 110+% 1974–83	used Trinidad currency 1935–51 (see Trinidad); West Indies/East Caribbean $4.80 = £1 stg, +3/8% and −7/16% 1951–76; East Caribbean $2.70 = US$1 1976–83
Liberia	1913–44		used West African currency (see Nigeria)
Libya [UK, France], 1951	1950–6	100% stg	Libyan £1 = £1 stg, ±1/4%
Malaya (part of Malaysia) [UK], 1963	1899–1942, 1946–67	110% stg	used Straits Settlement (Singapore) currency to 1939 (see Singapore); Malay $1 = 2s. 4d. stg, ±1/8% 1939–42, 1946–67
Maldive Islands (Maldives) [UK], 1965	1849?–1967		used Indian and Mauritius currency (see Mauritius)
Malta [UK], 1964	1949–65?	100+% stg	Maltese £1 = £1 stg
Mauritius [UK], 1964	1849–1967	33–50% coin + 50–67% Mauritius rupees and stg = 100% 1849–65; = 110% 1865–1934; 110% stg 1934–67	1 Mauritius rupee = 1 Indian rupee 1849–1934; 15 Mauritius rupees = £1 stg, ±1/2% 1934–67
New Zealand [UK], 1907	1850–6	min. 25% coin + max. 75% stg = 100%	New Zealand £1 = £1 stg
Nigeria [UK], 1960	1913–59	110% stg	West African £1 = £1 stg, ±1/2%

Country (current name) [colonial power], year independent	Years	Reserve ratio and assets	Exchange rate, exchange spread
North Borneo (part of Malaysia) [UK], 1963	1881?–1942, 1946–67	110% stg	Borneo $1 = Spanish $1 1881–1906 (may have been a currency board); Borneo $1 = 2s. 4d. stg 1906–52 (currency board for part or all of period); Malay $1 = 2s. 4d. stg, ±⅛% 1939–42, 1946–67
North Russia (part of Russia)	1918–20	75% stg + 25% roubles	40 roubles = £1 stg, ±1%
Northern Rhodesia (Zambia) [UK], 1964	1940–56	110% stg 1940–2; 100% stg + 10% Rhodesian £ 1942–7; min. 50% stg + max. 60% Rhodesian £ = 110% 1947–56	Rhodesian £1 = £1 stg, ±¼%
Nyasaland (Malawi) [UK], 1966	1940–56	110% stg 1940–2; 100% stg + 10% Rhodesian £ 1942–7; min. 50% stg+ max. 60% Rhodesian £ = 110% 1947–56	Rhodesian £1 = £1 stg, ±¼%
Oman	1970–4	100+% stg	1 rial Omani = £1 stg
Palestine (Israel) [UK], 1948	1927–48 (1927–51 in Gaza Strip)	110% stg	Palestine £1 = £1 stg, ±⅛%
Panama	1904–31?	100% silver coin + 15% US$ = 100% of gold value	1 balboa = US$1
Philippines [USA], 1946	1903–18, 1923–42, 1945–8	100% silver coin + 15–25% US$ = 100% of gold value 1903–8, 1923–42, 1945–8; 100% silver coin + 17.5% US$ + 17.5% pesos = 100% of gold value 1908–18	2 pesos = US$1, ±⅜% (cheques) or ±¾% (telegrams)
Qatar [UK], 1971	1966–73	100% gold and foreign exchange	1 Qatar/Dubai riyal = 0.16621 g gold

Country (current name) [colonial power], year independent	Years	Reserve ratio and assets	Exchange rate, exchange spread
St Helena [UK]	1970s	100+% stg	St Helena £1 = £1 stg
Sarawak (part of Malaysia) [UK], 1963	1927–42, 1946–67	110% stg	Sarawak $1 = 2s. 4d. stg 1927–52; Malay $1 = 2s. 4d. stg, ±⅛% 1952–67
Seychelles [UK], 1976	1849–1966?	100+% stg 1934–66	used Mauritius currency to 1936 (see Mauritius); 1 Seychelles rupee = 1s. 6d. stg, ±½%? 1936–66?
Sierra Leone [UK], 1961	1913–64	110% stg	West African £1 = £1 stg, ±½%
Singapore [UK], 1967	1899–1942, 1946–73	50–67% coin (incl. at least 10% silver) + 33–50% Indian rupees and stg*** = 105% 1899–23; 110% stg 1923–42, 1946–67; 100% gold and foreign exchange 1967–73	managed floating 1899–06; Straits $1 = 2s. 4d. stg, +1⅛% and −⅞% 1906–39; Malay $1 = 2s. 4d. stg, ±⅛% 1939–42, 1946–67; Singapore $1 = 2s. 8–7/10d. stg 1967–73
Southern Rhodesia (Zimbabwe) [UK], 1965	1940–56	110% stg 1940–2; 100% stg + 10% Rhodesian £ 1942–7; min. 50% stg + max. 60% Rhodesian £ = 110% 1947–56	Rhodesian £1 = £1 stg, ±¼%
Sudan [Egypt, UK], 1956	1957–60	50% stg + 50% Sudanese £	Sudanese £ = £1 6d. stg
Swaziland [UK], 1968	1974–86	100% South African rands	1 langeni = 1 South African rand, no spread
Tanganyika (Tanzania) [UK], 1961	1920–66	100%* stg	20 East African shillings = £1 stg, ±½%
Togoland (part of Ghana) [UK], 1957	1914–58	110% stg	West African £1 = £1 stg, ±½%

Country (current name) [colonial power], year independent	Years	Reserve ratio and assets	Exchange rate, exchange spread
Tonga [UK], 1970	1936–74	100+% stg and Australian £/$?	Tonga £1 = Australian £1, ±1¾% (cheques) or ±2½% (telegrams) 1936–66; 1 pa'anga = Australian $1 1966–74
Transjordan (Jordan) [UK], 1946	1927–64	110% stg	Palestine £1 = £1 stg, ±⅛% 1927–48; 1 Jordanian dinar = £1 stg, ±⅛% 1948–64
Trinidad and Tobago [UK], 1962	1935–64	100+% stg	(Trinidad) West Indies $4.80 = £1 stg 1935–51; West Indies $4.80 = £1 stg, +⅜% and −⁷⁄₁₆% 1951–64
Uganda [UK], 1962	1919–66	100% stg*	20 East African shillings = £1 stg, ±½%
Western Samoa [New Zealand], 1962	1920–73?	100% New Zealand £/$?	Western Samoa £1 = New Zealand £1 1920–67; 0.8076 tala = New Zealand $1 1967–73?
Windward Islands (Grenada, St Vincent and the Grenadines, St Lucia, Dominica) [UK], 1974–9	1935–83	110% stg 1951–64; 70% stg + 30% West Indies $ = 110% 1964–8; 100% stg = some West Indies $ = 110+% 1968–71; 90% stg + 10% East Caribbean $ = 110% 1971–4; 100% foreign exchange + some East Caribbean $ = 110+% 1974–83	used Trinidad currency 1935–51 (see Trinidad); West Indies/East Caribbean $4.80 = £1 stg, +⅜% and −⁷⁄₁₆% 1951–76; East Caribbean $2.70 = US$1 1976–83
Yemen Arab Republic (part of Yemen)	1964–71	100+% stg	3 Yemeni rials = £1 stg
Zanzibar (Tanzania) [UK], 1961	1936–66	100%* stg	20 East African shillings = £1 stg, ±½%

Source: Schuler 1992b: appendix, with corrections.

APPENDIX C

Key

Column 1 (Country, etc.):
[UK] indicates that the country is a current or former British colony or mandate.

Column 3 (Reserve ratio and assets):
A reserve ratio of '100+%' means that the ratio was 100% to 110%, although we could not find information on the precise ratio.
Arithmetic of the form '67% gold + 33% stg and US$ = 110%' means that the reserve ratio was 110%, divided in the proportion 67% gold to 33% pounds sterling and US dollars.
'Stg' means assets in currencies in the sterling area, excluding the domestic currency. Most sterling assets were held in sterling itself.
*The East African Currency Board always held 100 per cent marginal reserves, but did not hold 100 per cent total reserves until 1950; see note 101.
**These were margins of fluctuation in the exchange rate permitted during the breakup of the Bretton Woods system, not commission fees of the Hong Kong currency board.
***The Singapore currency board illegally and somewhat unwittingly held 8 per cent or so assets in Straits dollars until 1936 (King 1957: 17).

Column 4 (Exchange rate, exchange spread):
During the Bretton Woods era (1945–73), many currencies were officially defined in terms of gold but were actually linked to a foreign currency. In such cases the table lists the reserve currency rather than gold as the basis of the exchange rate. The composition of reserves and the exchange spread varied during the lives of some currency boards. The table lists the most characteristic values for the composition of reserves and the exchange spread. Exchange spreads listed are for banks and other large foreign exchange dealers. Exchange spreads for the public were often wider.
The following currency boards operated in more than one territory:
West African Currency Board – Cameroons, Gambia, Gold Coast, Nigeria, Sierra Leone, Togoland.
East African Currency Board – Aden, British Somaliland, Eritrea, Ethiopia, Italian Somaliland, Kenya, Tanganyika, Uganda, Zanzibar.
Southern Rhodesian (later Central African) Currency Board – Northern Rhodesia, Nyasaland, Southern Rhodesia.
Board of Commissioners of Currency, Malaya and British North Borneo – Brunei, Malaya, North Borneo, Sarawak, Singapore.
Palestine Currency Board – Gaza Strip, Palestine, Transjordan.
Board of Commissioners of Currency, British Caribbean Territories (Eastern Group) (later East Caribbean Currency Authority) – Barbados, British Guiana, Leeward Islands (Antigua and Barbuda, St Kitts and Nevis, Montserrat), Trinidad and Tobago, Windward Islands (Grenada, St Vincent and the Grenadines, St Lucia, and Dominica).
Bahrain Currency Board – Abu Dhabi, Bahrain.
Qatar/Dubai Currency Board – Dubai, Qatar.
Other currency boards operated in one territory only. The notes of some currency boards circulated extensively in nearby territories. Liberia, for example, used West African currency until 1944 because it had no official currency.

NOTES

1 Previous works by us that advocate currency boards include Hanke and Schuler (1990, 1991b,c,d), Hanke and Walters (1990), Schuler *et al.* (1991), and Selgin and Schuler (1990). Other economists who have advocated currency boards for Eastern Europe and the former Soviet Union include Cobb (1990, 1991) Friedman (1991), Gressel (1989), Hetzel (1990). Jordan (1991), Meltzer (1990), Schmieding (1992), Selgin (1992a), and Walters (1991, 1992a). Makinen (1992), Osband and Villanueva (1992), and Schwartz (1992a,b) also discuss the currency board system. Soros (1993) has proposed a scheme similar to a currency board.

2 The term 'extreme inflation' comes from Dornbusch *et al.* (1990).

3 GDP is the value of all goods and services produced for final consumption in a country within a given period, usually a year. It excludes income from foreign investments or payments to foreign investors.

4 We usually use statistics published by or based on statistics supplied by the Russian government. Readers should be aware that even conscientiously gathered statistics of recent economic conditions in Russia often have large margins of error, and that not all statistics are gathered conscientiously. Top officials of the Russian government have admitted to us in private conversation that the government has distorted some statistics to increase its likelihood of receiving foreign aid. In doing so, the Russian government is following an old precedent. Morgenstern (1963: 21) reports, 'When the Marshall Plan was being introduced, one of the chief European figures in its administration (who shall remain nameless) told me: "We shall produce any statistic that we think will help us to get as much money out of the United States as we possibly can. Statistics which we do not have, but which we need to justify our demands, we will simply fabricate." ' That is one reason we are sceptical of proposals for a 'new Marshall Plan' for Russia. On problems with interpreting official statistics, see Bush (1992), Marer *et al.* (1992), and Morgenstern (1963).

5 In many countries, a government agency other than the central bank issues coins. Coins are typically a very small proportion of the total money supply, and the agency issuing coins usually coordinates its policy with that of the central bank, so it typically has no independent influence on monetary policy.

6 By 'developing countries' we mean those classified by the World Bank as low- and middle-income economies. By 'developed countries' we mean those classified by the World Bank as high-income economies. The World Bank classifies Israel, Singapore, Hong Kong, the United Arab Emirates, and Kuwait as developing countries although they are high-income economies (World Bank 1992a: 218–19).

181

7 We make this definition of the money supply for ease of exposition. In practice, near-monies such as accounts at money market mutual funds (in the United States) or, to a lesser extent, credits by state enterprises to other state enterprises (in Russia) are almost as liquid and widely accepted in payment as deposits at commercial banks. To avoid such problems of definition, one can think of commercial banks as symbolizing all institutions that extend credit widely accepted as means of payment.

8 Another example of the opacity of central banking is the gold supposedly held by the State Bank of the USSR. To attract foreign loans, the State Bank for years lied about the quantity of gold in its possession. In September 1991, an adviser to the Soviet government revealed that most of the gold did not exist (Hiatt 1993a). Even the most respected central banks have similarly hidden their activities from public inspection. For example, Oskar Morgenstern (1963: 20–1), who researched the accuracy of central bank balance sheets, remarked that

> Central banks in many countries, the venerable Bank of England not excepted, have for decades published deliberately misleading statistics, as, for example, when part of the gold in their possession is put under 'other assets' and only part is shown as 'gold'. In democratic Great Britain before World War II, the Government's 'Exchange Equalization Account' suppressed for a considerable period all statistics about its gold holdings, although it became clear later that these exceeded the amount of gold shown to be held by the Bank of England at the time. This list could be greatly lengthened. If respectable governments falsify information for policy purposes, if the Bank of England lies and hides or falsifies data, then how can one expect minor operators in the financial world always to be truthful, especially when they know that the Bank of England and so many other central banks are not?

9 Examples of the conventional approach are Allison and Yavlinsky (1991: 44), Camdessus (1992), Fischer (1992: 89–94), Fischer and Gelb (1991), IMF *et al.* (1990, 1: 373–5), Lipton and Sachs (1992: 229–44, but see 258–9), Sachs and Lipton (1992: 29, 47), and World Bank (1992b: xxiii, 113). Other recent writings that assume that Russia must have a central bank include Angell (1989), Indjikian (1991: 51), McKinnon (1991: 143), Uno (1991: 167), the Shatalin plan (Yavlinski and Kushner 1991), and other Soviet or Russian reform plans, and, with a few exceptions, the essays in Brada and Claudon (1992), Claasen (1991), Clague and Rausser (1992), and Williamson (1991a).

10 For descriptions of the Polish reform programme and its results so far, see Lipton and Sachs (1990a, b) and OECD (1992). For a description of the somewhat similar Czechoslovak reform programme before Czechoslovakia divided into two countries, see Aghevli *et al.* (1992). For general descriptions and assessments of economic stabilization programmes designed with the help of the IMF, see Bruno (1992) and Tocqueville Institute (1992).

11 The description of the alternative approach here borrows liberally from Walters (1992b).

12 For more on hard and soft budget constraints and their relation to inflation, see Kornai (1992: 140–5, 548–52) and Nagoaka and Atiyas (1990).

13 Real interest rates in this book always mean *ex ante* real rates (the rates that lenders and borrowers expect to obtain), not *ex post* real rates (the rates that actually occur in retrospect).

14 The Russian government in 1992 was considering wage controls (an incomes

policy) to prevent the soft budget constraints of state enterprises from softening further (IMF 1992c: 30). The Polish government imposes wage controls on state enterprises (OECD 1992: 44–5).

15 Or, in the parallel currency approach to establishing a currency board, budget constraints tend to harden during a brief transition period until they are completely hard (see chapter 5).

16 Rybczynski (1991: 31) also argues that financial reform should be the first reform, although he does not advocate a currency board.

17 Some advocates of the conventional approach, for example Fischer and Gelb (1991: 98), have also stressed the need for corporatization.

18 See, for example, Edwards (1989) and Fischer and Gelb (1991: 101–4).

19 A survey released in September 1992 estimates that 20 million persons in Russia, Ukraine, and Belarus have contemplated emigration (Krol 1992).

20 Some economists reserve the term 'parallel currency' for a currency that circulates alongside another at a floating exchange rate, often illegally.

21 In accord with American usage, 'billion' in this book means a thousand million.

22 Part of the interregional variation results from subsidies provided by some local governments but not by others for some goods, particularly food.

23 Very high real interest rates are usually caused by exchange risk or political risk. A Russian currency board will tend to eliminate exchange risk with the reserve currency, but it will not eliminate political risk. Real interest rates will be high unless the Russian government establishes more secure property rights (see chapter 7).

24 Recent publications from the IMF (1992a: 16; 1992d: 52–3) obscure the distinction between a currency board and a central bank in part because they mistake the fixed exchange rate maintained by a typical currency board for the pegged exchange rates maintained by many central banks.

25 Fixed, pegged, and floating exchange rates are easiest to distinguish when currencies are fully convertible. The differences among them become somewhat blurred for partly convertible or inconvertible currencies, because foreign-exchange controls often are more important than exchange-rate arrangements in influencing the true market exchange rates of the currencies. A currency that has a pegged exchange rate and capital controls may behave like a floating currency in unrestricted foreign-exchange markets, such as the domestic unofficial market.

26 Several definitions of the real exchange rate exist; see Hutton (1992).

27 A recent essay on speculative attacks on currencies is Krugman and Rotemberg (1992 [1991]).

28 On the previous twelve realignments, see Fratianni and von Hagen (1992: 22).

29 On crawling pegs, see Williamson (1981). The IMF and the World Bank have suggested a pegged exchange rate as a possible future exchange rate arrangement for Russia, but have not distinguished between a hard peg and a crawling peg (Camdessus 1992: 342; World Bank 1992b: 30).

30 On the possibility of reducing the costs of a transition to low inflation by means of a parallel currency, see chapter 5. The economic costs of suddenly imposing hard budget constraints in Russia are probably a much less significant obstacle than the potential political costs.

31 An exceptionally good central bank may be able to keep inflation relatively low by targeting the price level, a measure of the money supply, or another statistic (for an example, see Jonung 1979). However, for a typical central bank such targets create political pressure for soft budget constraints, because the standards for evaluating their success are less transparent than for an

exchange rate target. Even some central banks that were formerly exceptionally good, such as the Bank of Sweden, have more recently had difficulty keeping inflation low.

Milton Friedman (1984: 46–53) has proposed a way of avoiding the problem of choosing a target: freeze the monetary base, abolish the central bank, and allow banks to issue currency competitively, like traveller's cheques. Unlike the currency board system, Friedman's proposal has not been extensively tested by historical practice. Schemes like it have been tried in a few cases, however. After the American Civil War, the American government froze the supply of government-issued 'greenbacks' as a prelude to returning to the gold standard. The government regulated but did not freeze the supply of notes issued competitively by commercial banks, which were convertible into greenbacks (Friedman and Schwartz 1963: 46–9).

32 On the reasons for the superiority of decentralized exchange when a sound currency exists, see Hayek (1975 [1935]), Lavoie (1985), and Mises (1981 [1932]).

33 The governments of Hungary and Poland limit some current-account transactions (IMF 1992g: 210–15, 395–400). For more on different types of foreign-exchange convertibility, see Greene and Isard (1991: 2–3).

34 This counts Belgium and Luxembourg separately, although their monetary systems are unified. The IMF statistics cited exclude some countries, such as Switzerland (which had full convertibility) and the former Soviet republics (which had inconvertible currencies, except for Estonia).

Even some developed countries that have full convertibility according to the criteria of the IMF impose hidden capital controls. German insurance companies, for instance, are forbidden to buy assets not denominated in German marks (Walters 1990: 86).

35 Bermudians are allowed to convert Bermuda $25,000 per person per year for foreign investment and are allowed to convert Bermuda $3,000 per person per trip without special permission. It is unclear what purpose capital controls serve, since the Bermuda Monetary Authority holds US dollar reserves of about 115 per cent of the monetary base.

British colonial currency boards that used the pound sterling as their reserve currency had full convertibility into sterling, but from 1939 to 1979 the British government limited the capital-account convertibility of sterling into third currencies, particularly the US dollar. The British government allowed a fairly free market in sterling–US dollar exchange in Hong Kong.

36 Recent events in Italy, especially the floating of the lira on 17 September 1992, which in effect devalued it against the German mark, indicate that the Italian government may have reached the limit of the market's willingness to hold more Italian government bonds.

37 For similar examples in Poland and Israel, see OECD (1992: 150) and Plessner (1988: 76–8).

38 New Zealand's experiment with a very independent central bank since 1989 has not yet lasted long enough to be declared a decisive success.

39 The German Bundesbank has more than 18,000 employees (Whitney 1992).

40 The *Communist Manifesto* declares that one step for achieving communism is 'Centralization of credit in the hands of the state, by means of a national bank with state capital and an exclusive monopoly' (Marx and Engels 1948 [1848]: 30). Marx and Engels had in mind a system where a single bank exercises central banking and commercial banking functions, not the current system in Western nations with a central bank and competing commercial banks. How-

ever, insofar as a central bank exerts control over commercial banks, it partly achieves the goal desired by Marx and Engels.

41 On the case for a fiscal constitution, see Buchanan and Wagner (1977). On a monetary constitution, see Grilli *et al.* (1991) and Yeager (1962, 1992).

42 Steve Hanke approved Yugoslavia's currency reform and watched it collapse in his capacity as personal economic advisor to the then deputy prime minister, Zivko Pregl. He first met Pregl in Vienna on 12–13 October 1989 to discuss ways to control Yugoslavia's inflation, and was Pregl's personal economic advisor from 1990 to 30 June 1991. Hanke, who was impressed with the success of Austria's passive monetary policy of pegging the schilling to the West German mark (Koren 1982), advised Pregl that a pegged exchange rate would be appropriate for Yugoslavia. The experience of Yugoslavia convinced Hanke that the only monetary arrangement that can control inflation in an economic and cultural setting such as Yugoslavia or Russia is a truly fixed exchange rate such as that enforced by a currency board. We advocated a currency board for Yugoslavia in Hanke and Schuler (1991c).

43 Measuring the economic growth of Russia is a contentious matter. For thoughts on the subject, see Gregory and Stuart (1986: 29–50), Nove (1989: 1–16, 402), and Nutter (1962).

44 All dates are according to the 'new style' (Gregorian) calendar. The 'old style' (Julian) calendar, which was 13 days behind the 'new style' calendar, did not become the official calendar in Russia until February 1918.

45 Shortly before the Bolshevik Revolution, Lenin (1964 [1917]: 106) had written:

> The big banks *are* the 'state apparatus' which we *need* to bring about socialism, and which we *take ready-made* from capitalism; our task here is merely to *lop off* what *capitalistically mutilates* this excellent apparatus, to make it *even bigger*, even more democratic, even more comprehensive. Quantity will be transformed into quality. A single State Bank, the biggest of the big, will constitute as much as nine-tenths of the *socialist* apparatus. This will be country-wide *book-keeping*, country-wide *accounting* of the production and distribution of goods, this will be, so to speak, something in the nature of the *skeleton* or socialist society [emphasis in original].

46 For a more detailed account of socialist financial systems in general, see Peebles (1991: 15–79). On the Soviet financial system, see Arnold (1937), Carr (1951–69), Garvy (1977), Holzman (1955), and Kuschpèta (1978).

47 On 17 November 1935 the Soviet government devalued the tourist exchange rate of the rouble 77 per cent, but the devaluation had no significant effect on Soviet citizens because the rouble was an inconvertible currency.

48 The *net* new credit created by the Central Bank of Russia to cancel enterprise arrears outstanding on 1 July 1992 was 181 billion roubles, according to the Central Bank (FBIS 1992u).

49 The government provides some forms of insurance, such as automobile insurance, and some small private insurance companies exist (IMF 1992c: 94).

50 On Russia's foreign debt, see IMF (1992b: 91–3; 1992c: 32–3), Uchitelle (1992b), and World Bank (1992b: 16, 54–7).

51 Russia became a member of the IMF on 1 June 1992, and a member of the World Bank on 16 June 1992 (IMF 1992c: 1, 36; World Bank 1992b; iii).

52 The law states: 'There is appropriated for an increase in the United States quota in the International Monetary Fund, the dollar equivalent of 8,608.5 million Special Drawing Rights, to remain available until expended and, among other uses, such funds may be used to support monetary stability in member

countries through the instrumentality of currency boards' (Public Law 102–391, 106 US Statutes at Large 1636).

Authorization to use the increase in the IMF quota to establish currency boards was the result of an amendment sponsored by Senator Phil Gramm, and co-sponsored by Senators Robert Dole, Steve Symms, Connie Mack, Alan Simpson, and Jesse Helms. Steve Hanke had previously discussed the currency board system with several of the sponsors of the amendment. The law took effect 6 October 1992.

53 This assumes that the ultimate reserves are used only in the currency board system and the reserve country, not elsewhere. In reality, ultimate reserves of some currencies are held outside of their country of origin; for example, US dollar notes are held extensively in Latin America.

54 For a general discussion of the role of a nominal anchor, see Bruno (1991).

55 Quotas and high tariffs also reduce the efficiency of arbitrage, which is one reason that the alternative approach to economic reform in Russia discussed in chapter 1 recommends deregulation of trade.

56 The Federal Reserve System will lend to government deposit insurance agencies whose funds are depleted. It is the ultimate lender of last resort in the American monetary system.

57 This information was supplied to us by Friedberg Commodity Management, Inc.

58 We advocated a currency board for Argentina in a publication written before the monetary reform of April 1991 (Hanke and Schuler 1991d). The November 1992 speculative attack on the peso reinforces the case for replacing the Banco Central with a currency board.

59 A currency board can conceivably hold foreign reserves of less than 100 per cent if the reserve ratio is fixed and binding. Chapter 8 explains why a reserve ratio of less than 100 per cent is likely to weaken the legitimacy of a currency board.

60 See Blowers and McLeod (1952), Caine (1950), Chalmers (1893), Clauson (1944), Crick (1965), Drake (1966, 1969), Edo (1975), Freris (1991), Ghose (1987), Greaves (1953), Jao (1974), Jao and King (1990), King (1957), Kratz (1966), Lee (1986), Loynes (1962), Nelson (1984), Newlyn and Rowan (1954), Sayers (1952), and Shannon (1951, 1952). Unpublished works that summarize the history of the currency board system include Hanke and Schuler (forthcoming), Schuler (1992b), and Schwartz (1992a).

61 The East Caribbean Currency Authority in effect devalued the East Caribbean dollar by approximately 30 per cent when it changed from sterling to the US dollar as its reserve currency in 1976. The devaluation was apparently intended to improve the competitiveness of exports. The assets of the East Caribbean Currency Board were more than sufficient to have supported the change of reserve currencies without a devaluation.

62 The Bank of Commerce and Credit International (BCCI), based in Abu Dhabi, failed in early July 1992. It had branches in Hong Kong, as well as in many countries with central banking systems. Depositors in Hong Kong, where the bank had the equivalent of US$1 billion in assets, may eventually recover as much as 70 per cent of their deposits. BCCI is the largest bank to have failed in any currency board system.

63 In 1991, only 11 of the 55 or so former currency board systems that reported to the IMF had full convertibility: Antigua and Barbuda, the Bahamas, Bahrain, Gambia, Kuwait, Malaysia, Maldives, Oman, Seychelles, Singapore, and the United Arab Emirates (IMF 1992e: 570–5).

NOTES

64 In some earlier writings we stated that the exchange rate could be set at the existing unofficial market rate if monetary conditions were so desperate that instant (that is, virtually overnight) reform seemed necessary. We now think that the parallel currency approach described later in this chapter is more efficient for rapidly establishing a sound domestic currency.

65 For recent articles on currency substitution, see *Revista de análisis económico* (1992).

66 Walters (1992b) has also advocated a parallel currency issued by a currency board in Russia. Selgin and Schuler (1990) and Schuler *et al.* (1991) suggested that Lithuania establish a currency board to issue a parallel currency to the rouble. Hanke *et al.* (1992a, 1992b) did likewise for Estonia (see chapter 4).

67 Typical monetary analysis, which relies on the quantity theory of money, does not apply to a system of parallel currencies. On the economics of parallel currencies, see Hayek (1978) and Vaubel (1978). (Earlier, Hayek [1937: 91–2] advocated a type of currency board system.)

68 It will be disadvantageous to receive payments in Central Bank rouble cheques if the Russian payments system remains inefficient.

69 No statistics are published for cash held by banks, which however does not seem to be large.

70 We have made a similar estimate before (Hanke and Schuler 1991b: 25). The calculation here values noncash roubles generously, as having equal value to cash roubles.

71 On other difficulties with estimating purchasing power parity, see Officer (1982: 5–22, 119–37). On the difficulty of estimating the fundamental equilibrium exchange rate, see Williamson (1991b: 397).

72 See Bordo and Jonung (1987: appendix) and the IMF's *International Financial Statistics*.

73 If no initial foreign reserves are available for the currency board from the IMF or from the Russian government, it still may be possible to establish the Russian currency board by an experimental method never used before. The currency board could offer a small premium on foreign notes for a short period during which the currency board would make one-way exchanges of its notes and coins for foreign notes, but not for foreign-currency deposits. The currency board would not pay reserve currency for its currency during the period that it paid the premium for foreign notes. For instance, after announcing a choice of reserve currency and an exchange rate with that currency, during a one-week period the currency board could offer to pay a premium of 2 per cent on all fully convertible foreign-currency notes offered to it by residents of Russia. (It could accept notes of other foreign currencies besides the reserve currency, then use them to buy reserve-currency assets.) To prevent arbitragers from using its offer for pure speculative gain, the currency board could limit the amount it allows each person to convert and could announce that it retains the right to shorten the period for conversions at the special rate.

The purpose of the limited conversion would be to encourage Russians to exchange for currency board roubles the foreign notes that they hoard in mattresses and under floorboards. The conversion would benefit the Russian government by allowing it to capture seigniorage that now accrues to foreign central banks. After the offer expired, the currency board would cease paying a premium and would open to make exchanges from its currency into the reserve currency. The currency board would soon recover the expense of the premium, from its net seigniorage. The currency board could secure a loan to ensure that its foreign reserves were 100 per cent from the start, but its net seigniorage would quickly enable it to repay the loan.

74 Gressel (1989) proposed that a Soviet currency board could set a fixed amount of roubles equal to one dollar plus one mark. The currency board proposed by Gressel would hold an equal number of dollars and marks as reserves. It is the simplest type of currency basket.

75 Angell (1989) and Wanniski (1990) have advocated a gold standard for Russia, but assume that a central bank rather than a currency board will issue the gold-backed rouble. Their proposals would rely on the Central Bank of Russia to maintain a hard pegged exchange rate, which the Central Bank is unlikely to do.

76 For more details on the operations of past currency boards mentioned in this chapter, see Hanke and Schuler (forthcoming) and Schuler (1992b).

77 The word 'seigniorage' comes from the French word *seigneur* (lord). Seigniorage was originally the difference between the face value and the bullion value of gold and silver coins. Feudal lords appropriated the difference as a type of tax by keeping it and dictating that their subjects should accept the coins at face value.

78 For some mathematics of seigniorage, see Osband and Villanueva (1992: appendix A). For an empirical study of seigniorage, see Fischer (1982).

79 Even the Hong Kong currency board system, the most notable remaining currency board system, has departed somewhat from orthodox currency board practices in recent years and adopted features that later could be used to establish a central bank. The currency board itself is orthodox, but it is part of an agency that also regulates commercial banks and controls the government's accumulated budget surpluses (Culp and Hanke 1992; Dodwell 1992; Freris 1991: 206–15). The Hong Kong government has since 1989 used the powers of the agency to act as a lender of last resort, and the agency could be converted into a central bank. The government has never offered convincing reasons for these deviations from the orthodox currency board system.

80 If the currency board also serves other former Soviet republics besides Russia, and their governments choose some members of the board of directors, the directors chosen by the IMF should not be citizens of those countries, either.

81 Inflation rates within the range should be tolerated because changing reserve currencies is costly for the economy. The 'menu costs' are probably small, but the cost of discovering an appropriate new structure of prices to reflect the new reserve currency is probably large. Readers who think that the proposed range for tolerating inflation is too large should compare it with actual inflation in Russia since 1990.

82 Because we think that appropriate rules for changing the reserve currency can be devised, we do not share the worry of Schwartz (1992b: 20, 23) that a reserve currency, once chosen, may cause disruptions if the reserve country becomes no longer an important trading partner of the currency board country. Anyway, for Russia those potential disruptions are small compared to the disruptions caused by the unsound condition of the rouble at present.

83 The recent World Bank report on the Russian economy (World Bank 1992b: 175–92) makes no mention of the deterrent to current production of oil caused by the promise of later liberalization of the price of oil. Nor do IMF officials advising the Russian government seem aware of the problem, despite an IMF working paper (Kumar and Osband 1991) that emphasizes it.

84 For example, the Russian government could privatize utilities, railroads, the mass media, and so on; sell portions of the electromagnetic spectrum to new

competitors in the television, radio, and telephone business; and further reduce subsidies and government capital investment, which were about 40 per cent of government spending in 1992 (FBIS 1992k).

85 Assessments of the profitability or unprofitability of state enterprises must consider whether prices of their inputs and outputs have been liberalized. Some currently profitable state enterprises will become unprofitable if energy prices are liberalized, and some currently unprofitable state enterprises may become profitable if prices of their outputs are liberalized.

86 The recent World Bank report on the Russian economy (World Bank 1992b: 111) is cautious about competition from foreign commercial banks.

87 In improbable circumstances, reserve requirements may not hinder financial intermediation (see Fry 1988: 108–25).

88 Broker and Schuijer (1991) describe the Western trend.

89 For the contrary opinion, see Long and Sagari (1991: 434–5).

90 For a similar proposal, see Hinds (1990: 74–8). See also Aghevli et al. (1992: 15) on the solution used in then-united Czechoslovakia in 1991. Mates (1992) opposes making enterprise arrears the responsibility of the government and giving government bonds to creditor state enterprises.

91 For ideas on reforming the payments system within its current framework, see Sachs and Lipton (1992: 45–6) and Summers (1992).

92 The best older criticism are Analyst (1953), Basu (1971: 54–66, 240–4), Hazlewood (1954), and Nevin (1961: 1–44, 67–71). See also some of the essays in Drake (1966). Recent criticisms include Bofinger (1991), Fieleke (1992), Fratianni et al. (1992: 42–3), Havrylyshyn and Williamson (1991: 39–40), and Schwartz (1992b: 18–21). For refutations, see Greaves (1953), King (1957: 61–99), and especially Ow (1985: 54–86).

93 A good recent exposition of the role of a central bank as a lender of last resort to commercial banks is Goodhart (1988: 96–102).

94 Dowd (1988) discusses the option clause in the context of 'free banking' (see chapter 8). For historical examples of the use of option clauses in free banking systems, see Jonung (1989) and White (1984: 26, 29–30). Hayek (1937: 92) mentions another option for a type of lender of last resort: the possibility of emergency note issue with less than 100 per cent foreign reserves in a system that otherwise had 100 per cent foreign reserves against note circulation. In Hayek's proposal it would be difficult to define the conditions of an emergency precisely enough to prevent the monetary policy of a currency board from becoming less rule-bound and more discretionary.

95 On the performance of floating exchange rates since the end of the Bretton Woods system of pegged exchange rates in 1973, see MacDonald (1988).

96 Milton Friedman (1991), the leading advocate of floating exchange rates for central banking systems, endorsed our proposal for a currency board for Estonia.

97 No generally agreed criteria exist for determining optimum currency areas (Kawai 1992). One criterion that has been suggested is that labour should be mobile within an optimum currency area. According to the criterion, Russia may not be part of an optimum currency area with any Western country because labour is not mobile between Russia and any serious potential reserve country; hence the currency board system is inappropriate for Russia.

   The experience of currency board systems has been that labour mobility with the reserve country is unimportant. For example, labour has not been mobile between Hong Kong and Britain or the United States, which have been Hong Kong's reserve countries, but Hong Kong has had rapid economic growth under the currency board system. Currency boards have encouraged trade and mobility of savings with their reserve countries, which seem to have offset lack of labour mobility with the reserve countries.

98 One way of providing competing currencies is to establish several currency boards, each with a fixed exchange rate to a different reserve currency (Culp and Hanke 1992).

99 The converse proposition is that in a contracting economy with a currency board, the money supply operates in an *inflationary* manner, which some critics of the currency board system may think is a desirable countercyclical response.

100 In chapter 6 it was suggested that solvent private commercial banks could be allowed to issue notes. Allowing commercial banks to issue notes would alleviate their need to reduce loans as a result of occasional increases in the public's demand to convert deposits into notes. To a commercial bank, deposits and notes issued by it are equivalent liabilities, like deposits and traveller's cheques (Selgin 1988b: 108–24). If the public wanted only to convert deposits into notes, not necessarily into reserves, commercial banks could meet the demand by paying the public with their own notes, and their total liabilities and their reserves would not change.

101 A possible exception is a case where it seems prohibitively expensive initially to acquire 100 per cent foreign reserves when converting a central bank into a currency board. In that case, the currency board could have a 100 per cent *marginal* reserve requirement. The currency board should be required to retain net seigniorage until its foreign reserves are 100 per cent of its notes and coins in circulation. The East African Currency Board, which served Kenya and the other British colonies in the region, operated in that fashion from 1920 to 1950. Near the beginning of its existence, the East African Currency Board reduced its foreign reserves below 100 per cent by accepting silver coins in Tanganyika, a colony recently captured from Germany, at their face value rather than at their lower bullion value (Newlyn and Rowan 1954: 58–60, 63–4). The real value of the monetary base in Russia is so small now that 100 per cent foreign reserves are feasible from the start. We oppose foreign reserves of less than 100 per cent for currency boards in general and for a Russian currency board in particular.

102 The World Bank has estimated Russia's 'external financing requirements' as $23 billion for 1992 and a comparable amount for 1993 (World Bank 1992b: 49–50).

103 The discussion assumes that the deposits of the public would remain unchanged, and that the public would not try to convert a large proportion of its deposits into notes and coins at the same time as it was converting currency board notes and coins into reserve currency.

If the Russian government obtains the initial foreign reserves by borrowing from the IMF, it would have to repay the IMF with funds other than the net seigniorage of the currency board, because net seigniorage would now be zero.

104 On the theory of free banking, see Dowd (1989, 1993), Glasner (1989), Selgin (1988b), and White (1989a). On historical experience with free banking, see Dowd (1992a), Jonung (1989), Smith (1990 [1936]), and White (1984, 1993).

105 For a somewhat more detailed account of the North Russian currency board, see Hanke and Schuler (1991a).

106 Evsey Domar, an economist of Russian origin, observed the proliferation of Russian currencies from a vantage point thousands of miles from North Russia. In a reminiscence of his life, he remarked,

To a future economist, Harbin [China] could offer valuable lessons, particularly in the field of money. The city had been built by the Russians in 1897 (or 1896) at the intersection of the Chinese Eastern Railway (an extension of the Trans-Siberian Railway) and a large navigable river (the Sungari). They forgot to provide the city with waterworks and a sewer, but not with their army, police, courts, and, of course, their paper currency, which circulated freely. After the February Revolution (1917) but before the October one, new notes appeared, called 'kerenski' in honor of the then head of the provisional government (A. F. Kerensky). The civil war gave birth to several White (anti-Communist) regimes, which promptly printed their own money. In time, these notes reached Harbin and were accepted at par. But as the fortunes of the White regimes waned, the populace became suspicious: Chinese merchants and peddlars still accepted the notes, provided that they looked absolutely perfect when held against the light; even a pinhole caused a rejection. (Why they applied this particular test I don't know; I have never heard of a similar case.) Anyhow, soon enough all these notes became worthless; in our downstairs closet, where firewood was stored, I found whole stacks of them.

(Domar 1992: 116)

107 Arnold (1937: 146–280) and Elster (1930) provide detailed accounts of the chervonets. Dohan (1991) and Rostowski and Shapiro (1992) provide recent summaries. For a general economic history of the period, see Carr (1951–69).

108 Statistics of the Soviet money supply in the 1920s must be interpreted with proper attention to changes in the economy. For example, the real supply of bank deposits in 1928 was 20 per cent of what it had been in 1914 because former deposit payments between businesses became book-entry transactions within state enterprises (Arnold 1937: 250–1).

109 The account that follows borrows liberally from Greenwood (1981, 1983a).

110 Only assumption 1 is necessary for the analysis of the money supply process in a currency board system, the other assumptions can be discarded, but the analysis then becomes much more complicated. See Hanke and Schuler (forthcoming), Ow (1985), and Walters and Hanke (1992) for details.

BIBLIOGRAPHY

Aghevli, Bijan B., Borensztein, Eduardo, and Willigen, Tessa van der (1992) *Stabilization and Structural Reform in the Czech and Slovak Federal Republic: First Stage*, Occasional Paper 92, Washington: International Monetary Fund.

Aglietta, Michel (1992) 'Payments systems for CIS interrepublic trade', *Studies on Soviet Economic Development*, 3, 5: 348–60.

Albright, Joseph (1991) 'Vodka becomes liquid currency, but supply's tight', *Atlanta Constitution*, 30 December: A17.

Alesina, Alberto (1989) 'Politics and business cycles in industrial democracies', *Economic Policy: A European Forum*, 4, 8, April: 57–98.

Alexeev, Michael, Gaddy, Clifford, and Leitzel, Jim (1991) 'The economics of the ruble overhang', *Communist Economies and Economic Transformation*, 3, 4: 467–79.

Allison, Graham, and Yavlinsky, Grigory (1991) *Window of Opportunity: The Grand Bargain for Democracy in the Soviet Union*, New York: Pantheon Books.

Analyst (1953) 'Currency and banking in Jamaica', *Social and Economic Studies*, 1: 41–53.

Anderson, Annelise (1992) 'The ruble problem: a competitive solution', Stanford, California: Hoover Institution.

Angell, Wayne D. (1989) 'Monetary policy in a centrally planned economy: restructuring toward a market-oriented socialist system', unpublished manuscript, Federal Reserve System Board of Governors, Washington.

Arnold, Arthur Z. (1937) *Banks, Credit, and Money in Soviet Russia*, New York: Columbia University Press.

Åslund, Anders (1991) *Gorbachev's Struggle for Economic Reform*, rev. ed., Ithaca, New York: Cornell University Press.

Åslund, Anders (1992) 'Prospects for a successful change of economic system in Russia', unpublished paper, Stockholm Institute of Soviet and East European Studies, 30 October.

Auerbach, Paul, Davison, Geoffrey, and Rostowski, Jacek (1992) 'Secondary currencies and high inflation: implications for monetary theory and policy', Discussion Paper 58, Centre for Economic Performance, London School of Economics, February.

Aukutsionek, Sergei, and Belyanova, Elena (1993) 'Russian credit markets remain distorted', *RFE/RL Research Report*, 2, 4, 22 January: 37–40.

Aven, Petr O. (1991) 'Economic policy and the reforms of Mikhail Gorbachev: a short history', in Merton J. Peck and Thomas J. Richardson (eds) *What Is to Be Done? Proposals for the Soviet Transition to the Market*: 179–206, New Haven: Yale University Press.

Balls, Edward (1993) ' "Bottom-up" style in fashion for ex-Soviet reform', *Financial Times*, 8 January: 3.

Barro, Robert J. and Gordon, David B. (1983) 'Rules, discretion and reputation in a model of monetary policy', *Journal of Monetary Economics*, 12, 2, July: 101–21.

Basu, S. K. (1971) *A Review of Current Banking Theory and Practice*, Calcutta: Macmillan.

BCRA (1992) Banco Central de la República Argentina, *Indicadores económicos*, June.

Bennett, Adam G. G. (1992) 'The operation of the Estonian currency board', International Monetary Fund Paper on Policy Analysis and Assessment 92/3.

Bernholz, Peter, and Gersbach, Hans (1992) 'The present monetary theory of advanced inflation: a failure?' *Journal of Institutional and Theoretical Economics*, 148, 4, December: 705–19.

Berreby, David (1992) 'The companies that make money from making money', *New York Times*, 23 August: F10.

Birman, Igor (1980) 'The financial crisis in the USSR', *Soviet Studies*, 32, 1, January: 84–105.

Birman, Igor (1990) 'The budget gap, excess money and reform', *Communist Economies*, 2, 1: 25–45.

Birnbaum, Eugene A. (1957) 'The cost of a foreign exchange standard or of the use of a foreign currency as the circulating medium', *International Monetary Fund Staff Papers*, 5, 3, February: 477–91.

Blanchard, Olivier, Dornbusch, Rudiger, Krugman, Paul, and Layard, Richard (1991) *Reform in Eastern Europe*, Cambridge, Massachusetts: MIT Press.

Bloomfield, Arthur I. (1939) *Monetary Policy under the International Gold Standard 1891–1914*, New York: Federal Reserve Bank of New York.

Blowers, G. A., and McLeod, A. N. (1952) 'Currency unification in Libya', *International Monetary Fund Staff Papers*, 2, 3, November: 439–67.

Boettke, Peter J. (1993) *Why Perestroika Failed: The Politics and Economics of Socialist Transformation*, London: Routledge.

Bofinger, Peter (1991) 'Options for the payments and exchange-rate system in Eastern Europe', *European Economy*, special edition 2: 243–62.

Bofinger, Peter (1992) 'The transition to convertibility in Eastern Europe: a monetary view', in John Williamson (ed.) *Currency Convertibility in Eastern Europe*: 116–38, Washington: Institute for International Economics.

Bordo, Michael D., and Jonung, Lars (1987) *The Long-Run Behavior of Velocity: The International Evidence*, Cambridge: Cambridge University Press.

Boughton, James M. (1992) 'The CFA franc: zone of fragile stability in Africa', *Finance and Development*, 29, 4, December: 34–6.

Boulton, Leyla (1992a) 'All roubles are free, but some are freer than others', *Financial Times*, 1 July: 2.

Boulton, Leyla (1992b) 'Russia's war on oil industry corruption', *Financial Times*, 23 September: 30.

Boulton, Leyla (1993) 'Former Soviet republics try to avert trade collapse', *Financial Times*, 22 January: 5.

Brabant, Jozef M. van (1991a) *Integrating Eastern Europe into the Global Economy: Convertibility Through a Payments Union*, Dordrecht, Netherlands: Kluwer Academic Publishers.

Brabant, Jozef M. van (1991b) 'Convertibility in Eastern Europe through a payments union', in John Williamson (ed.) *Currency Convertibility in Eastern Europe*: 63–95, Washington: Institute for International Economics.

Brabant, Jozef M. van (1992) 'Rouble', in Peter Newman, Murray Milgate, and

John Eatwell (eds) *The New Palgrave Dictionary of Money and Finance*, 3: 376–8, London: Macmillan.

Brada, Josef C. and Claudon, Michael P. (eds) (1992) *Reforming the Ruble: Monetary Aspects of Perestroika*, New York: New York University Press.

Brada, Josef C., *et al.* (1990) 'A phased plan for making the ruble convertible: a multilateral proposal', in Josef C. Brada and Michael P. Claudon (eds) *Reforming the Ruble: Monetary Aspects of Perestroika:* 93–131, New York: New York University Press.

Brainard, Lawrence J. (1991) 'Reform in Eastern Europe: creating a capital market', *Finance and the International Economy*, 4: 6–22, New York: Oxford University Press.

Broker, Günther, and Schuijer, Jan (1991) 'Diversification and deregulation in banking in the OECD countries', in Paul Marer and Salvatore Zechinni (eds) *The Transition to a Market Economy*, 2: 398–429, Paris: Organisation for Economic Cooperation and Development.

Bruno, Michael (1991) *High Inflation and the Nominal Anchors of an Open Economy*, Essays in International Finance 183, June, Princeton: International Finance Section, Department of Economics, Princeton University.

Bruno, Michael (1992) 'Stabilization and reform in Eastern Europe: a preliminary evaluation', *International Monetary Fund Staff Papers*, 39, 4, December: 741–77.

Buchanan, James M., and Wagner, Richard E. (1977) *Democracy in Deficit: The Political Legacy of Lord Keynes*, New York: Academic Press.

Bush, Keith (1992) 'The Russian budget deficit', *RFE/RL Research Report*, 1, 40, 9 October: 30–2.

[Caine, Sydney] (1950) *Monetary Systems of the Colonies*, London: The Banker.

Camdessus, Michel (1992) 'Monetary arrangements in Eastern Europe and the former Soviet Union', unpublished speech delivered at Bank of Greece colloquium on Monetary Integration in the Eastern European Economies, Athens, 9 October; excerpted in 'Monetary arrangements should promote price stability, says Camdessus', *IMF Survey*, 9 November: 341–3.

Cameron, Rondo *et al.* (1967) *Banking in the Early Stages of Industrialization: A Study in Comparative Economic History*, New York: Oxford University Press.

Cameron, Rondo (ed.) (1972) *Banking and Economic Development: Some Lessons of History*, New York: Oxford University Press.

Capie, Forrest (ed.) (1991) *Major Inflations in History*, Aldershot, England: Edward Elgar.

Carr, Edward Hallett (1951–69) *A History of Soviet Russia*, London: Macmillan.

Carrington, Samantha (1992) 'The remonetization of the Commonwealth of Independent States', *American Economic Review*, 82, 2, May: 22–6.

Chalmers, Robert C. (1893) *A History of Currency in the British Colonies*, London: Eyre and Spottiswoode for HMSO.

Claasen, Emil-Maria (ed.) (1991) *Exchange Rate Policies in Developing and Post-Socialist Countries*, San Francisco: International Center for Economic Growth/ Institute for Contemporary Studies Press.

Clague, Christopher, and Rausser, Gordon C. (eds) (1992) *The Emergence of Market Economies in Eastern Europe*, Oxford: Blackwell Publishers.

Clauson, G. L. M. (1944) 'The British colonial currency system', *Economic Journal*, 54, 213, April: 1–25.

Cobb, Joe (1990) 'The true achievement of state sovereignty: a currency for Lithuania', unpublished paper presented at a conference in Vilnius, 28 November.

Cobb, Joe (1991) 'Introducing a new, independent currency in a seceding USSR republic', unpublished paper, Arlington, Virginia.

Collier, Paul, and Joshi, Vijay (1989) 'Exchange-rate policy in developing countries', *Oxford Review of Economic Policy*, 5, 3, Autumn: 94–113.

Collyns, Charles (1983) *Alternatives to the Central Bank in the Developing World*, Occasional Paper 20, Washington: International Monetary Fund.

Commersant (English edition, Chicago).

Conant, Charles A. (1969 [1927]) *A History of Modern Banks of Issue*, 6th ed. rev., New York: Augustus M. Kelley.

Connolly, Michael (1985) 'On the optimal currency peg for developing countries', *Journal of Development Economics*, 18, 2–3, August: 555–9.

Congdon, T. G. (1985) *Economic Liberalisation in the Cone of Latin America*, Thames Essays 40, London: Trade Policy Research Centre.

Cooper, Richard (1991a) 'Opening the Soviet economy', in Merton J. Peck and Thomas J. Richardson (eds) *What Is to Be Done? Proposals for the Soviet Transition to the Market:* 116–32, New Haven: Yale University Press.

Cooper, Richard (1991b) 'Comment', in John Williamson (ed.) *Currency Convertibility in Eastern Europe:* 310–14, Washington: Institute for International Economics.

Corbett, Jenny, and Mayer, Colin (1991) 'Financial reform in Eastern Europe: progress with the wrong model', *Oxford Review of Economic Policy*, 7, 4, Winter: 57–75.

Corbo, Vittorio, de Melo, Jaime, and Tybout, James (1986) 'What went wrong with the recent reforms in the Southern Cone', *Economic Development and Cultural Change*, 34, 3, April: 607–40.

Coricelli, Fabrizio, and Rezende Rocha, Roberto de (1991) 'A comparative analysis of the Polish and Yugoslav programmes of 1990', in Paul Marer and Salvatore Zechinni (eds) *The Transition to a Market Economy*, 2: 189–243, Paris: Organisation for Economic Cooperation and Development.

Crick, W. F. (ed.) (1965) *Commonwealth Banking Systems*, Oxford: Clarendon Press.

Cukierman, Alex (1992) *Central Bank Strategy, Credibility, and Independence: Theory and Evidence*, Cambridge, Massachusetts: MIT Press.

Cukierman, Alex, Webb, Steven B., and Neyapti, Bilin (1992) 'Measuring the independence of central banks and its effect on policy outcomes', *World Bank Economic Review*, 6, 3, September: 353–98.

Culp, Christopher, and Hanke, Steve H. (1992) 'The Hong Kong linked rate mechanism: monetary lessons for economic development', unpublished paper, University of Chicago and Johns Hopkins University.

Dodwell, David (1992) 'New institutions offered to keep growth on track', *Financial Times*, 8 October: 4.

Dohan, Michael (1991) 'Comment', in John Williamson (ed.) *Currency Convertibility in Eastern Europe:* 318–28, Washington: Institute for International Economics.

Domar, Evsey D. (1992) 'How I tried to become an economist', in Michael Szenberg (ed.) *Eminent Economists: Their Life Philosophies:* 115–27, Cambridge: Cambridge University Press.

Dornbusch, Rudiger, Sturzenegger, Frederico, and Wolf, Holger (1990) 'Extreme inflation: dynamics and stabilization', *Brookings Papers on Economic Activity*, 2: 1–64, 77–84.

Dowd, Kevin (1988) 'Option clauses and the stability of a laisser faire monetary system', *Journal of Financial Services Research*, 1, 4, December: 319–33.

Dowd, Kevin (1989) *The State and the Monetary System*, New York: St Martin's Press.

195

Dowd, Kevin (ed.) (1992a) *The Experience of Free Banking*, London: Routledge.

Dowd, Kevin (1992b) 'Money and the market: what role for government?' unpublished paper, University of Nottingham, forthcoming in *Cato Journal*, 12, 3, Winter 1993.

Dowd, Kevin (1993) *Laissez-Faire Banking*, London: Routledge.

Drake, P. J. (ed.) (1966) *Money and Banking in Malaya and Singapore*, Singapore: Malayan Publications.

Drake, P. J. (1969) *Financial Development in Malaya and Singapore*, Canberra: Australian National University Press.

Economist (1992a) 'Behind the facade', *The Economist*, 19 September: 96.

Economist (1992b) 'Hand over the money', *The Economist*, 17 October: 95.

Economist (1992c) 'Fools' gold', *The Economist*, 5 December: 73.

Edo, Michael E. (1975) 'Currency and banking legislation in the Arabian Peninsula', *International Monetary Fund Staff Papers*, 22, 2, July: 510–38.

Edwards, Sebastian (1989) 'On the sequencing of structural reforms', Organisation for Economic Cooperation and Development, Department of Economics and Statistics, Working Paper 70, September.

Edwards, Sebastian (1991) 'Capital and current account liberalization and real exchange rates in developing countries', in Emil-Maria Classen (ed.) *Exchange Rate Policies in Developing and Post-Socialist Countries:* 243–75, San Francisco: International Center for Economic Growth/Institute for Contemporary Studies Press.

Eesti Pank (1992a) Regulations for Foreign Exchange Market, 18 June.

Eesti Pank (1992b) Foreign Currency Statutes of Estonia, Appendix to Eesti Pank board meeting, 18 June.

Ellman, Michael (1991) 'Convertibility of the rouble', *Cambridge Journal of Economics*, 15, 4, December: 481–97.

Ellman, Michael (1992) 'Money in the 1980s: from disequilibrium to collapse', in Michael Ellman and Vladimir Kontorovich (eds) *The Disintegration of the Soviet Economic System*, London: Routledge.

Elster, Karl (1930) *Vom rubel zum Tscherwonjez: zur Geschichte der sowjet-Währung*, Jena: Gustav Fischer.

Estonia (1992) Monetary Reform Committee of the Republic of Estonia, Decree 030, 17 June.

FBIS (1992a) 'No restrictions on hard currency exchange', Tallinn Radio Tallinn Network, 20 June, trans. in US Foreign Broadcast Information Service *Daily Report, Central Eurasia*, FBIS-SOV–92–124, 26 June: 95–6.

FBIS (1992b) 'Central bank aide on purchasing hard currency', *Izvestiya*, 30 July: 2, trans. in US Foreign Broadcast Information Service *Daily Report, Central Eurasia*, FBIS-SOV–92–150, 4 August.

FBIS (1992c) 'Nizhniy Novgorod to issue own currency', Moscow Russian Television Network, 8 August, trans. in US Foreign Broadcast Information Service *Daily Report, Central Eurasia*, 8 August: 49.

FBIS (1992d) 'Central bank to open commercial bank accounts', Interfax Business Report, 9 August, reprinted in US Foreign Broadcast Information Service *Daily Report, Central Eurasia*, FBIS-SOV–92–154, 10 August: 40.

FBIS (1992e) 'Central bank attempts measures to balance interrepublic payments', *Rossiyskaya Gazeta*, 14 August: 2, trans. in US Foreign Broadcast Information Service *Report, Central Eurasia*, FBIS-USR–92–111, 30 August: 1.

FBIS (1992f) 'Gerashchenko on monetary, credit policy', *Komosomolskaya Pravda*, 1 September: 1–2, trans. in US Foreign Broadcast Information Service *Report, Central Eurasia*, FBIS-USR–92–116, 11 September: 9–11.

FBIS (1992g) 'Dniester Republic sets up banking network', Moscow Radio Rossii Network, 14 September, trans. in US Foreign Broadcast Information Service *Daily Report, Central Eurasia*, FBIS-SOV–92–179, 15 September: 33.

FBIS (1992h) 'Bank tying savings deposit rates to inflation', Moscow Central Television First Program, 10 September, trans. in US Foreign Broadcast Information Service *Daily Report, Central Eurasia*, FBIS-SOV–92–181, 17 September: 27–8.

FBIS (1992i) 'Probe into Chechen banking affair continues; central bank official on improving financial transactions', *Rossiyskaya Gazeta*, 25 August: 1, 3, trans. in US Foreign Broadcast Information Service *Report, Central Eurasia*, FBIS-USR–92–120, 19 September: 39–42.

FBIS (1992j) 'Government owes central bank 1.2 billion [sic] rubles', Interfax, 22 September, reprinted in US Foreign Broadcast Information Service *Daily Report, Central Eurasia*, FBIS-SOV–92–185, 23 September: 27.

FBIS (1992k) 'Law on budget system for 1992', *Rossiyskaya Gazeta*, 21 August: 4, trans. in US Foreign Broadcast Information Service *Report, Central Eurasia*, FBIS-USR–92–121, 24 September: 59–64.

FBIS (1992l) 'Bank, government disagree on credit policy', Interfax, 23 September, reprinted in US Foreign Broadcast Information Service *Daily Report, Central Eurasia*, FBIS-SOV–92–188, 28 September: 17–18.

FBIS (1992m) 'Government grants more credits than planned', Interfax, 30 September, reprinted in US Foreign Broadcast Information Service *Daily Report, Central Eurasia*, FBIS-SOV–92–191, 1 October: 19–20.

FBIS (1992n) 'Nechayev expresses optimism about economy', *Nezavisimaya Gazeta*, 30 September: 1, trans. in US Foreign Broadcast Information Service *Daily Report, Central Eurasia*, FBIS-SOV–92–191, 1 October: 20–1.

FBIS (1992o) 'Aven: export duties to replace quotas', Itar-Tass, 7 October, reprinted in US Foreign Broadcast Information Service *Daily Report, Central Eurasia*, FBIS-SOV–92–195, 7 October: 10.

FBIS (1992p) 'Nechayev predicts slowing of economic slump', Itar-Tass, 14 October, reprinted in US Foreign Broadcast Information Service *Daily Report, Central Eurasia*, FBIS-SOV–92–200, 15 October: 27–8.

FBIS (1992q) 'Central bank warns of devaluation, economic crisis', *Baltic Independent*, 25 September: 4, reprinted in US Foreign Broadcast Information Service *Report, Central Eurasia*, FBIS-USR–92–131, 16 October: 124.

FBIS (1992r) 'Prices rise 46 percent since currency introduced', Itar-Tass, 27 October, reprinted in US Foreign Broadcast Information Service *Daily Report, Central Eurasia*, FBIS-SOV–92–209, 28 October: 72–3.

FBIS (1992s) 'Jan-Sep economic performance summarized', *Rossiyskaya Gazeta*, 4 November, first edition: 1, 4, trans. in US Foreign Broadcast Information Service *Daily Report, Central Eurasia*, FBIS-SOV–92–214, 4 November: 37–41.

FBIS (1992t) 'Cost of living increases 7.7 percent in October', Baltfax, 6 November, reprinted in US Foreign Broadcast Information Service *Daily Report, Central Eurasia*, FBIS-SOV–92–217, 9 November: 55–6.

FBIS (1992u) 'Central bank finishes state business debt reconciliation', Interfax, 11 December, reprinted in US Foreign Broadcast Information Service *Daily Report, Central Eurasia*, FBIS-SOV–92–240, 14 December: 11.

FBIS (1992v) 'Profiles of Estonia's seized banks', *Baltic Independent*, 27 November: 6, reprinted in US Foreign Broadcast Information Service *Report, Central Eurasia*, FBIS-USR–92–165, 25 December: 117.

FBIS (1992w) 'Failed banks getting no help', *Baltic Independent*, 4–10 December:

4, reprinted in US Foreign Broadcast Information Service *Report, Central Eurasia*, FBIS-USR–92–165, 25 December: 117–18.

FBIS (1993a) 'Russian bank for reconstruction, development set up', Itar-Tass, 5 January, reprinted in US Foreign Broadcast Information Service *Daily Report, Central Eurasia*, FBIS-SOV–93–003, 6 January: 20.

FBIS (1993b) 'Russian 1992 economic performance reported', *Rossiyskaya Gazeta*, 3 February: 5, trans. in US Foreign Broadcast Information Service *Daily Report, Central Eurasia*, FBIS-SOV–93–021, 3 February: 21–4.

FBIS (1993c) 'Federov says savings bank to increase interest rates', Interfax, 9 February, reprinted in US Foreign Broadcast Information Service *Daily Report, Central Eurasia*, FBIS-SOV–93–026, 10 February: 26.

FBIS (1993d) 'Economics ministry presents 1992 data', Interfax, 10 February, reprinted in US Foreign Broadcast Information Service *Daily Report, Central Eurasia*, FBIS-SOV–93–027, 11 February: 17.

FBIS (1993e) 'Russian Federation 1992 economic data', *Ekonomika i zhizn*, January: 13–15, trans. in US Foreign Broadcast Information Service *Report, Central Eurasia*, FBIS-USR–93–020, 25 February: 23–36.

FBIS (1993f) 'Credit policy eyed', Interfax, 25 February, reprinted in US Foreign Broadcast Information Service *Daily Report, Central Eurasia*, FBIS-SOV–93–037, 26 February: 21.

FBIS (1993g) 'Central bank's influence on foreign currency exchange', *Kommersant*, 1–7 February: 10, trans. in US Foreign Broadcast Information Service *Report, Central Eurasia*, FBIS-USR–93–022, 26 February: 21–3.

Federov, Boris (1991) 'Convertibility of the ruble', in John Williamson (ed.) *Currency Convertibility in Eastern Europe:* 281–93, Washington: Institute for International Economics.

Feige, Edgar L. (1990) 'Perestroika and socialist privatization: What is to be done? And how?' *Comparative Economic Studies*, 32, 3, Fall: 1–54.

Fenton, Paul, and Murray, John (1992) 'Optimum currency areas: a cautionary tale', unpublished paper, Bank of Canada, September.

Fieleke, Norman S. (1992) 'The quest for sound money: currency boards to the rescue?' *New England Economic Review* (Federal Reserve Bank of Boston), November-December: 14–24.

Filatochev, Igor, and Bradshaw, Ray (1992) 'The Soviet hyperinflation: its origins and impact throughout the former republics', *Soviet Studies*, 44, 5: 439–59.

Fischer, Stanley (1982) 'Seigniorage and the case for a national money', *Journal of Political Economy*, 90, 2, April: 295–313.

Fischer, Stanley (1992) 'Stabilization and economic reform in Russia', *Brookings Papers on Economic Activity*, 1: 77–111, 125–6.

Fischer, Stanley, and Gelb, Alan (1991) 'The process of socialist economic transformation', *Journal of Economic Perspectives*, 4, 5, Fall: 91–105.

Fisher, Irving (1935) *100% Money*, New York: Adelphi Press.

Fitzgerald, Randall (1988) *When Government Goes Private*, New York: Universe Books.

FO (1918a) Great Britain, Foreign Office, *General Correspondence, Russia*, 3295, Wilmington, Delaware: Scholarly Resources, microfilm.

FO (1918b) Great Britain, Foreign Office, *General Correspondence, Russia*, 3344, Wilmington, Delaware: Scholarly Resources, microfilm.

FO (1919a) Great Britain, Foreign Office, *General Correspondence, Russia*, 3969, Wilmington, Delaware: Scholarly Resources, microfilm.

FO (1919b) Great Britain, Foreign Office, General Correspondence, Russia, 3970, Wilmington, Delaware: Scholarly Resources, microfilm.

Fratianni, Michele, Davidson, Lawrence S., and von Hagen, Jürgen (1992) 'Proposal for monetary and fiscal reforms in the Baltic republics', *G–7 Report*, Summer: 37–50.

Fratianni, Michele, and von Hagen, Jürgen (1992) *The European Monetary System and European Monetary Unity*, Boulder, Colorado: Westview Press.

Freeland, Chrystia (1993) ' "Mini-Opec" formed to tackle CIS energy crisis', *Financial Times*, 3 March 1993: 24 (box by John Lloyd).

Freris, Andrew (1991) *The Financial Markets of Hong Kong*, London: Routledge.

Friedman, Milton (1948) 'A monetary and fiscal framework for economic stability', *American Economic Review*, 38, 3: September, 245–64.

Friedman, Milton (1960) *A Program for Monetary Stability*, New York: Fordham University Press.

Friedman, Milton (1984) 'Monetary policy in the 1980s', in John H. Moore (ed.) *To Promote Prosperity: US Domestic Policy in the Mid–1980s*, Stanford, California: Hoover Institution Press.

Friedman, Milton (1988 [1953]) 'The case for flexible exchange rates', in Leo Melamed (ed.) *The Merits of Flexible Exchange Rates: An Anthology*: 3–42, Fairfax, Virginia: George Mason University Press.

[Friedman, Milton] (1991) 'Milton Friedman m fl: "Precis vad Estland behöver" ', *Dagens Industri* (Stockholm), 17 December: 9.

Friedman, Milton, and Schwartz, Anna Jacobson (1963) *A Monetary History of the United States*, Princeton: Princeton University Press.

Fry, Maxwell J. (1988) *Money, Interest, and Banking in Economic Development*, Baltimore: Johns Hopkins University Press.

Fry, Maxwell J., and Nuti, D. Mario (1992) 'Monetary and exchange-rate policies during Eastern Europe's transition: some lessons from further east', *Oxford Review of Economic Policy*, 8, 1, Spring: 27–43.

Garvy, George (1977) *Money, Financial Flows, and Credit in the Soviet Union*, Cambridge, Massachusetts: Ballinger Publishing Co. for National Bureau of Economic Research.

Ghose, T. K. (1987) *The Banking System of Hong Kong*, Singapore: Butterworths.

Glasner, David (1989) *Free Banking and Monetary Reform*, Cambridge: Cambridge University Press.

Goldstein, Morris, Isard, Peter, Masson, Paul R., and Taylor, Mark P. (1992) *Issues in the Evolving International Monetary System*, Occasional Paper 96, Washington: International Monetary Fund.

Goodhart, Charles (1988) *The Evolution of Central Banks*, Cambridge, Massachusetts: MIT Press.

Greaves, Ida C. (1953) *Colonial Monetary Conditions*, London: HMSO.

Greene, Joshua E., and Isard, Peter (1991) *Currency Convertibility and the Transformation of Centrally Planned Economies*, Occasional Paper 81, Washington: International Monetary Fund.

Greenhouse, Steven (1993) 'Monetary fund criticizes Russia on inflation', *New York Times*, 4 February: A13.

Greenwood, John G. (1981) 'Time to blow the whistle', *Asian Monetary Monitor*, 5, 4, July-August: 15–33.

Greenwood, John G. (1983a) 'How to rescue the HK$: three practical proposals', *Asian Monetary Monitor* 7, 5, September–October: 11–39.

Greenwood, John G. (1983b) 'The stabilisation of the Hong Kong dollar', *Asian Monetary Monitor* 7, 6, November–December: 9–37.

Greenwood, John G. (1984) 'Why the HK$/US$ linked rate system should not be changed', *Asian Monetary Monitor* 8, 6, November–December.

Greenwood, John G., and Gressel, Daniel L. (1988) 'How to tighten up the linked rate mechanism', *Asian Monetary Monitor* 12, 1, January–February: 2–13.

Gregory, Paul R., and Stuart, Robert C. (1986) *Soviet Economic Structure and Performance*, 3rd ed., New York: Harper and Row.

Gressel, Daniel (1989) 'Soviet macroeconomic imbalances during perestroika', unpublished paper, G.T. Capital Management, San Francisco, 15 November.

Grilli, Vittorio, Masciandro, Donato, and Tabellini, Guido (1991) 'Political and monetary institutions and public financial policies in the industrial countries', *Economic Policy: A European Forum*, 13, October: 341–76, 383–92.

Hanke, Steve H. (ed.) (1987) *Privatization and Economic Development*, San Francisco: International Center for Economic Growth.

Hanke, Steve H. (1991) 'Reflections on Yugoslavia's transition to a market economy', Fairfax, Virginia: Atlas Economic Research Foundation.

Hanke, Steve H., Jonung, Lars, and Schuler, Kurt (1992a) *Rahareform vabale eestile: valuutafondi lahendus*, trans. by Avo Viiol, Tartu, Estonia: Tartu Ülikool.

Hanke, Steve H., Jonung, Lars, and Schuler, Kurt (1992b) *Monetary Reform for a Free Estonia: A Currency Board Solution*, Stockholm: SNS Förlag.

Hanke, Steve H., and Schuler, Kurt (1990) 'Keynes and currency reform: some lessons for Eastern Europe', *Journal of Economic Growth*, 4, 2: 10–16.

Hanke, Steve H., and Schuler, Kurt (1991a) 'Keynes's Russian currency board', in Steve H. Hanke and Alan A. Walters (eds) *Capital Markets and Development*: 43–63, San Francisco: Institute for Contemporary Studies Press.

Hanke, Steve H., and Schuler, Kurt (1991b) 'Currency Boards for Eastern Europe', Heritage Lectures 355, Washington: Heritage Foundation.

Hanke, Steve H., and Schuler, Kurt (1991c) *Monetary Reform and the Development of a Yugoslav Market Economy*, London: Centre for Research into Communist Economies.

Hanke, Steve H., and Schuler, Kurt (1991d) *¿Banco central o caja de conversión?* Buenos Aires: Fundación República.

Hanke, Steve H., and Schuler, Kurt (forthcoming) *Currency Boards and Economic Development*.

Hanke, Steve, and Walters, Alan (1990) 'Reform begins with a currency board', *Financial Times*, 21 February: 17.

Hanke, Steve H., and Walters, Alan A. (1991a) 'Confidence and the liberal economic imperative', in Steve H. Hanke and Alan A. Walters (eds) *Capital Markets and Development*: 347–53, San Francisco: Institute for Contemporary Studies Press.

Hanke, Steve H., and Walters, Alan A. (1991b) 'Financial and capital markets in developing countries', in Steve H. Hanke and Alan A. Walters (eds) *Capital Markets and Development*: 25–42, San Francisco: Institute for Contemporary Studies Press.

Hanke, Steve H., and Walters, Alan A. (1991c) 'Discussion', in Steve H. Hanke and Alan A. Walters (eds) *Capital Markets and Development*: 187–202, San Francisco: Institute for Contemporary Studies Press.

Hansson, Ardo (1992) 'Estonian currency reform: progress report and future policies', unpublished paper, Stockholm Institute of Soviet and East European Studies, 7 August.

Hansson, Ardo, and Sachs, Jeffrey (1992) 'Crowning the Estonian kroon', *Transition* (World Bank Transition and Macro-Adjustment Division, Country Economics Department), 3, 9, October: 1–3.

Havrylyshyn, Oleh, and Williamson, John (1991) *From Soviet disUnion to Eastern*

Economic Community? Policy Analyses in International Economics 35, October, Washington: Institute for International Economics.

Hayek, F. A. (ed.) (1975 [1935]) *Collectivist Economic Planning*, Clifton, New Jersey: Augustus M. Kelley Publishers.

Hayek, F. A. (1937) *Monetary Nationalism and International Stability*, London: Longmans, Green and Co.

Hayek, F. A. (1978) *Denationalisation of Money – The Argument Refined: An Analysis of the Theory and Practice of Concurrent Currencies*, 2nd ed., Hobart Paper Special 70, London: Institute of Economic Affairs.

Hays, Laurie (1992a) 'Despite muddled economic policy in Russia, IMF is giving Yeltsin a hearty endorsement', *Wall Street Journal*, 1 September: A11.

Hays, Laurie (1992b) 'As ruble slides in Moscow trading, the dollar finds takers at any price', *Wall Street Journal*, 7 October: A13.

Hazlewood, Arthur (1954) 'The economics of colonial monetary arrangements', *Social and Economic Studies*, 3, 3–4, December: 291–315.

Hetzel, Robert (1990) 'Free enterprise and central banking in formerly communist countries', *Federal Reserve Bank of Richmond Economic Review*, July: 13–19.

Hiatt, Fred (1993a) 'Soviets hid gold loss for years', *Washington Post*, 3 February: A2.

Hiatt, Fred (1993b) 'The $6 billion Russia never got to spend', *Washington Post*, 1 March: 12.

Hinds, Manuel (1990) 'Issues in the introduction of market forces in East European economies', World Bank Report IDP–0057, April.

Holzman, Franklyn D. (1955) *Soviet Taxation: The Fiscal and Monetary Problems of a Planned Economy*, Cambridge, Massachusetts: Harvard University Press.

Holzman, Franklyn D. (1991) 'Moving towards ruble convertibility', *Comparative Economic Studies*, 33, 3, Fall: 3–66.

Hong Kong (1992) Government Information Services, *Hong Kong in Statistics*, Hong Kong: Government Printer.

Hutton, J. P. (1992) 'Real exchange rates', in Peter Newman, Murray Milgate, and John Eatwell (eds) *The New Palgrave Dictionary of Money and Finance*, 3: 303–5, London: Macmillan.

Ickes, Barry W., and Ryterman, Randi (1992) 'The interenterprise arrears crisis in Russia', *Post-Soviet Affairs*, 6, 4, October–December: 331–61.

IMF (1991) 'Yugoslavia: recent economic developments', unpublished paper prepared by N. Weerasinghe, P. Thomsen, D. Hardy, M. Gilman, and J. Horne, European Department, 25 February.

IMF (1992a) International Monetary Fund, *Common Issues and Interrepublic Relations in the Former U.S.S.R.*, prepared under the direction of John Odling-Smee, April, Washington: International Monetary Fund.

IMF (1992b) International Monetary Fund, *The Economy of the Former USSR in 1991*, prepared under the direction of John Odling-Smee, April, Washington: International Monetary Fund.

IMF (1992c) International Monetary Fund, *Russian Federation*, prepared under the direction of John Odling-Smee, April, Washington: International Monetary Fund.

IMF (1992d) International Monetary Fund, *Annual Report, 1992*, Washington: International Monetary Fund.

IMF (1992e) International Monetary Fund, *Annual Report on Exchange Arrangements and Exchange Restrictions*, Washington: International Monetary Fund.

IMF (1992f) International Monetary Fund, *International Financial Statistics*, September.

IMF (1992g) International Monetary Fund, *World Economic Outlook*, October.

IMF *et al.* (1990) International Monetary Fund, International Bank for Reconstruction and Development, Organisation for Economic Cooperation and Development, and European Bank for Reconstruction and Development, *The Economy of the USSR: Summary and Recommendations*, Washington: published jointly.

IMF *et al.* (1991) International Monetary Fund, International Bank for Reconstruction and Development, Organisation for Economic Cooperation and Development, and European Bank for Reconstruction and Development, *A Study of the Soviet Economy*, 3 v., Paris: Organisation for Economic Cooperation and Development.

Indjikian, Rouben (1991) 'Ruble convertibility and the Soviet economic reform: an interdependent paradigm', *Finance and the International Economy*, 4: 37–61, New York: Oxford University Press.

Institute of International Finance (1992) *USSR/CIS Country Report*, 7 February.

Ironside, William Edmund (1953) *Archangel: 1918–1919*, London: Constable.

Jack, Andrew (1992) 'Russia needs $500m to train accountants', *Financial Times*, 19 October: 4.

Jao, Y. C. (1974) *Banking and Currency in Hong Kong*, London: Macmillan.

Jao, Y. C. (1992) 'Recent trends in currency substitution', *Asian Monetary Monitor*, 16, 4, July–August: 12–21.

Jao, Y. C., and King, F. H. H. (1990) *Money in Hong Kong: Historical Perspective and Contemporary Analysis*, Hong Kong: Centre of Asian Studies, University of Hong Kong.

Jonung, Lars (1979) 'Knut Wicksell's norm of price stabilization and Swedish monetary policy in the 1930s', *Journal of Monetary Economics*, 5, 4, October: 459–96.

Jonung, Lars (1984) 'Swedish experience under the classical gold standard 1873–1913', in Michael D. Bordo and Anna J. Schwartz (eds) *A Retrospective on the Classical Gold Standard: 361–99*, Chicago: University of Chicago Press for National Bureau of Economic Research.

Jonung, Lars (1989) 'The economics of private money: the experience of private notes in Sweden 1831–1902', Research Report 282, Stockholm School of Economics.

Jordan, Jerry (1991) 'Fiscal and monetary policies during the transition from socialism to capitalism', unpublished paper, First Interstate Bancorp, Los Angeles.

Kawai, Masahiro (1992) 'Optimum currency areas', in Peter Newman, Murray Milgate, and John Eatwell (eds) *The New Palgrave Dictionary of Money and Finance*, 3: 78–81, London: Macmillan.

Kazmin, Andrei I., and Tsimailo, Andrei V. (1991) 'Toward the convertible ruble: the case for a parallel currency', in John Williamson (ed.) *Currency Convertibility in Eastern Europe: 294–309*, Washington: Institute for International Economics.

Kenen, Peter (1991) 'Comment', in John Williamson (ed.) *Currency Convertibility in Eastern Europe: 139–42*, Washington: Institute for International Economics.

Keynes, John Maynard (1971 [1913]) *Indian Currency and Finance*, in *The Collected Writings of John Maynard Keynes*, 1, London: Macmillan.

Keynes, John Maynard (1971 [1923]) *A Tract on Monetary Reform*, in *The Collected Writings of John Maynard Keynes*, 4, London: Macmillan.

Keynes, John Maynard (1983 [1913]) '[Review of] *Departmental Committee on Matters Affecting Currency of the British West African Colonies and Protectorates. Report; Minutes of Evidence*', in Donald Moggridge (ed.) *The Collected Writings of John Maynard Keynes*, 11: 383–4, London: Macmillan.

King, Frank H. H. (1957) *Money in British East Asia*, London: HMSO.

Koren, Stephan (1982) 'Austrian monetary and exchange rate policies', in Sven W. Arndt (ed.) *The Political Economy of Austria*, Washington: American Enterprise Institute.

Kornai, János (1990) *The Road to a Free Economy: Shifting from a Socialist System; The Example of Hungary*, New York: W. W. Norton and Co.

Kornai, János (1992) *The Socialist System: The Political Economy of Socialism*, Princeton: Princeton University Press.

Kratz, Joachim W. (1966) 'The East African Currency Board', *International Monetary Fund Staff Papers*, 13, 2, July: 229–55.

Krol, Ronald van de (1992) 'Survey claims 20m in CIS want to emigrate', *Financial Times*, 30 September: 3.

Krugman, Paul R., and Rotemberg, Julio (1992 [1991]) 'Speculative attacks on target zones', in Paul R. Krugman, *Currencies and Crises*, Cambridge, Massachusetts: MIT Press.

Kumar, Manmohan S., and Osband, Kent (1991) 'Energy pricing in the Soviet Union', International Monetary Fund Working Paper 91/125, December.

Kuschpèta, O. (1978) *The Banking and Credit System of the USSR*, Leiden: Martinus Nijhoff.

Kydland, Finn E., and Prescott, Edward C. (1977) 'Rules rather than discretion: the inconsistency of optimal plans', *Journal of Political Economy*, 85, 3, June: 473–92.

Laidler, David (1982) *Monetarist Perspectives*, Cambridge, Massachusetts: Harvard University Press.

Lavoie, Don C. (1985) *Rivalry and Central Planning: The Socialist Calculation Debate Reconsidered*, Cambridge: Cambridge University Press.

Lee, Sheng-Yi (1986) *The Monetary and Banking Development of Singapore*, rev. ed., Singapore: Singapore University Press.

Lenin, V. I. (1964 [1917]) 'Can the Bolsheviks retain state power?' in V. I. Lenin, *Collected Works*, 26: 87–136, London: Lawrence and Wishart.

Lindsey, David E., and Wallich, Henry C. (1987) 'Monetary policy', in John Eatwell, Murray Milgate, and Peter Newman (eds) *The New Palgrave: A Dictionary of Economics*, 3: 508–15, London: Macmillan.

Lipton, David, and Sachs, Jeffrey (1990a) 'Creating a market economy in Eastern Europe: the case of Poland', *Brookings Papers on Economic Activity*, 1: 75–133, 146–7.

Lipton, David, and Sachs, Jeffrey (1990b) 'Privatization in Eastern Europe: the case of Poland', *Brookings Papers on Economic Activity*, 2: 293–333, 340–1.

Lipton, David, and Sachs, Jeffrey D. (1992) 'Prospects for Russia's economic reforms', *Brookings Papers on Economic Activity*, 2: 213–65, 281–3.

Lloyd, John (1992) 'Russian oil and gas fields out for tender', *Financial Times*, 29 September: 7.

Lloyd, John (1993) 'Russia adopts a crisis plan to avert collapse', *Financial Times*, 21 January: 2.

Lloyd, John, and Volkov, Dmitry (1992) 'Yeltsin bows to fierce anti-reform backlash', *Financial Times*, 7 October: 2.

Long, Millard, and Sagari, Silvia B. (1991) 'Financial reform in the European economies in transition', in Paul Marer and Salvatore Zechinni (eds) *The Transition to a Market Economy*, 2: 430–42, Paris: Organisation for Economic Cooperation and Development.

Loynes, J. B. (1962) *The West African Currency Board 1912–1962*, London: West African Currency Board.

MacDonald, Ronald (1988) *Floating Exchange Rates: Theories and Evidence*, London: Unwin Hyman.

McKinnon, Ronald (1991) *The Order of Economic Liberalization: Financial Control in the Transition to a Market Economy*, Baltimore: Johns Hopkins University Press.

Makinen, Gail (1992) 'A currency board as an alternative to a central bank', US Library of Congress, Congressional Research Service Paper 92–937E, 1 December.

Marer, Paul, Arvay, Janos, O'Connor, John, Schrenk, Martin, and Swanson, Daniel (1992) *Historically Planned Economies: A Guide to the Data*, Washington: World Bank.

Marnie, Sheila (1993) 'The unresolved question of land reform in Russia', *RFE/RL Research Report*, 2, 7, 12 February: 35–7.

Marx, Karl, and Engels, Frederick (1948 [1848]) *The Communist Manifesto*, New York: International Publishers.

Mates, Neven (1992) 'Does the government have to clean bank balance sheets in transitional economies?' *Communist Economies and Economic Transformation*, 4, 3: 395–409.

Meltzer, Allan (1990) 'Monetary reform in the U.S.S.R.', unpublished speech presented at a conference in Moscow, 17 September.

Meltzer, Allan (1992) 'The Fed at seventy-five', in Michael T. Belongia (ed.) *Monetary Policy on the Fed's 75th Anniversary: Proceedings of the Fourteenth Annual Conference of the Federal Reserve Bank of St Louis*: 3–65, Boston: Kluwer.

Michalopoulos, Constantine, and Tarr, David (1992) *Trade and Payments Arrangements for States of the Former USSR*, Studies of Economies in Transformation 2, Washington: World Bank.

Mises, Ludwing von (1981 [1932]) *Socialism*, 2nd ed., trans. by J. Kahane, Indianapolis: Liberty Classics.

Morgenstern, Oskar (1963) *On the Accuracy of Economic Observations*, 2nd ed., Princeton: Princeton University Press.

Moore, Des (ed.) (1992) *Can Monetary Policy Be Made to Work? Papers Presented at the IPA Monetary Policy Conference*, Jolimont, Australia: Institute of Public Affairs, Economic Policy Unit.

Mundell, Robert A. (1961) 'A theory of optimum currency areas', *American Economic Review*, 51, 3, September: 657–65.

Nagoaka, Sadao, and Atiyas, Izak (1990) 'Tightening the soft budget constraint in reforming socialist economies', World Bank Industry and Energy Department Working Paper 35, May.

Nash, Nathaniel (1992) 'Argentina amid crisis over economic policies', *New York Times*, 16 November: D3.

National Bank of Yugoslavia (1991) Research Department, *Yugoslavia: Statistical Survey*, 6, June.

Nelson, William Evan (1984) 'The imperial administration of currency and British banking in the Straits Settlements, 1867–1908', unpublished Ph.D. dissertation, Duke University.

Nevin, Edward (1961) *Capital Funds in Underdeveloped Countries*, New York: St Martin's Press.

Neurrisse, André (1987) *Le franc CFA*, Paris: Librairie Générale de Droit et de Jurisprudence.

Newlyn, W. T., and Rowan, D. C. (1954) *Money and Banking in British Colonial Africa: A Study of the Monetary and Banking Systems of Eight British African Territories*, Oxford: Clarendon Press.

Niskanen, William A. (1991) 'The soft infrastructure of a market economy', *Cato Journal*, 11, 2, Fall: 233–8.

Norman, Peter (1991) 'Bank of England training E. Europe central bankers', *Financial Times*, 16 September: 1.

Norman, Peter (1992) 'The day Germany planted a currency time bomb', *Financial Times*, 12/13 December: 2.

Norman, Peter, and Barber, Lionel (1992) 'The monetary tragedy of errors that led to currency chaos', *Financial Times*, 11 December: 2.

Nove, Alec (1989) *An Economic History of the U.S.S.R.*, 2nd ed., London: Penguin Books.

Nuti, Domenico Mario (1991) 'Comment', in John Williamson (ed.) *Currency Convertibility in Eastern Europe:* 48–55, Washington: Institute for International Economics.

Nutter, G. Warren (1962) *The Growth of Industrial Production in the Soviet Union*, Princeton: Princeton University Press.

[Odling-Smee, John] (1992a) 'The Russia file: phasing in the assistance; interview with IMF department director John Odling-Smee', *Transition* (World Bank Transition and Macro-Adjustment Division, Country Economics Department), 3, 7, July-August: 4–6.

Odling-Smee, John (1992b) 'Letter to the editor: IMF comment on Sachs and Hansson's recent article on the Estonian kroon', *Transition* (World Bank Transition and Macro-Adjustment Division, Country Economics Department), 3, 10, November: 9.

Officer, Lawrence H. (1982) *Purchasing Power Parity and Exchange Rates: Theory, Evidence and Relevance*, Greenwich, Connecticut: JAI Press.

OECD (1992) Organisation for Economic Co-operation and Development, *Poland 1992*, Paris: Organisation for Economic Co-operation and Development.

Osband, Kent, and Villanueva, Delano (1992) 'Independent currency authorities: an analytic primer', International Monetary Fund Working Paper 92/50, July, published in *International Monetary Fund Staff Papers*, 40, 1, March 1993: 202–16.

Osiris Conseil (1992) *Banking in Russia, Guide 1993*, Paris: Osiris Conseil.

Ow, Chwee Huay (1985) 'The currency board monetary system – the case of Singapore and Hong Kong', unpublished Ph.D. dissertation, Johns Hopkins University.

Patrick, Hugh T. (1990) 'The financial development of Taiwan, Korea, and Japan: a framework for consideration of issues', unpublished paper presented at Academica Sinica Institute of Economics Conference on Financial Development in Japan, Korea, and Taiwan, 27–28 August.

Peebles, Gavin (1991) *A Short History of Socialist Money*, Sydney: Allen and Unwin.

Persson, Torsten, and Tabellini, Guido (1990) *Macroeconomic Policy, Credibility and Politics*, Chur, Switzerland: Harwood Academic Publishers.

Piot, Olivier (1992) 'La zone franc', *Le Monde*, 10 November: 32.

Pirie, Madsen (1988) *Privatization*, Aldershot, England: Wildwood House.

Pleskovic, Boris, and Sachs, Jeffrey (1992) 'Currency reform in Slovenia: the tolar standing tall', *Transition* (World Bank Transition and Macro-Adjustment Division, Country Economics Department), 3, 8, September: 6–8.

Plessner, Yakir (1988) 'Israel's monetary policy', in Alvin Rabushka and Steve H. Hanke (eds) *Toward Growth: A Blueprint for Economic Rebirth in Israel*, Jerusalem: Institute for Advanced Strategic and Political Studies.

Pollak, Jacques (1991) 'Convertibility: the indispensable element in the transition process', in John Williamson (ed.) *Currency Convertibility in Eastern Europe:* 21–30, Washington: Institute for International Economics.

Revista de análisis económico (1992) special issue on convertibility and currency substitution, 7, 1, June.

RFE/RL (1992) 'Roskomstat releases third quarter results', *RFE/RL Research Report*, 1, 45, 13 November: 56.

Rhodes, Benjamin D. (1988) *The Anglo-American Winter War with Russia, 1918–1919: A Diplomatic and Military Tragicomedy*, New York: Greenwood Press.

Roberts, Paul Craig, and LaFollette, Karen (1990) *Meltdown: Inside the Soviet Economy*, Washington: Cato Institute.

Rostowski, Jacek (1992) 'The benefits of currency substitution during high inflation and stabilization', *Revista de análisis económico*, 7, 1, June: 91–107.

Rostowski, Jacek, and Shapiro, Judith (1992) 'Secondary currencies in the Russian hyperinflation of 1921–24', Discussion Paper 59, Centre for Economic Performance, London School of Economics, January.

Rothbard, Murray N. (1962) 'The case for a 100 percent gold dollar', in Leland B. Yeager (ed.) *In Search of a Monetary Constitution:* 94–136, Cambridge, Massachusetts: Harvard University Press.

Rubinfien, Elisabeth (1992) 'Russia offers privatization plan amid turmoil, currency chaos', *Wall Street Journal*, 2 October: A10.

Russian Economic Trends (London).

Rybczynski, Tad M. (1991) 'The sequencing of reform', *Oxford Review of Economic Policy*, 7, 4, Winter: 26–34.

Sachs, Jeffrey, and Lipton, David (1992) 'Russia: towards a market-based monetary system', *Central Banking*, Summer: 29–53.

Sayers, R. S. (ed.) (1952) *Banking in the British Commonwealth*, London: Oxford University Press.

Schmieding, Holger (1992) 'Lending stability to Europe's emerging market economies: on the potential importance of the EC and the ECU for the transformation process in Central and Eastern Europe', unpublished Ph.D. dissertation, Christian-Albrechts Universität, Kiel, Germany, published in Kieler Studien, Tübingen: J. C. B. Mohr (Paul Siebeck).

Schuler, Kurt (1992a) 'The world history of free banking', in Kevin Dowd (ed.) *The Experience of Free Banking:* 7–47, London: Routledge.

Schuler, Kurt (1992b) 'Currency boards', unpublished Ph.D. dissertation, George Mason University.

Schuler, Kurt, Selgin, George, and Sinkey, Joseph, Jr. (1991) 'Replacing the rouble in Lithuania: real change versus pseudoreform', Cato Institute Policy Analysis 163, 28 October.

Schwartz, Anna J. (1992a) 'Currency boards: their past, present, and possible future', unpublished paper, National Bureau of Economic Research.

Schwartz, Anna J. (1992b) *Do Currency Boards Have a Future?* Occasional Paper 88, London: Institute of Economic Affairs.

Selgin, George A. (1988a) 'A free banking approach to reforming Hong Kong's monetary system', *Asian Monetary Monitor*, 12, 1, January–February: 14–24.

Selgin, George A. (1988b) *The Theory of Free Banking: Money Supply Under Competitive Note Issue*, Totowa, New Jersey: Rowman and Littlefield.

Selgin, George (1992a) 'The ECU could stabilize eastern currencies', *Wall Street Journal*, 9 January: A12.

Selgin, George (1992b) 'On ensuring the acceptability of a new fiat money', unpublished paper, University of Georgia, 11 November, forthcoming in *Journal of Money, Credit, and Banking*.

Selgin, George A., and Schuler, Kurt (1990) 'A proposal for reforming Lithuania's monetary system', unpublished paper, University of Georgia and George Mason University, 14 November.

Senik-Leygonie, Claudia, and Hughes, Gordon (1992) 'Industrial profitability and trade among the former Soviet republics', *Economic Policy: A European Forum*, 15, October: 353–77, 386.

Sesit, Michael R. (1992) 'Europe central banks said to have lost up to $6 billion trying to help currencies', *Wall Street Journal*, 1 October: C1.

Shannon, H. A. (1951) 'Evolution of the colonial sterling exchange standard', *International Monetary Fund Staff Papers*, 1, 3, April: 334–54.

Shannon, H. A. (1952) 'The modern colonial sterling exchange standard', *International Monetary Fund Staff Papers*, 2, 2, April: 318–62.

Shapiro, Joshua (1993) 'Australia's plastic bills: durable and hard to counterfeit', *New York Times*, 7 February: F9.

Shelton, Judy (1989) *The Coming Soviet Crash: Gorbachev's Desperate Pursuit of Credit in Western Financial Markets*, New York: Free Press.

Shmelev, Nikolai, and Popov, Vladimir (1989) *The Turning Point: Revitalizing the Soviet Economy*, New York: Doubleday.

Siebert, Horst (ed.) (1992) *The Transformation of Socialist Economies: Symposium 1991*, 2 v., Tübingen: J. C. B. Mohr (Paul Siebeck).

Sieburger, Marlis (1991) 'Aktuelle Probleme des sowjetischen Finanzsystems: Interdependenz von Bankenreform und Budgetdefizit', Berichte des Bundesinstitut für ostwissenschaftliche und internationale Studien 35, Köln.

Simons, Henry (1934) *A Positive Program for Laissez Faire: Some Proposals for a Liberal Economic Policy*, Chicago: University of Chicago Press.

Smith, Vera (1990 [1936]) *The Rationale of Central Banking and the Free Banking Alternative*, Indianapolis: Liberty Press.

Solimano, Andrés (1991) 'On economic transformation in East-Central Europe: a historical and international perspective', World Bank Working Paper 677, May.

Soros, George (1993) 'A social safety net for Russia', *Washington Post*, 4 January: A21.

Spring-Rice, D. (1919) 'The North Russian currency', *Economic Journal*, 29, 115, September: 280–9.

Sudetic, Chuck (1991) 'Financial scandal rocks Yugoslavia', *New York Times*, 10 January: A5.

Sudetic, Chuck (1993) 'A Belgrade banker makes big profits from trade sanctions', *New York Times*, 16 February: A3.

Summers, Bruce J. (1992) 'Russian payment institutions and the medium of exchange function of the rouble', unpublished paper, Federal Reserve Bank of Richmond, 8 October.

Talley, Samuel H., and Mas, Ignacio (1990) 'Deposit insurance in developing countries', World Bank Working Paper 548, November.

Taylor, Dean (1982) 'Official intervention in the foreign exchange market, or, bet against the central bank', *Journal of Political Economy*, 90, 2, April: 356–68.

Tocqueville Institute (1992) 'IMF conditionality 1980–1991', unpublished paper, Alexis de Tocqueville Institute.

Uchitelle, Louis (1992a) 'Russians line up for gas as refineries sit on cheap oil', *New York Times*, 12 July: E4.

Uchitelle, Louis (1992b) 'New man, old burden: Moscow owes $86 billion', *New York Times*, 16 December: A14.

Uno, Kimio (1991) 'Privatization and the creation of a commercial banking system', in Merton J. Peck and Thomas J. Richardson (eds) *What Is to Be Done? Proposals for the Soviet Transition to the Market:* 149–78, New Haven: Yale University Press.

Vaubel, Roland (1978) *Strategies for Currency Unification: The Economics of Currency Competition and the Case for a European Parallel Currency*, Kieler Studien 156, Tübingen: J. C. B. Mohr (Paul Siebeck).

Volcker, Paul (1990) 'The role of central banks', in Federal Reserve Bank of Kansas City, *Central Banking Issues in Emerging Market Economies: A Symposium Sponsored by the Federal Reserve Bank of Kansas City:* 1–8, Kansas City: Federal Reserve Bank of Kansas City.

Vuylsteke, Charles (1988) 'Techniques of privatization of state-owned enterprises', 1, World Bank Technical Paper 88.

Wallich, Christine (1992) *Fiscal Decentralization: Intergovernmental Relations in Russia*, Studies of Economies in Transformation 6, Washington: World Bank.

Walters, Alan A. (1987) 'Currency boards', in Peter Newman, Murray Milgate, and John Eatwell (eds) *The New Palgrave: A Dictionary of Economics*, 1: 740–2, London: Macmillan.

Walters, Alan (1990) *Sterling in Danger: The Economic Consequences of Pegged Exchange Rates*, London: Fontana/Collins.

Walters, Alan (1991) 'A hard rouble for Boris', *London Evening Standard*, 22 November.

Walters, Alan A. (1992a) 'A hard ruble for the new republics', *National Review*, 3 February: 34–6.

Walters, Alan (1992b) 'The frontiers of reform: errors and omissions', *AIG World Markets Advisory* (AIG Trading Corp.), September: 1, 3–5.

Walters, Alan A., and Hanke, Steve H. (1992) 'Currency boards', in Peter Newman, Murray Milgate, and John Eatwell (eds) *The New Palgrave Dictionary of Money and Finance*, 1: 558–61, London: Macmillan.

Wanniski, Jude (1990) 'Save perestroika with monetary deflation', *Wall Street Journal*, 16 May: 20.

White, Lawrence H. (1984) *Free Banking in Britain: Theory, Experience and Debate 1800–1845*, Cambridge: Cambridge University Press.

White, Lawrence H. (1989a) *Competition and Currency: Essays on Free Banking and Money*, New York: New York University Press.

White, Lawrence H. (1989b) 'Fix or float? The international monetary dilemma', in Lawrence H. White, *Competition and Currency: Essays on Free Banking and Money:* 137–47, New York: New York University Press.

White, Lawrence H. (ed.) (1993) *Free Banking*, 3 v., Aldershot, UK: Edward Elgar.

Whitlock, Erik (1992) 'A borrower and a lender be: interenterprise debt in Russia', *RFE/RL Research Report*, 1, 40, 9 October: 33–8.

Whitlock, Erik (1993) 'New Russian government to continue economic reform?' *RFE/RL Research Report*, 2, 3, 15 January: 23–7.

Whitney, Craig R. (1992) 'Bundesbank: sound money bastion', *New York Times*, 22 October: D1, D9.

Williamson, John (ed.) (1981) *Exchange Rate Rules: The Theory, Performance and Prospects of the Crawling Peg*, New York: St Martin's Press.

Williamson, John (ed.) (1991a) *Currency Convertibility in Eastern Europe*, Washington: Institute for International Economics.

Williamson, John (1991b) 'The economic opening of Eastern Europe', in John Williamson (ed.) *Currency Convertibility in Eastern Europe:* 363–431, Washington: Institute for International Economics.

Williamson, John (1992) *Trade and Payments after Soviet Disintegration*, Policy Analyses in International Economics 37, June, Washington: Institute for International Economics.

World Bank (1992a) *World Development Report 1992: Development and the Environment*, Oxford: Oxford University Press.

World Bank (1992b) *Russian Economic Reform: Crossing the Threshold of Structural Change*, Washington: World Bank.

World Bank (1992c) *Statistical Handbook: States of the Former USSR*, prepared by Country Department III, Europe and Central Asia region, under the supervision of Misha V. Belkindas, Studies of Economies in Transformation 3, Washington: World Bank.

Yavlinski, Grigori, and Kushner, David S. (1991) *500 Days: Transition to the Market*, New York; St Martin's Press.

Yeager, Leland B. (1976) *International Monetary Relations: Theory, History, and Policy*, New York: Harper and Row.

Yeager, Leland B. (ed.) (1962) *In Search of a Monetary Constitution*, Cambridge, Massachusetts: Harvard University Press.

Yeager, Leland (1992) 'Monetary constitutions', in Peter Newman, Murray Milgate, and John Eatwell (eds) *The New Palgrave Dictionary of Money and Finance*, 2: 731–4, London: Macmillan.

Yeager, Leland, and associates (1981) *Experiences with Stopping Inflation*, Washington: American Enterprise Institute.

Zhurek, Stefan (1993) 'Commodity exchanges in Russia: success or failure?' *RFE/RL Research Report*, 2, 6, 5 February: 41–4.

INDEX

clearing *see* payments
clearing union 33–4, 58–9
clearinghouse 119
closed economy 135
Cobb, Joe 181 n1
coins 4–6, 57, 108, 181 n5; *see also* notes
collateral 54, 125
Collier, Paul 29
colonial currency boards *see* British
colonial currency boards
colonialism 141
commercial banks: and cash
convertibility 31; in central banking 4,
7, 69, 71–2; in currency board system
5–10, 14–15, 63–4, 66–7 (Figures
4.1–2), 104–7, 163–71; defined 5;
foreign 81, 121, 123, 134; in Hong
Kong 138; as issuers of notes 111–12,
145, 184 n31, 190 n100; and lender
of last resort 14–15, 133–4; and
money supply 6–7, 30, 64–6, 71–2,
163–71, 182 n7; and monetary reform
85, 94–5, 97, 110–13, 120–7;
nonstate 53–4, 122, 124; regulation of
120–3, 189 n86; restructuring 123–4,
189 n90; state 15, 51–4, 122–3; in
Russia 42, 51–6, 59, 94; in
Yugoslavia 40–1; *see also* bank
failures
commercial credit 118
Commissariat of Finance 151–3, 155
commission fees 74, 105, 161
commitment of currency board 110
commodity convertibility *see*
convertibility
commodity exchanges 22, 56
Communism 43–4, 150
Communist Party 24, 154
competing currencies 111–13, 190 n8;
see also free banking; parallel
currency
competition 12, 13, 32, 39; in banking
system 53–4, 120–1, 126
Conant, Charles A. 26
confiscation of money 46, 124
Congdon, T.G. 79
Congress of People's Deputies 47, 154
Connolly, Michael 28
constitution, for currency board 160–2
consumer prices *see* inflation; prices
consumer's surplus 112
contracts 28, 91–2, 111, 125, 127–8,

161–2; *see also* indexation; option
clause
conventional approach *see* economic
reform, conventional approach
conversion of Central Bank of Russia
into currency board 84–7, 89–9, 119,
126–7
convertibility: in Argentina 73; cash 31,
32, 56, 127; of CFA franc 79; and
central banking 8, 183 nn33–4; 186
n63; of chervonets 44, 153–4; and
currency board system 8, 34–5, 81–2,
104, 142; commodity 31–2; in
Estonia 76; foreign-exchange 31–2,
44; full 32–5; of rouble 42–5, 49,
56–9, 95; types of 30–2, 183 n25; *see
also* capital controls; cash circuit
Cooper, Richard 88
cooperative banks 5, 44, 53; *see also*
commercial banks
copper currency 42, 88
Corbett, Jenny 122
Corbo, Vittorio 33
corporatization 13 (Table 1.2), 17, 52,
123, 183 n17
correspondent accounts 58 *see also*
bilateral accounts
Council of Ministers 47, 50
crawling peg 28, 135, 183 n29
credibility: of Central Bank of Russia
23–4, 61; of central banks 9–10,
23–5, 73, 74–5, 79; of chervonets 155;
of commercial banks 120; of
currency boards 9–10, 25, 90–1, 110,
141; defined 9–10; in economic
reform 17–18; and exchange rates
25–30; of reserve currency 100–1
Crick, W. F. 186 n60
Cukierman, Alex 37
Culp, Christopher 68, 188 n79, 190 n98
currency *see* cash; coins; money
supply; notes
currency basket *see* basket of currencies
currency board, currency board
system: advocates of 181 n1; defined
5; central banks that mimic 72–9;
constitution, model 160–2;
converting Central Bank of Russia
into 84–7, 94–9, 119, 126–7;
contrasted with central bank 4–11,
25, 30, 33, 36–7, 39–40, 183 n24; and
economic reform 11–19; establishing
84–102, 186 n52, 188 n80; history

equilibrium 38, 65–7, 71–2, 165–6,
168–9, 171
Estonia 49, 58, 72, 74–6, 79, 189 n96
European Currency Unit, 75, 100–2
Eurocurrency markets 107, 134
European Monetary System 27–8, 141,
183 n28
European Payments Union 33–4
exchange rates: in Argentina 73–4; in
Bretton Woods system 180; and
central banks 70–2; and credibility
25–30; and currency board system
65, 69, 80–1, 86–7, 92; in Estonia 74,
76; fixed 7, 14, 18, 25–30, 65, 69, 86,
136–7; floating 7, 28–30, 70–2, 84–5,
136–7, 189 n95; foreign 47 (Table
3.1), 59–60; forward 111;
fundamental equilibrium 96–7; and
indexation 2; interrepublican 57–9;
nominal 86, 92; pegged 7, 14–15,
25–8, 61; real 26–7, 81, 86, 96–7, 136;
in Russia currently 47 (Table 3.1),
49, 56–61; in Russia historically 42–3,
148, 152–3; and Russian currency
board 84–6, 93, 95–7, 103–4, 110–11,
113–14, 161–2, 187 n64; setting
86–7; types 7, 25, 183 n25; and wages
and prices 128–30; in Yugoslavia
40–1; see also parallel currency
expectations: of inflation 24, 28, 61,
136; and money supply 70–1;
rational, 38
exchange risk 18, 25, 30, 73–4, 134, 136
expenses of a currency board 5, 106,
108–9, 154
exports 26–7, 32–3, 65–8, 70–2, 80; of
oil 116–17
extreme inflation see inflation, extreme

failures see bank failures; state
enterprises, restructuring of
Falkland Islands 35, 81–2
Faroe Islands 35, 82, 174
Fed funds 69, 101
Federal Reserve System, US 11, 69, 100,
126, 140–1, 143, 186 n56
Federov, Boris 16
Fenton, Paul 137
Fieleke, Norman S. 189 n92
financial statement 161
First World War 26, 43, 65, 146, 149
fiscal honeymoon 118

Fischer, Stanley 96, 182 n9, 183
nn17–18, 188 n78
Five-Year Plan 44, 154
fixed exchange rate see exchange rates,
fixed
flexibility: of central bank 36–40, 129;
of real prices 3, 132
floating exchange rate see exchange
rates, floating
flow cost of dollarization 144
Foreign Office, British 147, 150
forced tender 88, 91, 128, 162
foreign aid 22, 49–50 (Table 3.3), 60,
142, 156
foreign commercial banks see
commercial banks, foreign
foreign currency: in central banking 29;
and convertibility 31–3; in currency
board system 5, 85, 92, 125, 137,
165–7; in Russia currently 3, 22, 49
(Table 3.3), 59–60, 90; in Russia
historically 89, 151–2; in Slovenia
98; see also dollarization; exchange
rates; reserves
foreign-currency deposits 48 (Table
3.2), 128
foreign debt 49–50 (Table 3.3), 60, 128,
185 n50
foreign domination 102, 141
foreign exchange 59–60, 127–8, 142; see
also exchange rates; interrepublican
exchange
foreign-exchange controls see capital
controls; convertibility
foreign investment: in currency board
systems 65, 69, 80, 169; in Russia
currently 26, 32–34; in Russian
currency board system 86, 100, 128
foreign reserves see reserves
foreign trade see convertibility; exports;
trade
forward exchange 111
France 60, 79, 141
French franc 79
Fratianni, Michele 183 n28, 189 n92
fraud 56, 92, 121
free banking 145
Freeland, Chrystia 116
freezing deposits 124
Freris, Andrew 112, 133, 186 n60, 188
n79
Friedman, Milton 38, 137, 181 n1, 184
n31, 189 n96

insurance 185 n49
Inter-State Bank 58
interbank lending 64, 133
interest *see* seigniorage
interest rates: in Argentina 73–4; on
  currency board's reserves 107–9,
  140; in currency board system 65–9,
  120, 124–5, 137–8, 165; and
  exchange rates 26–7; in Estonia 75;
  in Germany 40, 75, 100; and money
  supply 65–9; and option clause 134;
  real 13, 24–5, 28–9, 130, 182 n13,
  183 n23; in reserve currency, 100–1;
  in Russia 13, 35–6, 47, 50–1, 53–4,
  122; in Yugoslavia 40–1
International Monetary Fund (IMF): as
  author only 8, 23, 29, 34–5, 46–8,
  53–4, 56–9, 73, 79, 121–2, 135, 182
  n9, 183 n14, 185 n49, 185 n50; and
  central banking 36–7; and currency
  board system 183 n24; and economic
  reform 11, 16; and Estonia 76; and
  Russia 49–50, 60–2, 116, 183 n29,
  185 n51, 188 n83; and Russian
  currency board 62, 98–9, 106, 110,
  142, 185 n52, 190 n103; and
  Yugoslavia 40
interrepublican exchange 56–8, 62, 127
investment reserve, of currency boards
  108, 139
Ireland 141, 175
Irish punt, 27
Ironside, William Edmund 149
Isard, Peter 16, 32, 184 n33
Israel 24, 177, 184 n37
Italy 35, 60, 184 n36

Jack, Andrew 55
jail sentences 122
Jamaica 104, 175
Jao, Y. C. 137, 186 n60
Japan 43, 60, 137
Japanese yen 34, 42, 81, 111, 137
Jonung, Lars 69, 183 n31, 187 nn66, 72,
  189 n94, 190 n104
Jordan 110, 141, 179
Jordan, Jerry 181 n1
Joshi, Vijay 29

Kawai, Masahiro 137, 189 n97
Kazmin, Andrei I. 90
Kenen, Peter 34

Kerensky, Alexander F. 43, 146, 150,
  191 n106
Keynes, John Maynard 23, 146–8
King, Frank H. H. 34, 81, 144, 180, 186
  n60, 189 n92
Koren, Stephen 185 n42
Kornai, János 182 n12
Kratz, Joachim W. 105, 107, 186 n60
Krol, Roland van de 183 n19
Krugman, Paul R. 183 n27
Kumar, Manmohan S. 117, 188 n83
Kuschpèta, O. 185 n46
Kydland, Finn E. 27, 38

labour: as factor of production 26,
  32–3, 119; mobility 189 n97;
  productivity 15, 18, 68
lags 30, 37, 70–1
Laidler, David 38
land 17, 26, 32, 33, 124, 125, 130
large economy 135
Lavoie, Don C. 184 n32
law *see* constitution; contracts; legal
  tender; property rights
Law on State Enterprise 45
League of Nations 80
Lee, Sheng-Yi 77, 186 n60
legal tender: in currency board system
  91, 128, 162; in Estonia 74; in Russia
  in 1920s 151
lender of last resort: in Argentina 73;
  central banks as 9, 14–15, 33, 69,
  133–4; Central Bank of Russia as
  14–15, 51; and currency board
  system 9, 116, 118, 122–3, 126,
  133–4; and dollarization 143; in
  Estonia 75; in Hong Kong 188 n79;
  in United States 69–70
Lenin, V. I. 185 n45; *see also* Bolsheviks
liabilities: of Central Bank of Russia
  85–7; of commercial banks 123–4,
  163–4; of currency board 7–8, 10,
  77–8, 109; of state enterprises 119
liberalization *see* prices, deregulation
  vs. liberalization
Libyan Currency Board 110, 176
Lindsey, David E. 30
Lipton, David 36, 55–6, 74, 119, 182
  nn9–10, 189 n91
liquid reserve of currency boards 108
lira, Italian 27, 35, 184 n36
Lithuania 187 n66
Lloyd, John 59, 117, 144